The Taxpayer Advocate Service Is Here To Help You

What is the Taxpayer Advocate Service?
The Taxpayer Advocate Service (TAS) is an *independent* organization within the Internal Revenue Service (IRS) that helps taxpayers and protects taxpayer rights. Our job is to ensure that every taxpayer is treated fairly and that you know and understand your rights under the *Taxpayer Bill of Rights*.

What can the Taxpayer Advocate Service do for you?
We can help you resolve problems that you can't resolve with the IRS. And our service is free. If you qualify for our assistance, your advocate will be with you at every turn and do everything possible. TAS can help you if:
- Your problem is causing financial difficulty for you, your family, or your business.
- You face (or your business is facing) an immediate threat of adverse action.
- You've tried repeatedly to contact the IRS but no one has responded, or the IRS hasn't responded by the date promised.

How can you reach us?
We have offices in *every state, the District of Columbia, and Puerto Rico*. Your local advocate's number is at *www.TaxpayerAdvocate.irs.gov*, at *IRS.gov/advocate*, and in your local directory. You can also call us at 1-877-777-4778.

How can you learn about your taxpayer rights?
The Taxpayer Bill of Rights describes ten basic rights that all taxpayers have when dealing with the IRS. Our Tax Toolkit at *www.TaxpayerAdvocate.irs.gov* can help you understand *what these rights mean to you* and how they apply. These are *your* rights. Know them. Use them.

How else does the Taxpayer Advocate Service help taxpayers?
TAS works to resolve large-scale problems that affect many taxpayers. If you know of one of these broad issues, please report it to us at *IRS.gov/sams*.

Low Income Taxpayer Clinics Help Taxpayers

Low Income Taxpayer Clinics (LITCs) are independent from the IRS. Some serve individuals whose income is below a certain level and who need to resolve a tax problem. These clinics provide professional representation before the IRS or in court on audits, appeals, tax collection disputes, and other issues for free or for a small fee. Some clinics provide information about taxpayer rights and responsibilities in many different languages for individuals who speak English as a second language. For more information, and to find a clinic near you, read the LITC page on *IRS.gov/litc* or IRS *Publication 4134, Low Income Taxpayer Clinic List*. You can also get this publication at your local IRS office or by calling 1-800-829-3676.

Suggestions for Improving the IRS

Taxpayer Advocacy Panel

Have a suggestion for improving the IRS and do not know who to contact? The Taxpayer Advocacy Panel (TAP) is a diverse group of citizen volunteers who listen to taxpayers, identify taxpayers' issues, and make suggestions for improving IRS service and customer satisfaction. The panel is demographically and geographically diverse, with at least one member from each state, the District of Columbia, and Puerto Rico. Contact TAP at *www.improveirs.org* or 1-888-912-1227 (toll-free).

Affordable Care Act—What You Need To Know

Requirement To Reconcile Advance Payments of the Premium Tax Credit

The premium tax credit helps pay premiums for health insurance purchased from the Marketplace. Eligible individuals may have advance payments of the premium tax credit made on their behalf directly to the insurance company.

If you or a family member enrolled in health insurance through the Marketplace and advance payments of the premium tax credit were made to your insurance company to reduce your monthly premium payment, you must attach **Form 8962** to your return to **reconcile** (compare) the advance payments with your premium tax credit for the year.

The Marketplace is required to send **Form 1095-A** by **January 31, 2017,** listing the advance payments and other information you need to complete **Form 8962.**

1. You will need **Form 1095-A** from the Marketplace.

2. Complete **Form 8962** to claim the credit and to reconcile your advance credit payments.

3. Include **Form 8962** with your **1040, 1040A,** or **1040NR.** (Do not include Form 1095-A.)

Health Coverage Individual Responsibility Payment Increased

If you or someone in your household didn't have qualifying health care coverage or qualify for a coverage exemption for one or more months of 2016, the amount of your shared responsibility payment may be larger this year than it was last year. For 2016, you must:

  OR   OR

Report Health Care Coverage	**Claim a Coverage Exemption**	**Make a Shared Responsibility Payment**
Check the Full-year coverage box on **line 61** to indicate that you, your spouse (if filing jointly), and anyone you can or do claim as a dependent had qualifying health care coverage throughout 2016.	Attach **Form 8965** to claim an exemption from the requirement to have health care coverage. For more information, go to *IRS.gov/form8965.*	Make a shared responsibility payment if, for any month in 2016, you, your spouse (if filing jointly), or anyone you can or do claim as a dependent didn't have coverage and don't qualify for a coverage exemption. For more information, go to *IRS.gov/srp.*

Health Coverage Reporting

- If you or someone in your family had health coverage in 2016, the provider of that coverage is required to send you a **Form 1095-A, 1095-B,** or **1095-C** (with Part III completed), that lists individuals in your family who were enrolled in the coverage and shows their months of coverage. You may use this information to help complete **line 61.** You should receive the **Form 1095-A** by early **February 2017** and **Form 1095-B** or **1095-C** by early **March 2017,** if applicable. You do not need to wait to receive your Form 1095-B or 1095-C to file your return. You may rely on other information about your coverage to complete line 61. Do not include Form 1095-A, Form 1095-B, or Form 1095-C with your tax return.

- If you or someone in your family was an employee in 2016, the employer may be required to send you a **Form 1095-C. Part II** of **Form 1095-C** shows whether your employer offered you health insurance coverage and, if so, information about the offer. You should receive **Form 1095-C** by early **March 2017.** This information may be relevant if you purchased health insurance coverage for 2016 through the Health Insurance Marketplace and wish to claim the premium tax credit on **line 69.** However, you do not need to wait to receive this form to file your return. You may rely on other information received from your employer. If you don't wish to claim the premium tax credit for 2016, you don't need the information in **Part II** of **Form 1095-C.** For more information on who is eligible for the premium tax credit, see the Instructions for Form 8962.

1040

THIS BOOKLET DOES NOT CONTAIN INSTRUCTIONS FOR ANY FORM 1040 SCHEDULES

INSTRUCTIONS

2016

 is the fast, safe, and free way to prepare and *e-file* your taxes. See *IRS.gov/freefile*.

Get a faster refund, reduce errors, and save paper. For more information on **IRS** Free File and *e-file*, see *Free Software Options for Doing Your Taxes* in these instructions or go to *IRS.gov/freefile*.

2016 TAX CHANGES

See *What's New* in these instructions.

FUTURE DEVELOPMENTS

For the latest information about developments related to Form 1040 and its instructions, such as legislation enacted after they were published, go to *IRS.gov/form1040*.

Department of the Treasury **Internal Revenue Service** IRS.gov

Dec 15, 2016   Cat. No. 24811V

Department
of the
Treasury

**Internal
Revenue
Service**

Table of Contents

Free Software Options for Doing Your Taxes

Why have 49 million Americans used Free File?

- *Security*—Free File uses the latest encryption technology to safeguard your information.
- *Flexible Payments*—File early; pay by April 18, 2017.
- *Greater Accuracy*—Fewer errors mean faster processing.
- *Quick Receipt*—Get an acknowledgment that your return was received and accepted.
- *Go Green*—Reduce the amount of paper used.
- *It's Free*—through *IRS.gov/freefile*.
- *Faster Refunds*—Join the eight in 10 taxpayers who get their refunds faster by using direct deposit and *e-file*.

 Do Your Taxes for Free

If your adjusted gross income was $64,000 or less in 2016, you can use free tax software to prepare and *e-file* your tax return. Earned more? Use Free File Fillable Forms.

Free File. This public-private partnership, between the IRS and tax software providers, makes approximately a dozen brand name commercial software products and *e-file* available for free. Seventy percent of the nation's taxpayers are eligible.

Just visit *IRS.gov/freefile* for details. Free File combines all the benefits of *e-file* and easy-to-use software at no cost. Guided questions will help ensure you get all the tax credits and deductions you are due. It's fast, safe, and free.

You can review each software provider's criteria for free usage or use an online tool to find which free software products match your situation. Some software providers offer state tax return preparation for free.

Free File Fillable Forms. The IRS offers electronic versions of IRS paper forms that also can be *e-filed* for free. Free File Fillable Forms is best for people experienced in preparing their own tax returns. There are no income limitations. Free File Fillable Forms does basic math calculations. It supports only federal tax forms.

Free Tax Help Available Nationwide

Volunteers are available in communities nationwide providing free tax assistance to low to moderate income (generally under $54,000 in adjusted gross income) and elderly taxpayers (age 60 and older). At selected sites, taxpayers can input and electronically file their own tax return with the assistance of an IRS-certified volunteer.

See *How To Get Tax Help* near the end of these instructions for additional information or visit IRS.gov (Keyword: VITA) for a VITA/TCE site near you!

IRS.gov is the gateway to all electronic services offered by the IRS, as well as the spot to download forms at *IRS.gov/forms*.

Make your tax payments electronically—it's easy.

You can make electronic payments online, by phone, or from a mobile device. Paying electronically is safe and secure. The IRS uses the latest encryption technology and does not store the bank account number you use to submit your payment. When you use any of the IRS electronic payment options, it puts you in control of paying your tax bill and gives you peace of mind. You determine the payment date, and you will receive an immediate confirmation from the IRS. It's easy, secure, and much quicker than mailing in a check or money order. Go to *IRS.gov/payments* to see all your electronic payment options.

What's New

Due date of return. File Form 1040 by April 18, 2017. The due date is April 18, instead of April 15, because of the Emancipation Day holiday in the District of Columbia—even if you do not live in the District of Columbia.

Service at local IRS offices by appointment. Many issues can be resolved conveniently on IRS.gov with no waiting. However, if you need help from an IRS Taxpayer Assistance Center (TAC) you need to call to schedule an appointment. Go to *IRS.gov/taclocator* to find the location and telephone number of your local TAC.

Delayed refunds for returns claiming certain credits. Due to changes in the law, the IRS can't issue refunds before February 15, 2017, for returns that claim the earned income credit or the additional child tax credit. This delay applies to the entire refund, not just the portion associated with these credits. Although the IRS will begin releasing refunds for returns that claim these credits on February 15, because of the time it generally takes banking or financial systems to process deposits, it is unlikely that your refund will arrive in your bank account or on a debit card before the week of February 27 (assuming your return has no processing issues and you elect direct deposit).

If you filed your return before February 15, you can check *Where's My Refund* on IRS.gov (*IRS.gov/refunds*) a few days after February 15 for your projected deposit date. *Where's My Refund* and the IRS2Go phone app remain the best ways to check the status of any refund.

Delivery services. Eight delivery services have been added to the list of designated private delivery services. For the complete list see *Private Delivery Services.*

Cash payment option. There is a new option for taxpayers who want to pay their taxes in cash. For details, see *Pay by Cash* under *Amount You Owe* in the instructions for line 78.

Educator expenses. You may be able to deduct certain expenses for professional development courses you have taken related to the curriculum you teach or to the students you teach. See the instructions for line 23.

Olympic and Paralympic medals and USOC prize money. If you receive Olympic and Paralympic medals and United States Olympic Committee prize money, the value of the medals and the amount of the prize money may be nontaxable. See the instructions for line 21 for more information.

Child tax credit and additional child tax credit may be disallowed. If you take the child tax credit or the additional child tax credit even though you aren't eligible, you may not be able to take these credits for up to 10 years. For more information, see the Instructions for Schedule 8812.

American opportunity credit may be disallowed. If you take the American opportunity credit even though you aren't eligible, you may not be able to take this credit for up to 10 years. For more information, see the Instructions for Form 8863.

Health coverage tax credit (HCTC). The HCTC is a tax credit that pays a percentage of health insurance premiums for certain eligible taxpayers and their qualifying family members. The HCTC is a separate tax credit with different eligibility rules than the premium tax credit. You may have received monthly advance payments of the HCTC beginning in July 2016. For information on how to report these payments or on the HCTC generally, see the Instructions for Form 8885.

Get Transcript Online. The Get Transcript Online tool on IRS.gov is available again to get a copy of your tax transcripts and similar documents. To guard against fraud, you will now need to go through a two-step authentication process in order to use the online tool. For more information, go to *IRS.gov/transcript*.

Electronic Filing PIN. Electronic Filing PIN, an IRS-generated PIN used to verify your signature on your self-prepared, electronic tax return, is no longer available. To validate your signature, you must use your prior-year adjusted gross income or prior-year self-select PIN. See *Electronic Return Signatures*, later.

Individual taxpayer identification number (ITIN) renewal. If you were assigned an ITIN before January 1, 2013, or if you have an ITIN that you haven't included on a tax return in the last three consecutive years, you may need to renew it. For more information, see the Instructions for Form W-7.

Personal exemption amount increased for certain taxpayers. Your personal exemption is increased to $4,050. But the amount is reduced if your adjusted gross income is more than $155,650 if married filing separately; $259,400 if single; $285,350 if head of household; or $311,300 if married filing jointly or qualifying widow(er). See the instructions for line 42.

Limit on itemized deductions. You may not be able to deduct all of your itemized deductions if your adjusted gross income is more than $155,650 if married filing separately; $259,400 if single; $285,350 if head of household; or $311,300 if married filing jointly or qualifying widow(er).

Standard deduction for head of household filing status. For 2016, the standard deduction for head of household filing status has increased to $9,300. The other standard deduction amounts are unchanged.

Secure access. To combat identity fraud, the IRS has upgraded its identity verification process for certain self-help tools on IRS.gov. To find out what types of information new users will need, go to *IRS.gov/secureaccess*.

Filing Requirements

 Have you tried IRS *e-file?* It's the fastest way to get your refund and it's free if you are eligible. Visit IRS.gov for details.

Do You Have To File?

Use Chart A, B, or C to see if you must file a return. U.S. citizens who lived in or had income from a U.S. possession should see Pub. 570. Residents of Puerto Rico can use *Tax Topic 901* to see if they must file.

 Even if you do not otherwise have to file a return, you should file one to get a refund of any federal income tax withheld. You should also file if you are eligible for any of the following credits.

- *Earned income credit.*
- *Additional child tax credit.*
- *American opportunity credit.*
- *Credit for federal tax on fuels.*
- *Premium tax credit.*
- *Health coverage tax credit.*

See Pub. 501 for details. Also see Pub. 501 if you do not have to file but received a Form 1099-B (or substitute statement).

Requirement to reconcile advance payments of the premium tax credit. If you, your spouse with whom you are filing a joint return, or a dependent was enrolled in coverage through the Marketplace for 2016 and advance payments of the premium tax credit were made for this coverage, you must file a 2016 return and attach Form 8962. You (or whoever enrolled you) should have received Form 1095-A from the Marketplace with information about your coverage and any advance payments.

You must attach Form 8962 even if someone else enrolled you, your spouse, or your dependent. If you are a dependent who is claimed on someone else's 2016 return, you do not have to attach Form 8962.

Exception for certain children under age 19 or full-time students. If certain conditions apply, you can elect to include on your return the income of a child who was under age 19 at the end of 2016 or was a full-time student under age 24 at the end of 2016. To do so, use Form 8814. If you make this election, your child doesn't have to file a return. For details, use *Tax Topic 553* or see Form 8814.

A child born on January 1, 1993, is considered to be age 24 at the end of 2016. Do not use Form 8814 for such a child.

Resident aliens. These rules also apply if you were a resident alien. Also, you may qualify for certain tax treaty benefits. See Pub. 519 for details.

Nonresident aliens and dual-status aliens. These rules also apply if you were a nonresident alien or a dual-status alien and both of the following apply.

- You were married to a U.S. citizen or resident alien at the end of 2016.
- You elected to be taxed as a resident alien.

See Pub. 519 for details.

 Specific rules apply to determine if you are a resident alien, nonresident alien, or dual-status alien. Most nonresident aliens and dual-status aliens have different filing requirements and may have to file Form 1040NR or Form 1040NR-EZ. Pub. 519 discusses these requirements and other information to help aliens comply with U.S. tax law.

When and Where Should You File?

File Form 1040 by **April 18, 2017.** (The due date is April 18, instead of April 15, because of the Emancipation Day holiday in the District of Columbia—even if you do not live in the District of Columbia.) If you file after this date, you may have to pay interest and penalties. See *Interest and Penalties,* later.

If you were serving in, or in support of, the U.S. Armed Forces in a designated combat zone or contingency operation, you may be able to file later. See Pub. 3 for details.

If you *e-file* your return, there is no need to mail it. However, if you choose to mail it, filing instructions and addresses are at the end of these instructions.

What if You Can't File on Time?

You can get an automatic 6-month extension if, no later than the date your return is due, you file Form 4868. For details, see Form 4868. Instead of filing Form 4868, you can apply for an automatic extension by making an electronic payment by the due date of your return.

 An automatic 6-month extension to file doesn't extend the time to pay your tax. If you do not pay your tax by the original due date of your return, you will owe interest on the unpaid tax and may owe penalties. See Form 4868.

If you are a U.S. citizen or resident alien, you may qualify for an automatic extension of time to file without filing Form 4868. You qualify if, on the due date of your return, you meet one of the following conditions.

- You live outside the United States and Puerto Rico and your main place of business or post of duty is outside the United States and Puerto Rico.
- You are in military or naval service on duty outside the United States and Puerto Rico.

This extension gives you an extra 2 months to file and pay the tax, but interest will be charged from the original due date of the return on any unpaid tax. You must include a statement showing that you meet the requirements. If you are still unable to file your return by the end of the 2-month period, you can get an additional 4 months if, no later than June 15, 2017, you file Form 4868. This 4-month extension of time to file doesn't extend the time to pay your tax. See Form 4868.

Private Delivery Services

If you choose to mail your return, you can use certain private delivery services designated by the IRS to meet the "timely mailing treated as timely filing/paying" rule for tax returns and payments. These private delivery services include only the following.

• DHL Express 9:00, DHL Express 10:30, DHL Express 12:00, DHL Express Worldwide, DHL Express Envelope, DHL Import Express 10:30, DHL Import Express 12:00, DHL Import Express Worldwide.

• UPS Next Day Air Early AM, UPS Next Day Air, UPS Next Day Air Saver, UPS 2nd Day Air, UPS 2nd Day Air A.M., UPS Worldwide Express Plus, and UPS Worldwide Express.

• FedEx First Overnight, FedEx Priority Overnight, FedEx Standard Overnight, FedEx 2 Day, FedEx International Next Flight Out, FedEx International Priority, FedEx International First, and FedEx International Economy.

For more information, go to IRS.gov and enter "private delivery service" in the search box. The search results will direct you to the IRS mailing address to use if you are using a private delivery service. You will also find any updates to the list of designated private delivery services.

The private delivery service can tell you how to get written proof of the mailing date.

Chart A—For Most People

IF your filing status is . . .	AND at the end of 2016 you were*. . .	THEN file a return if your gross income** was at least . . .
Single (see the instructions for line 1)	under 65 65 or older	$10,350 11,900
Married filing jointly*** (see the instructions for line 2)	under 65 (both spouses) 65 or older (one spouse) 65 or older (both spouses)	$20,700 21,950 23,200
Married filing separately (see the instructions for line 3)	any age	$4,050
Head of household (see the instructions for line 4)	under 65 65 or older	$13,350 14,900
Qualifying widow(er) with dependent child (see the instructions for line 5)	under 65 65 or older	$16,650 17,900

*If you were born on January 1, 1952, you are considered to be age 65 at the end of 2016. (If your spouse died in 2016 or if you are preparing a return for someone who died in 2016, see Pub. 501.)

**Gross income means all income you received in the form of money, goods, property, and services that isn't exempt from tax, including any income from sources outside the United States or from the sale of your main home (even if you can exclude part or all of it). Do not include any social security benefits unless (a) you are married filing a separate return and you lived with your spouse at any time in 2016 or (b) one-half of your social security benefits plus your other gross income and any tax-exempt interest is more than $25,000 ($32,000 if married filing jointly). If (a) or (b) applies, see the instructions for lines 20a and 20b to figure the taxable part of social security benefits you must include in gross income. Gross income includes gains, but not losses, reported on Form 8949 or Schedule D. Gross income from a business means, for example, the amount on Schedule C, line 7, or Schedule F, line 9. But, in figuring gross income, do not reduce your income by any losses, including any loss on Schedule C, line 7, or Schedule F, line 9.

***If you didn't live with your spouse at the end of 2016 (or on the date your spouse died) and your gross income was at least $4,050, you must file a return regardless of your age.

Chart B—For Children and Other Dependents (See the instructions for line 6c to find out if someone can claim you as a dependent.)

If your parent (or someone else) can claim you as a dependent, use this chart to see if you must file a return.

In this chart, **unearned income** includes taxable interest, ordinary dividends, and capital gain distributions. It also includes unemployment compensation, taxable social security benefits, pensions, annuities, and distributions of unearned income from a trust. **Earned income** includes salaries, wages, tips, professional fees, and taxable scholarship and fellowship grants. **Gross income** is the total of your unearned and earned income.

Single dependents. Were you **either** age 65 or older **or** blind?

☐ **No.** You must file a return if **any** of the following apply.
- Your unearned income was over $1,050.
- Your earned income was over $6,300.
- Your gross income was more than the **larger** of—
  - $1,050, or
  - Your earned income (up to $5,950) plus $350.

☐ **Yes.** You must file a return if **any** of the following apply.
- Your unearned income was over $2,600 ($4,150 if 65 or older **and** blind).
- Your earned income was over $7,850 ($9,400 if 65 or older **and** blind).
- Your gross income was more than the **larger** of—
  - $2,600 ($4,150 if 65 or older **and** blind), or
  - Your earned income (up to $5,950) plus $1,900 ($3,450 if 65 or older **and** blind).

Married dependents. Were you **either** age 65 or older **or** blind?

☐ **No.** You must file a return if **any** of the following apply.
- Your unearned income was over $1,050.
- Your earned income was over $6,300.
- Your gross income was at least $5 and your spouse files a separate return and itemizes deductions.
- Your gross income was more than the **larger** of—
  - $1,050, or
  - Your earned income (up to $5,950) plus $350.

☐ **Yes.** You must file a return if **any** of the following apply.
- Your unearned income was over $2,300 ($3,550 if 65 or older **and** blind).
- Your earned income was over $7,550 ($8,800 if 65 or older **and** blind).
- Your gross income was at least $5 and your spouse files a separate return and itemizes deductions.
- Your gross income was more than the **larger** of—
  - $2,300 ($3,550 if 65 or older **and** blind), or
  - Your earned income (up to $5,950) plus $1,600 ($2,850 if 65 or older **and** blind).

Chart C—Other Situations When You Must File

You must file a return if any of the five conditions below apply for 2016.

1. You owe any special taxes, including any of the following.
  a. Alternative minimum tax.
  b. Additional tax on a qualified plan, including an individual retirement arrangement (IRA), or other tax-favored account. But if you are filing a return only because you owe this tax, you can file **Form 5329** by itself.
  c. Household employment taxes. But if you are filing a return only because you owe this tax, you can file **Schedule H** by itself.
  d. Social security and Medicare tax on tips you didn't report to your employer or on wages you received from an employer who didn't withhold these taxes.
  e. Recapture of first-time homebuyer credit. See the instructions for line 60b.
  f. Write-in taxes, including uncollected social security and Medicare or RRTA tax on tips you reported to your employer or on group-term life insurance and additional taxes on health savings accounts. See the instructions for line 62.
  g. Recapture taxes. See the instructions for lines 44, 60b, and line 62.

2. You (or your spouse, if filing jointly) received health savings account, Archer MSA, or Medicare Advantage MSA distributions.

3. You had net earnings from self-employment of at least $400.

4. You had wages of $108.28 or more from a church or qualified church-controlled organization that is exempt from employer social security and Medicare taxes.

5. Advance payments of the premium tax credit were made for you, your spouse, or a dependent who enrolled in coverage through the Marketplace. You or whoever enrolled you should have received Form(s) 1095-A showing the amount of the advance payments.

Where To Report Certain Items From 2016 Forms W-2, 1095, 1097, 1098, and 1099

File electronically. You may be eligible for free tax software that will take the guesswork out of preparing your return. Free File makes available free brand-name software and free *e-file*. Visit *IRS.gov/freefile* for details.

If any federal income tax withheld is shown on these forms, include the tax withheld on Form 1040, line 64. If any state or local income tax withheld is shown on these forms and you deduct state and local income taxes on Schedule A, line 5, include the tax withheld in your deduction on that line.

Form	Item and Box in Which It Should Appear	Where To Report
W-2	Wages, tips, other compensation (box 1)	Form 1040, line 7
	Allocated tips (box 8)	See *Wages, Salaries, Tips, etc.*
	Dependent care benefits (box 10)	Form 2441, Part III
	Adoption benefits (box 12, code T)	Form 8839, line 20
	Employer contributions to an Archer MSA (box 12, code R)	Form 8853, line 1
	Employer contributions to a health savings account (box 12, code W)	Form 8889, line 9
	Uncollected social security and Medicare or RRTA tax (box 12, code A, B, M, or N)	See the instructions for Form 1040, line 62
W-2G	Gambling winnings (box 1)	Form 1040, line 21 (Schedule C or C-EZ for professional gamblers)
1095-A	Advance payment of premium tax credit (line 33, column c)	See Form 8962 and its instructions
1097-BTC	Bond tax credit	See Form 8912 and its instructions
1098	Mortgage interest (box 1)	Schedule A, line 10, but first see the instructions on Form 1098*
	Refund of overpaid interest (box 4)	Form 1040, line 21, but first see the instructions on Form 1098*
	Mortgage insurance premiums (box 5)	See the instructions for Schedule A, line 13*
	Points (box 6)	Schedule A, line 10, but first see the instructions on Form 1098*
1098-C	Contributions of motor vehicles, boats, and airplanes	Schedule A, line 17
1098-E	Student loan interest (box 1)	See the instructions for Form 1040, line 33*
1098-MA	Homeowner mortgage payments (box 3)	Schedule A, but first see the instructions on Form 1098-MA
1098-T	Qualified tuition and related expenses (box 1)	See the instructions for Form 1040, line 34, or Form 1040, line 50; but first see the instructions on Form 1098-T*
1099-A	Acquisition or abandonment of secured property	See Pub. 4681
1099-B	Sales price of stocks, bonds, etc. (box 1d), cost or other basis (box 1e), and adjustments (boxes 1f and 1g)	Form 8949 or Schedule D, whichever applies; see the Instructions for Form 8949
	Aggregate profit or (loss) on contracts (box 11)	Form 6781, line 1
	Bartering (box 13)	See Pub. 525
1099-C	Canceled debt (box 2)	See Pub. 4681
1099-DIV	Total ordinary dividends (box 1a)	Form 1040, line 9a
	Qualified dividends (box 1b)	See the instructions for Form 1040, line 9b
	Total capital gain distributions (box 2a)	Form 1040, line 13, or, if required, Schedule D, line 13
	Unrecaptured section 1250 gain (box 2b)	See the instructions for Schedule D, line 19
	Section 1202 gain (box 2c)	See *Exclusion of Gain on Qualified Small Business (QSB) Stock* in the instructions for Schedule D
	Collectibles (28%) gain (box 2d)	See the instructions for Schedule D, line 18
	Nondividend distributions (box 3)	See the instructions for Form 1040, line 9a
	Investment expenses (box 5)	Schedule A, line 23
	Foreign tax paid (box 6)	Form 1040, line 48, or Schedule A, line 8; but first see the instructions for line 48
	Exempt-interest dividends (box 10)	Form 1040, line 8b
	Specified private activity bond interest dividends (box 11)	Form 6251, line 12
1099-G	Unemployment compensation (box 1)	See the instructions for Form 1040, line 19
	State or local income tax refunds, credits, or offsets (box 2)	See the instructions for Form 1040, line 10, and if box 8 on Form 1099-G is checked, see the box 8 instructions
	RTAA payments (box 5)	Form 1040, line 21
	Taxable grants (box 6)	Form 1040, line 21*
	Agriculture payments (box 7)	See the Instructions for Schedule F or Pub. 225*
	Market gain (box 9)	See the Instructions for Schedule F

If the item relates to an activity for which you are required to file Schedule C, C-EZ, E, or F or Form 4835, report the taxable or deductible amount allocable to the activity on that schedule or form instead.

Form	Item and Box in Which It Should Appear	Where To Report
1099-INT	Interest income (box 1)	See the instructions on Form 1099-INT
	Early withdrawal penalty (box 2)	Form 1040, line 30
	Interest on U.S. savings bonds and Treasury obligations (box 3)	See the instructions on Form 1099-INT and the instructions for Form 1040, line 8a
	Investment expenses (box 5)	Schedule A, line 23
	Foreign tax paid (box 6)	Form 1040, line 48, or Schedule A, line 8; but first see the instructions for line 48
	Tax-exempt interest (box 8)	Form 1040, line 8b
	Specified private activity bond interest (box 9)	Form 6251, line 12
	Market discount (box 10)	Form 1040, line 8a
	Bond premium (box 11), bond premium on Treasury obligations (box 12), and bond premium on tax-exempt bond (box 13)	See the instructions on Form 1099-INT and Pub. 550
1099-K	Payment card and third party network transactions	Schedule C, C-EZ, E, or F
1099-LTC	Long-term care and accelerated death benefits	See Pub. 525 and the Instructions for Form 8853
1099-MISC	Rents (box 1)	See the Instructions for Schedule E*
	Royalties (box 2)	See the Instructions for Schedule E* (for timber, coal, and iron ore royalties, see Pub. 544)*
	Other income (box 3)	Form 1040, line 21*
	Nonemployee compensation (box 7)	Schedule C, C-EZ, or F; but if you were not self-employed, see the instructions on Form 1099-MISC
	Excess golden parachute payments (box 13)	See the instructions for Form 1040, line 62
	Other (boxes 5, 6, 8, 9, 10, 14, and 15b)	See the instructions on Form 1099-MISC
1099-OID	Original issue discount (box 1) Other periodic interest (box 2)	See the instructions on Form 1099-OID
	Early withdrawal penalty (box 3)	Form 1040, line 30
	Market discount (box 5)	Form 1040, line 8a
	Acquisition premium (box 6)	See the instructions on Form 1099-OID and Pub. 550
	Original issue discount on U.S. Treasury obligations (box 8)	See the instructions on Form 1099-OID
	Investment expenses (box 9)	Schedule A, line 23
	Bond premium (box 10)	See the instructions on Form 1099-OID and Pub. 550
1099-PATR	Patronage dividends and other distributions from a cooperative (boxes 1, 2, 3, and 5)	Schedule C, C-EZ, or F or Form 4835; but first see the instructions on Form 1099-PATR
	Domestic production activities deduction (box 6)	Form 8903, line 23
	Credits and other deductions (boxes 7, 8, and 10)	See the instructions on Form 1099-PATR
	Patron's AMT adjustment (box 9)	Form 6251, line 27
1099-Q	Qualified education program payments	See the instructions for Form 1040, line 21
1099-QA	Distributions from ABLE accounts	See the instructions for line 21, Form 5329, and Pub. 907
1099-R	Distributions from IRAs**	See the instructions for Form 1040, lines 15a and 15b
	Distributions from pensions, annuities, etc.	See the instructions for Form 1040, lines 16a and 16b
	Capital gain (box 3)	See the instructions on Form 1099-R
	Disability income with code 3 in box 7	See the instructions for Form 1040, line 7
1099-S	Gross proceeds from real estate transactions (box 2)	Form 4797, Form 6252, Form 8824, or Form 8949
	Buyer's part of real estate tax (box 5)	See the instructions for Schedule A, line 6*
1099-SA	Distributions from health savings accounts (HSAs)	Form 8889, line 14a
	Distributions from MSAs***	Form 8853
SSA-1099	Social security benefits	See the instructions for lines 20a and 20b
RRB-1099	Railroad retirement benefits	See the instructions for lines 20a and 20b

*If the item relates to an activity for which you are required to file Schedule C, C-EZ, E, or F or Form 4835, report the taxable or deductible amount allocable to the activity on that schedule or form instead.

**This includes distributions from Roth, SEP, and SIMPLE IRAs.

***This includes distributions from Archer and Medicare Advantage MSAs.

Line Instructions for Form 1040

You may be eligible for free tax software that will take the guesswork out of preparing your return. Free File makes available free brand-name software and free *e-file*. Visit *IRS.gov/freefile* for details.

Section references are to the Internal Revenue Code.

Name and Address

Print or type the information in the spaces provided. If you are married filing a separate return, enter your spouse's name on line 3 instead of below your name.

 TIP *If you filed a joint return for 2015 and you are filing a joint return for 2016 with the same spouse, be sure to enter your names and SSNs in the same order as on your 2015 return.*

Name Change

If you changed your name because of marriage, divorce, etc., be sure to report the change to the Social Security Administration (SSA) before filing your return. This prevents delays in processing your return and issuing refunds. It also safeguards your future social security benefits.

Address Change

If you plan to move after filing your return, use Form 8822 to notify the IRS of your new address.

P.O. Box

Enter your box number only if your post office doesn't deliver mail to your home.

Foreign Address

If you have a foreign address, enter the city name on the appropriate line. Do not enter any other information on that line, but also complete the spaces below that line. Do not abbreviate the country name. Follow the country's practice for entering the postal code and the name of the province, county, or state.

Death of a Taxpayer

See *Death of a Taxpayer* under *General Information,* later.

Social Security Number (SSN)

An incorrect or missing SSN can increase your tax, reduce your refund, or delay your refund. To apply for an SSN, fill in Form SS-5 and return it, along with the appropriate evidence documents, to the Social Security Administration (SSA). You can get Form SS-5 online at *www.socialsecurity.gov*, from your local SSA office, or by calling the SSA at 1-800-772-1213. It usually takes about 2 weeks to get an SSN once the SSA has all the evidence and information it needs.

Check that both the name and SSN on your Forms 1040, W-2, and 1099 agree with your social security card. If they do not, certain deductions and credits on your Form 1040 may be reduced or disallowed and you may not receive credit for your social security earnings. If your Form W-2 shows an incorrect SSN or name, notify your employer or the form-issuing agent as soon as possible to make sure your earnings are credited to your social security record. If the name or SSN on your social security card is incorrect, call the SSA.

IRS Individual Taxpayer Identification Numbers (ITINs) for Aliens

If you are a nonresident or resident alien and you do not have and are not eligible to get an SSN, you must apply for an ITIN. It takes about 7 weeks to get an ITIN.

If you already have an ITIN, enter it wherever your SSN is requested on your tax return.

Make sure your ITIN has not expired. ITINs that have not been included on a U.S. federal tax return at least once in the last three consecutive years will expire. In addition, ITINs that were as-signed before 2013 will expire according to an annual schedule, regardless of use. Expired ITINs must be renewed in order to avoid delays in processing your return.

An ITIN is for tax use only. It doesn't entitle you to social security benefits or change your employment or immigration status under U.S. law.

For more information on ITINs, including application, expiration, and renewal, see Form W-7 and its instructions.

If you receive an SSN after previously using an ITIN, stop using your ITIN. Use your SSN instead. Visit a local IRS office or write a letter to the IRS explaining that you now have an SSN and want all your tax records combined under your SSN. Details about what to include with the letter and where to mail it are at *IRS.gov/ITINinfo*.

Nonresident Alien Spouse

If your spouse is a nonresident alien, he or she must have either an SSN or an ITIN if:

- You file a joint return,
- You file a separate return and claim an exemption for your spouse, or
- Your spouse is filing a separate return.

Presidential Election Campaign Fund

This fund helps pay for Presidential election campaigns. The fund reduces candidates' dependence on large contributions from individuals and groups and places candidates on an equal financial footing in the general election. The fund also helps pay for pediatric medical research. If you want $3 to go to this fund, check the box. If you are filing a joint return, your spouse can also have $3 go to the fund. If you check a box, your tax or refund won't change.

Need more information or forms? Visit IRS.gov.

Filing Status

Check only the filing status that applies to you. The ones that will usually give you the lowest tax are listed last.

- Married filing separately.
- Single.
- Head of household.
- Married filing jointly.
- Qualifying widow(er) with dependent child.

For information about marital status, see Pub. 501.

 More than one filing status can apply to you. You can choose the one that will give you the lowest tax.

Line 1

Single

You can check the box on line 1 if any of the following was true on December 31, 2016.

- You were never married.
- You were legally separated according to your state law under a decree of divorce or separate maintenance. But if, at the end of 2016, your divorce wasn't final (an interlocutory decree), you are considered married and can't check the box on line 1.
- You were widowed before January 1, 2016, and didn't remarry before the end of 2016. But if you have a dependent child, you may be able to use the qualifying widow(er) filing status. See the instructions for line 5.

Line 2

Married Filing Jointly

You can check the box on line 2 if any of the following apply.

- You were married at the end of 2016, even if you didn't live with your spouse at the end of 2016.
- Your spouse died in 2016 and you didn't remarry in 2016.
- You were married at the end of 2016, and your spouse died in 2017 before filing a 2016 return.

A married couple filing jointly report their combined income and deduct their combined allowable expenses on one return. They can file a joint return even if only one had income or if they didn't live together all year. However, both persons must sign the return. Once you file a joint return, you can't choose to file separate returns for that year after the due date of the return.

Joint and several tax liability. If you file a joint return, both you and your spouse are generally responsible for the tax and interest or penalties due on the return. This means that if one spouse doesn't pay the tax due, the other may have to. Or, if one spouse doesn't report the correct tax, both spouses may be responsible for any additional taxes assessed by the IRS. You may want to file separately if:

- You believe your spouse isn't reporting all of his or her income, or
- You do not want to be responsible for any taxes due if your spouse doesn't have enough tax withheld or doesn't pay enough estimated tax.

See the instructions for line 3. Also see *Innocent Spouse Relief* under *General Information,* later.

Nonresident aliens and dual-status aliens. Generally, a married couple can't file a joint return if either spouse is a nonresident alien at any time during the year. However, if you were a nonresident alien or a dual-status alien and were married to a U.S. citizen or resident alien at the end of 2016, you can elect to be treated as a resident alien and file a joint return. See Pub. 519 for details.

Line 3

Married Filing Separately

If you are married and file a separate return, you generally report only your own income, exemptions, deductions, and credits. Generally, you are responsible only for the tax on your own income. Different rules apply to people in community property states; see Pub. 555.

However, you will usually pay more tax than if you use another filing status for which you qualify. Also, if you file a separate return, you can't take the student loan interest deduction, the tuition and fees deduction, the education credits, or the earned income credit. You also can't take the standard deduction if your spouse itemizes deductions.

Be sure to enter your spouse's SSN or ITIN on Form 1040. If your spouse doesn't have and isn't required to have an SSN or ITIN, enter "NRA."

 You may be able to file as head of household if you had a child living with you and you lived apart from your spouse during the last 6 months of 2016. See Married persons who live apart.

Line 4

Head of Household

This filing status is for unmarried individuals who provide a home for certain other persons. You are considered unmarried for this purpose if any of the following applies.

- You were legally separated according to your state law under a decree of divorce or separate maintenance at the end of 2016. But if, at the end of 2016, your divorce wasn't final (an interlocutory decree), you are considered married.
- You are married but lived apart from your spouse for the last 6 months of 2016 and you meet the other rules under *Married persons who live apart.*
- You are married to a nonresident alien at any time during the year and you do not choose to treat him or her as a resident alien.

Check the box on line 4 only if you are unmarried (or considered unmarried) and either *Test 1* or *Test 2* applies.

Test 1. You paid over half the cost of keeping up a home that was the main home for all of 2016 of your parent whom you can claim as a dependent on line 6c, except under a multiple support agreement (see the line 6c instructions). Your parent didn't have to live with you.

Test 2. You paid over half the cost of keeping up a home in which you lived and in which one of the following also lived for more than half of the year (if half or less, see *Exception to time lived with you*).

1. Any person whom you can claim as a dependent on line 6c. But do not include:

a. Your child whom you claim as your dependent because of the rule for *Children of divorced or separated parents* in the line 6c instructions,

b. Any person who is your dependent only because he or she lived with you for all of 2016, or

c. Any person you claimed as a dependent under a multiple support agreement. See the line 6c instructions.

2. Your unmarried qualifying child who isn't your dependent.

3. Your married qualifying child who isn't your dependent only because you can be claimed as a dependent on line 6c of someone else's 2016 return.

4. Your qualifying child who, even though you are the custodial parent, isn't your dependent because of the rule for *Children of divorced or separated parents* in the line 6c instructions.

If the child isn't claimed as your dependent on line 6c, enter the child's name on line 4. If you do not enter the name, it will take us longer to process your return.

Qualifying child. To find out if someone is your qualifying child, see Step 1 of the line 6c instructions.

Dependent. To find out if someone is your dependent, see the instructions for line 6c.

Exception to time lived with you. Temporary absences by you or the other person for special circumstances, such as school, vacation, business, medical care, military service, or detention in a juvenile facility, count as time lived in the home. Also see *Kidnapped child* in the line 6c instructions, if applicable.

If the person for whom you kept up a home was born or died in 2016, you still may be able to file as head of household. If the person is your qualifying child, the child must have lived with you for more than half the part of the year he or she was alive. If the person is anyone else, see Pub. 501.

Keeping up a home. To find out what is included in the cost of keeping up a home, see Pub. 501.

If you used payments you received under Temporary Assistance for Needy Families (TANF) or other public assistance programs to pay part of the cost of keeping up your home, you can't count them as money you paid. However, you must include them in the total cost of keeping up your home to figure if you paid over half the cost.

Married persons who live apart. Even if you were not divorced or legally separated at the end of 2016, you are considered unmarried if all of the following apply.

• You lived apart from your spouse for the last 6 months of 2016. Temporary absences for special circumstances, such as for business, medical care, school, or military service, count as time lived in the home.

• You file a separate return from your spouse.

• You paid over half the cost of keeping up your home for 2016.

• Your home was the main home of your child, stepchild, or foster child for more than half of 2016 (if half or less, see *Exception to time lived with you*, earlier).

• You can claim this child as your dependent or could claim the child except that the child's other parent can claim him or her under the rule for *Children of divorced or separated parents* in the line 6c instructions.

Adopted child. An adopted child is always treated as your own child. An adopted child includes a child lawfully placed with you for legal adoption.

Foster child. A foster child is any child placed with you by an authorized placement agency or by judgment, decree, or other order of any court of competent jurisdiction.

Line 5

Qualifying Widow(er) With Dependent Child

You can check the box on line 5 and use joint return tax rates for 2016 if all of the following apply.

1. Your spouse died in 2014 or 2015 and you didn't remarry before the end of 2016.

2. You have a child or stepchild you can claim as a dependent on line 6c. This doesn't include a foster child.

3. This child lived in your home for all of 2016. If the child didn't live with you for the required time, see *Exception to time lived with you*, later.

4. You paid over half the cost of keeping up your home.

5. You could have filed a joint return with your spouse the year he or she died, even if you didn't actually do so.

If your spouse died in 2016, you can't file as qualifying widow(er) with dependent child. Instead, see the instructions for line 2.

Adopted child. An adopted child is always treated as your own child. An adopted child includes a child lawfully placed with you for legal adoption.

Dependent. To find out if someone is your dependent, see the instructions for line 6c.

Exception to time lived with you. Temporary absences by you or the child for special circumstances, such as school, vacation, business, medical care, military service, or detention in a juvenile facility, count as time lived in the home. Also see *Kidnapped child* in the line 6c instructions, if applicable.

A child is considered to have lived with you for all of 2016 if the child was born or died in 2016 and your home was the child's home for the entire time he or she was alive.

Keeping up a home. To find out what is included in the cost of keeping up a home, see Pub. 501.

If you used payments you received under Temporary Assistance for Needy Families (TANF) or other public assistance programs to pay part of the cost of keeping up your home, you can't count them as money you paid. However, you must include them in the total cost of keeping up your home to figure if you paid over half the cost.

Exemptions

You usually can deduct $4,050 on line 42 for each exemption you can take.

Line 6b

Spouse

Check the box on line 6b if either of the following applies.

1. Your filing status is married filing jointly and your spouse can't be claimed as a dependent on another person's return.

2. You were married at the end of 2016, your filing status is married filing separately or head of household, and both of the following apply.

a. Your spouse had no income and isn't filing a return.

Need more information or forms? Visit IRS.gov.

b. Your spouse can't be claimed as a dependent on another person's return.

If your filing status is head of household and you check the box on line 6b, enter the name of your spouse on the dotted line next to line 6b. Also, enter your spouse's social security number in the space provided at the top of your return. If you became divorced or legally separated during 2016, you can't take an exemption for your former spouse.

Death of your spouse. If your spouse died in 2016 and you didn't remarry by the end of 2016, check the box on line 6b if you could have taken an exemption for your spouse on the date of death. For other filing instructions, see *Death of a Taxpayer* under *General Information,* later.

Line 6c—Dependents

Dependents and Qualifying Child for Child Tax Credit

Follow the steps below to find out if a person qualifies as your dependent, qualifies you to take the child tax credit, or both. If you have more than four dependents, check the box to the left of line 6c and include a statement showing the information required in columns (1) through (4).

Step 1 Do You Have a Qualifying Child?

A qualifying child is a child who is your...

Son, daughter, stepchild, foster child, brother, sister, stepbrother, stepsister, half brother, half sister, or a descendant of any of them (for example, your grandchild, niece, or nephew)

AND

was ...

Under age 19 at the end of 2016 and younger than you (or your spouse, if filing jointly)

or

Under age 24 at the end of 2016, a student (defined later), and younger than you (or your spouse, if filing jointly)

or

Any age and permanently and totally disabled (defined later)

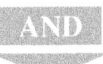

AND

Who didn't provide over half of his or her own support for 2016 (see Pub. 501)

AND

Who isn't filing a joint return for 2016
or is filing a joint return for 2016 only to claim a refund of withheld income tax or estimated tax paid (see Pub. 501 for details and examples)

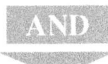

AND

Who lived with you for more than half of 2016. If the child didn't live with you for the required time, see *Exception to time lived with you*, later.

 If the child meets the conditions to be a qualifying child of any other person (other than your spouse if filing jointly) for 2016, see Qualifying child of more than one person, *later.*

1. Do you have a child who meets the conditions to be your qualifying child?
   ☐ **Yes.** Go to Step 2.   ☐ **No.** Go to Step 4.

Step 2 Is Your Qualifying Child Your Dependent?

1. Was the child a U.S. citizen, U.S. national, U.S. resident alien, or a resident of Canada or Mexico? (See Pub. 519 for the definition of a U.S. national or U.S. resident alien. If the child was adopted, see *Exception to citizen test,* later.)

   ☐ **Yes.** Continue   ☐ **No.**
   You can't claim this child as a dependent.

2. Was the child married?

   ☐ **Yes.** See *Married person,* later.   ☐ **No.** Continue

3. Could you, or your spouse if filing jointly, be claimed as a dependent on someone else's 2016 tax return? See Steps 1, 2, and 4.

   ☐ **Yes.** You can't claim any dependents. Go to Form 1040, line 7.   ☐ **No.** You can claim this child as a dependent. Complete Form 1040, line 6c, columns (1) through (3) for this child. Then, go to Step 3.

Step 3 Does Your Qualifying Child Qualify You for the Child Tax Credit?

1. Was the child under age 17 at the end of 2016?

   ☐ **Yes.** Continue   ☐ **No.**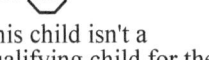
   This child isn't a qualifying child for the child tax credit.

2. Was the child a U.S. citizen, U.S. national, or U.S. resident alien? (See Pub. 519 for the definition of a U.S. national or U.S. resident alien. If the child was adopted, see *Exception to citizen test,* later.)

   ☐ **Yes.** This child is a qualifying child for the child tax credit. Check the box on Form 1040, line 6c, column (4).   ☐ **No.**
   This child isn't a qualifying child for the child tax credit.

Need more information or forms? Visit IRS.gov.

Step 4 Is Your Qualifying Relative Your Dependent?

A qualifying relative is a person who is your...

Son, daughter, stepchild, foster child, or a descendant of any of them (for example, your grandchild)

or

Brother, sister, half brother, half sister, or a son or daughter of any of them (for example, your niece or nephew)

or

Father, mother, or an ancestor or sibling of either of them (for example, your grandmother, grandfather, aunt, or uncle)

or

Stepbrother, stepsister, stepfather, stepmother, son-in-law, daughter-in-law, father-in-law, mother-in-law, brother-in-law, or sister-in-law

or

Any other person (other than your spouse) who lived with you all year as a member of your household if your relationship didn't violate local law. If the person didn't live with you for the required time, see *Exception to time lived with you*, later.

Who wasn't a qualifying child (see Step 1) of any taxpayer for 2016. For this purpose, a person isn't a taxpayer if he or she isn't required to file a U.S. income tax return **and** either doesn't file such a return or files only to get a refund of withheld income tax or estimated tax paid. See Pub. 501 for details and examples.

Who had gross income of less than $4,050 in 2016. If the person was permanently and totally disabled, see *Exception to gross income test*, later.

For whom you provided over half of his or her support in 2016. But see *Children of divorced or separated parents*, *Multiple support agreements*, and *Kidnapped child*, later.

1. Does any person meet the conditions to be your qualifying relative?

☐ **Yes.** Continue ☐ **No.** (STOP)

Go to Form 1040, line 7.

2. Was your qualifying relative a U.S. citizen, U.S. national, U.S. resident alien, or a resident of Canada or Mexico? (See Pub. 519 for the definition of a U.S. national or U.S. resident alien. If your qualifying relative was adopted, see *Exception to citizen test*, later.)

☐ **Yes.** Continue ☐ **No.** (STOP)
You can't claim this person as a dependent.

3. Was your qualifying relative married?

☐ **Yes.** See *Married person*, later. ☐ **No.** Continue ↘

4. Could you, or your spouse if filing jointly, be claimed as a dependent on someone else's 2016 tax return? See Steps 1, 2, and 4.

☐ **Yes.** (STOP)
You can't claim any dependents. Go to Form 1040, line 7.

☐ **No.** You can claim this person as a dependent. Complete Form 1040, line 6c, columns (1) through (3). Do not check the box on Form 1040, line 6c, column (4).

Definitions and Special Rules

Adopted child. An adopted child is always treated as your own child. An adopted child includes a child lawfully placed with you for legal adoption.

Adoption taxpayer identification numbers (ATINs). If you have a dependent who was placed with you for legal adoption and you do not know his or her SSN, you must get an ATIN for the dependent from the IRS. See Form W-7A for details. If the dependent isn't a U.S. citizen or resident alien, apply for an ITIN instead, using Form W-7.

If you didn't have an SSN (or ITIN) by the due date of your 2016 return (including extensions), you can't claim the child tax credit on either your original or an amended 2016 return, even if you later get an SSN (or ITIN). Also, no child tax credit is allowed on your original or an amended 2016 return with respect to a child who didn't have an SSN, ATIN, or ITIN by the due date of your return (including extensions), even if that child later gets one of those numbers.

If you apply for an ATIN or an ITIN on or before the due date of your 2016 return (including extensions) and the IRS issues you an ATIN or an ITIN as a result of the application, the IRS will consider your ATIN or ITIN as issued on or before the due date of your return.

Children of divorced or separated parents. A child will be treated as the qualifying child or qualifying relative of his or her noncustodial parent (defined later) if all of the following conditions apply.

1. The parents are divorced, legally separated, separated under a written separation agreement, or lived apart at all times during the last 6 months of 2016 (whether or not they are or were married).

2. The child received over half of his or her support for 2016 from the parents (and the rules on *Multiple support agreements*, later, do not apply). Support of a child received from a parent's spouse is treated as provided by the parent.

3. The child is in custody of one or both of the parents for more than half of 2016.

4. Either of the following applies.

a. The custodial parent signs Form 8332 or a substantially similar statement that he or she won't claim the child as a dependent for 2016, and the noncustodial parent includes a copy of the form or statement with his or her return. If the divorce decree or separation agreement went into effect after 1984 and before 2009, the noncustodial parent may be able to include certain pages from the decree or agreement instead of Form 8332. See *Post-1984 and pre-2009 decree or agreement* and *Post-2008 decree or agreement*.

b. A pre-1985 decree of divorce or separate maintenance or written separation agreement between the parents provides that the noncustodial parent can claim the child as a dependent, and the noncustodial parent provides at least $600 for support of the child during 2016.

If conditions (1) through (4) apply, only the noncustodial parent can claim the child for purposes of the dependency exemption (line 6c) and the child tax credits (lines 52 and 67). However, this doesn't allow the noncustodial parent to claim head of household filing status, the credit for child and dependent care expenses, the exclusion for dependent care benefits, the earned income credit, or the health coverage tax credit. See Pub. 501 for details.

Example. Even if conditions (1) through (4) are met and the custodial parent signs Form 8332 or a substantially similar statement that he or she will not claim the child as a dependent for 2016, this doesn't allow the noncustodial parent to claim the child as a qualifying child for the earned income credit. The custodial parent or another taxpayer, if eligible, can claim the child for the earned income credit.

Custodial and noncustodial parents. The custodial parent is the parent with whom the child lived for the greater number of nights in 2016. The noncustodial parent is the other parent. If the child was with each parent for an equal number of nights, the custodial parent is the parent with the higher adjusted gross income. See Pub. 501 for an exception for a parent who works at night, rules for a child who is emancipated under state law, and other details.

Post-1984 and pre-2009 decree or agreement. The decree or agreement must state all three of the following.

1. The noncustodial parent can claim the child as a dependent without regard to any condition, such as payment of support.

2. The other parent won't claim the child as a dependent.

3. The years for which the claim is released.

The noncustodial parent must include all of the following pages from the decree or agreement.
- Cover page (include the other parent's SSN on that page).
- The pages that include all the information identified in (1) through (3) above.

- Signature page with the other parent's signature and date of agreement.

 You must include the required information even if you filed it with your return in an earlier year.

Post-2008 decree or agreement. If the divorce decree or separation agreement went into effect after 2008, the noncustodial parent can't include pages from the decree or agreement instead of Form 8332. The custodial parent must sign either Form 8332 or a substantially similar statement the only purpose of which is to release the custodial parent's claim to an exemption for a child, and the noncustodial parent must include a copy with his or her return. The form or statement must release the custodial parent's claim to the child without any conditions. For example, the release must not depend on the noncustodial parent paying support.

Release of exemption revoked. A custodial parent who has revoked his or her previous release of a claim to exemption for a child must include a copy of the revocation with his or her return. For details, see Form 8332.

Exception to citizen test. If you are a U.S. citizen or U.S. national and your adopted child lived with you all year as a member of your household, that child meets the requirement to be a U.S. citizen in Step 2, question 1; Step 3, question 2; and Step 4, question 2.

Exception to gross income test. If your relative (including a person who lived with you all year as a member of your household) is permanently and totally disabled (defined later), certain income for services performed at a sheltered workshop may be excluded for this test. For details, see Pub. 501.

Exception to time lived with you. Temporary absences by you or the other person for special circumstances, such as school, vacation, business, medical care, military service, or detention in a juvenile facility, count as time the person lived with you. Also see *Children of divorced or separated parents*, earlier, or *Kidnapped child*, later.

If the person meets all other requirements to be your qualifying child but was born or died in 2016, the person is considered to have lived with you for more than half of 2016 if your home was this person's home for more than half the time he or she was alive in 2016.

Any other person is considered to have lived with you for all of 2016 if the person was born or died in 2016 and your home was this person's home for the entire time he or she was alive in 2016.

Foster child. A foster child is any child placed with you by an authorized placement agency or by judgment, decree, or other order of any court of competent jurisdiction.

Kidnapped child. If your child is presumed by law enforcement authorities to have been kidnapped by someone who isn't a family member, you may be able to take the child into account in determining your eligibility for head of household or qualifying widow(er) filing status, the dependency exemption, the child tax credit, and the earned income credit (EIC). For details, see Pub. 501 (Pub. 596 for the EIC).

Married person. If the person is married and files a joint return, you can't claim that person as your dependent. However, if the person is married but doesn't file a joint return or files a joint return only to claim a refund of withheld income tax or estimated tax paid, you may be able to claim him or her as a dependent. (See Pub. 501 for details and examples.) In that case, go to Step 2, question 3 (for a qualifying child) or Step 4, question 4 (for a qualifying relative).

Multiple support agreements. If no one person contributed over half of the support of your relative (or a person who lived with you all year as a member of your household) but you and another person(s) provided more than half of your relative's support, special rules may apply that would treat you as having provided over half of the support. For details, see Pub. 501.

Permanently and totally disabled. A person is permanently and totally disabled if, at any time in 2016, the person can't engage in any substantial gainful activity because of a physical or mental condition and a doctor has determined that this condition has lasted or can be expected to last continuously for at least a year or can be expected to lead to death.

Qualifying child of more than one person. Even if a child meets the conditions to be the qualifying child of more than one person, only one person can claim the child as a qualifying child for all of the following tax benefits, unless the special rule for *Children of divorced or separated parents,* described earlier, applies.

1. Dependency exemption (line 6c).

2. Child tax credits (lines 52 and 67).

3. Head of household filing status (line 4).

4. Credit for child and dependent care expenses (line 49).

5. Exclusion for dependent care benefits (Form 2441, Part III).

6. Earned income credit (lines 66a and 66b).

No other person can take any of the six tax benefits just listed unless he or she has a different qualifying child. If you and any other person can claim the child as a qualifying child, the following rules apply.

• If only one of the persons is the child's parent, the child is treated as the qualifying child of the parent.

• If the parents file a joint return together and can claim the child as a qualifying child, the child is treated as the qualifying child of the parents.

• If the parents do not file a joint return together but both parents claim the child as a qualifying child, the IRS will treat the child as the qualifying child of the parent with whom the child lived for the longer period of time in 2016. If the child lived with each parent for the same amount of time, the IRS will treat the child as the qualifying child of the parent who had the higher adjusted gross income (AGI) for 2016.

• If no parent can claim the child as a qualifying child, the child is treated as the qualifying child of the person who had the highest AGI for 2016.

• If a parent can claim the child as a qualifying child but no parent does so claim the child, the child is treated as the qualifying child of the person who had the highest AGI for 2016, but only if that person's AGI is higher than the highest AGI of any parent of the child who can claim the child.

Example. Your daughter meets the conditions to be a qualifying child for both you and your mother. Your daughter doesn't meet the conditions to be a qualifying child of any other person, including her other parent. Under the rules just described, you can claim your daughter as a qualifying child for all of the six tax benefits just listed for which you otherwise qualify. Your mother can't claim any of those six tax benefits unless she has a different qualifying child. However, if your mother's AGI is higher than yours and you do not claim your daughter as a qualifying child, your daughter is the qualifying child of your mother.

For more details and examples, see Pub. 501.

If you will be claiming the child as a qualifying child, go to Step 2. Otherwise, stop; you can't claim any benefits based on this child.

Social security number. You must enter each dependent's social security number (SSN). Be sure the name and SSN entered agree with the dependent's social security card. Otherwise, at the time we process your return, we may disallow the exemption claimed for the dependent and reduce or disallow any other tax benefits (such as the child tax credit) based on that dependent. If the name or SSN on the dependent's social security card isn't correct or you need to get an SSN for your dependent, contact the Social Security Administration. See *Social Security Number (SSN),* earlier. If your dependent won't have a number by the date your return is due, see *What if You Can't File on Time?* earlier.

If your dependent child was born and died in 2016 and you do not have an SSN for the child, enter "Died" in column (2) and include a copy of the child's birth certificate, death certificate, or hospital records. The document must show the child was born alive.

If you didn't have an SSN (or ITIN) by the due date of your 2016 return (including extensions), you can't claim the child tax credit on either your original or an amended 2016 return, even if you later get an SSN (or ITIN). Also, no child tax credit is allowed on your original or an amended 2016 return with respect to a child who didn't have an SSN, ATIN, or ITIN by the due date of your return (including extensions), even if that child later gets one of those numbers.

If you apply for an ATIN or an ITIN on or before the due date of your 2016 return (including extensions) and the IRS issues you an ATIN or an ITIN as a result of the application, the IRS will consider your ATIN or ITIN as issued on or before the due date of your return.

Student. A student is a child who during any part of 5 calendar months of 2016 was enrolled as a full-time student at a school, or took a full-time, on-farm training course given by a school or a state, county, or local government agency. A school includes a technical, trade, or mechanical school. It doesn't include an on-the-job training course, correspondence school, or school offering courses only through the Internet.

Income

Generally, you must report all income except income that is exempt from tax by law. For details, see the following instructions, especially the instructions for lines 7 through 21. Also see Pub. 525.

Foreign-Source Income

You must report unearned income, such as interest, dividends, and pensions, from sources outside the United States unless exempt by law or a tax treaty. You must also report earned income, such as wages and tips, from sources outside the United States.

If you worked abroad, you may be able to exclude part or all of your foreign earned income. For details, see Pub. 54 and Form 2555 or 2555-EZ.

Foreign retirement plans. If you were a beneficiary of a foreign retirement plan, you may have to report the undistributed income earned in your plan. However, if you were the beneficiary of a Canadian registered retirement plan, see Rev. Proc. 2014-55, 2014-44 I.R.B. 753, available at *IRS.gov//irb/ 2014-44_IRB/ar10.html*, to find out if you can elect to defer tax on the undistributed income.

Report distributions from foreign pension plans on lines 16a and 16b.

Foreign accounts and trusts. You must complete Part III of Schedule B if you:
- Had a foreign account, or
- Received a distribution from, or were a grantor of, or a transferor to, a foreign trust.

Foreign financial assets. If you had foreign financial assets in 2016, you may have to file Form 8938. See Form 8938 and its instructions.

Chapter 11 Bankruptcy Cases

If you are a debtor in a chapter 11 bankruptcy case, income taxable to the bankruptcy estate and reported on the estate's income tax return includes:
- Earnings from services you performed after the beginning of the case (both wages and self-employment income), and
- Income from property described in section 541 of title 11 of the U.S. Code

that you either owned when the case began or that you acquired after the case began and before the case was closed, dismissed, or converted to a case under a different chapter.

Because this income is taxable to the estate, do not include this income on your own individual income tax return. The only exception is for purposes of figuring your self-employment tax. For that purpose, you must take into account all your self-employment income for the year from services performed both before and after the beginning of the case. Also, you (or the trustee, if one is appointed) must allocate between you and the bankruptcy estate the wages, salary, or other compensation and withheld income tax reported to you on Form W-2. A similar allocation is required for income and withheld income tax reported to you on Forms 1099. You must also include a statement that indicates you filed a chapter 11 case and that explains how income and withheld income tax reported to you on Forms W-2 and 1099 are allocated between you and the estate. For more details, including acceptable allocation methods, see Notice 2006-83, 2006-40 I.R.B. 596, available at *IRS.gov/irb/2006-40_IRB/ar12.html*.

Community Property States

Community property states are Arizona, California, Idaho, Louisiana, Nevada, New Mexico, Texas, Washington, and Wisconsin. If you and your spouse lived in a community property state, you must usually follow state law to determine what is community income and what is separate income. For details, see Form 8958 and Pub. 555.

Nevada, Washington, and California domestic partners. A registered domestic partner in Nevada, Washington, or California generally must report half the combined community income of the individual and his or her domestic partner. See Form 8958 and Pub. 555.

Rounding Off to Whole Dollars

You can round off cents to whole dollars on your return and schedules. If you do round to whole dollars, you must round all amounts. To round, drop amounts under 50 cents and increase amounts from 50 to 99 cents to the next dollar. For example, $1.39 becomes $1 and $2.50 becomes $3.

If you have to add two or more amounts to figure the amount to enter on a line, include cents when adding the amounts and round off only the total.

Line 7

Wages, Salaries, Tips, etc.

Enter the total of your wages, salaries, tips, etc. If a joint return, also include your spouse's income. For most people, the amount to enter on this line should be shown in box 1 of their Form(s) W-2. But the following types of income must also be included in the total on line 7.
- All wages received as a household employee. An employer is not required to provide a Form W-2 to you if he or she paid you wages of less then $2,000 in 2016. If you received wages as a household employee and you didn't receive a Form W-2 because an employer paid you less than $2,000 in 2016, enter "HSH" and the amount not reported to you on a Form W-2 in the space to the left of line 7. For information on employment taxes for household employees, see *Tax Topic 756*.
- Tip income you didn't report to your employer. This should include any allocated tips shown in box 8 on your Form(s) W-2 unless you can prove that your unreported tips are less than the amount in box 8. Allocated tips aren't included as income in box 1. See Pub. 531 for more details. Also include the value of any noncash tips you received, such as tickets, passes, or other items of value. Although you do not report these noncash tips to your employer, you must report them on line 7.

 You may owe social security and Medicare or railroad retirement (RRTA) tax on unreported tips. See the instructions for line 58.

- Dependent care benefits, which should be shown in box 10 of your Form(s) W-2. But first complete Form 2441 to see if you can exclude part or all of the benefits.
- Employer-provided adoption benefits, which should be shown in box 12 of your Form(s) W-2 with code T. But see the Instructions for Form 8839 to find out if you can exclude part or all of the benefits. You may also be able to exclude amounts if you adopted a child

Need more information or forms? Visit IRS.gov.

with special needs and the adoption became final in 2016.

• Scholarship and fellowship grants not reported on Form W-2. Also, enter "SCH" and the amount on the dotted line next to line 7. However, if you were a degree candidate, include on line 7 only the amounts you used for expenses other than tuition and course-related expenses. For example, amounts used for room, board, and travel must be reported on line 7.

• Excess salary deferrals. The amount deferred should be shown in box 12 of your Form W-2, and the "Retirement plan" box in box 13 should be checked. If the total amount you (or your spouse if filing jointly) deferred for 2016 under all plans was more than $18,000 (excluding catch-up contributions as explained later), include the excess on line 7. This limit is (a) $12,500 if you have only SIMPLE plans, or (b) $21,000 for section 403(b) plans if you qualify for the 15-year rule in Pub. 571. Although designated Roth contributions are subject to this limit, do not include the excess attributable to such contributions on line 7. They are already included as income in box 1 of your Form W-2.

A higher limit may apply to participants in section 457(b) deferred compensation plans for the 3 years before retirement age. Contact your plan administrator for more information.

If you were age 50 or older at the end of 2016, your employer may have allowed an additional deferral (catch-up contributions) of up to $6,000 ($3,000 for section 401(k)(11) and SIMPLE plans). This additional deferral amount isn't subject to the overall limit on elective deferrals.

 You can't deduct the amount deferred. It isn't included as income in box 1 of your Form W-2.

• Disability pensions shown on Form 1099-R if you have not reached the minimum retirement age set by your employer. But see *Insurance Premiums for Retired Public Safety Officers* in the instructions for lines 16a and 16b. Disability pensions received after you reach minimum retirement age and other payments shown on Form 1099-R (other than payments from an IRA*) are repor-

ted on lines 16a and 16b. Payments from an IRA are reported on lines 15a and 15b.

• Corrective distributions from a retirement plan shown on Form 1099-R of excess salary deferrals and excess contributions (plus earnings). But do not include distributions from an IRA* on line 7. Instead, report distributions from an IRA on lines 15a and 15b.

• Wages from Form 8919, line 6.

This includes a Roth, SEP, or SIMPLE IRA.

Were You a Statutory Employee?

If you were, the "Statutory employee" box in box 13 of your Form W-2 should be checked. Statutory employees include full-time life insurance salespeople and certain agent or commission drivers, traveling salespeople, and homeworkers. If you have related business expenses to deduct, report the amount shown in box 1 of your Form W-2 on Schedule C or C-EZ along with your expenses.

Missing or Incorrect Form W-2?

Your employer is required to provide or send Form W-2 to you no later than January 31, 2017. If you do not receive it by early February, use *Tax Topic 154* to find out what to do. Even if you do not get a Form W-2, you must still report your earnings on line 7. If you lose your Form W-2 or it is incorrect, ask your employer for a new one.

Line 8a

Taxable Interest

Each payer should send you a Form 1099-INT or Form 1099-OID. Enter your total taxable interest income on line 8a. But you must fill in and attach Schedule B if the total is over $1,500 or any of the other conditions listed at the beginning of the Schedule B instructions apply to you.

For more details about reporting taxable interest, including market discount on bonds and adjustments for amortizable bond premium, see Pub. 550.

Interest credited in 2016 on deposits that you couldn't withdraw because of the bankruptcy or insolvency of the financial institution may not have to be included in your 2016 income. For details, see Pub. 550.

 If you get a 2016 Form 1099-INT for U.S. savings bond interest that includes amounts you reported before 2016, see Pub. 550.

Line 8b

Tax-Exempt Interest

If you received any tax-exempt interest, such as from municipal bonds, each payer should send you a Form 1099-INT. Your tax-exempt interest should be shown in box 8 of Form 1099-INT. Enter the total on line 8b. However, if you acquired a tax-exempt bond at a premium, only report the net amount of tax-exempt interest on line 8b (that is, the excess of the tax-exempt interest received during the year over the amortized bond premium for the year). See Pub. 550 for more information. Also include on line 8b any exempt-interest dividends from a mutual fund or other regulated investment company. This amount should be shown in box 10 of Form 1099-DIV.

Do not include interest earned on your IRA, health savings account, Archer or Medicare Advantage MSA, or Coverdell education savings account.

Line 9a

Ordinary Dividends

Each payer should send you a Form 1099-DIV. Enter your total ordinary dividends on line 9a. This amount should be shown in box 1a of Form(s) 1099-DIV.

You must fill in and attach Schedule B if the total is over $1,500 or you received, as a nominee, ordinary dividends that actually belong to someone else.

Nondividend Distributions

Some distributions are a return of your cost (or other basis). They won't be taxed until you recover your cost (or other basis). You must reduce your cost (or other basis) by these distributions. After you get back all of your cost (or other basis), you must report these distributions as capital gains on Form 8949. For details, see Pub. 550.

Dividends on insurance policies are a partial return of the premiums you paid. Do not report them as dividends. Include them in income on line 21 only if they exceed the total of all net premiums you paid for the contract.

Line 9b

Qualified Dividends

Enter your total qualified dividends on line 9b. Qualified dividends are also included in the ordinary dividend total required to be shown on line 9a. Qualified dividends are eligible for a lower tax rate than other ordinary income. Generally, these dividends are shown in box 1b of Form(s) 1099-DIV. See Pub. 550 for the definition of qualified dividends if you received dividends not reported on Form 1099-DIV.

Exception. Some dividends may be reported as qualified dividends in box 1b of Form 1099-DIV but aren't qualified dividends. These include:

• Dividends you received as a nominee. See the Schedule B instructions.

• Dividends you received on any share of stock that you held for less than 61 days during the 121-day period that began 60 days before the ex-dividend date. The ex-dividend date is the first date following the declaration of a dividend on which the purchaser of a stock isn't entitled to receive the next dividend payment. When counting the number of days you held the stock, include the day you disposed of the stock but not the day you acquired it. See the examples that follow. Also, when counting the number of days you held the stock, you can't count certain days during which your risk of loss was diminished. See Pub. 550 for more details.

• Dividends attributable to periods totaling more than 366 days that you received on any share of preferred stock held for less than 91 days during the 181-day period that began 90 days before the ex-dividend date. When counting the number of days you held the stock, you can't count certain days during which your risk of loss was diminished. See Pub. 550 for more details. Preferred dividends attributable to periods totaling less than 367 days are subject to the 61-day holding period rule just described.

• Dividends on any share of stock to the extent that you are under an obligation (including a short sale) to make related payments with respect to positions in substantially similar or related property.

• Payments in lieu of dividends, but only if you know or have reason to know that the payments aren't qualified dividends.

Example 1. You bought 5,000 shares of XYZ Corp. common stock on July 8, 2016. XYZ Corp. paid a cash dividend of 10 cents per share. The ex-dividend date was July 16, 2016. Your Form 1099-DIV from XYZ Corp. shows $500 in box 1a (ordinary dividends) and in box 1b (qualified dividends). However, you sold the 5,000 shares on August 11, 2016. You held your shares of XYZ Corp. for only 34 days of the 121-day period (from July 9, 2016, through August 11, 2016). The 121-day period began on May 17, 2016 (60 days before the ex-dividend date), and ended on September 14, 2016. You have no qualified dividends from XYZ Corp. because you held the XYZ stock for less than 61 days.

Example 2. The facts are the same as in Example 1 except that you bought the stock on July 15, 2016 (the day before the ex-dividend date), and you sold the stock on September 16, 2016. You held the stock for 63 days (from July 16, 2016, through September 16, 2016). The $500 of qualified dividends shown in box 1b of Form 1099-DIV are all qualified dividends because you held the stock for 61 days of the 121-day period (from July 16, 2016, through September 14, 2016).

Example 3. You bought 10,000 shares of ABC Mutual Fund common stock on July 8, 2016. ABC Mutual Fund paid a cash dividend of 10 cents a share. The ex-dividend date was July 16, 2016. The ABC Mutual Fund advises you that the part of the dividend eligible to be treated as qualified dividends equals 2 cents a share. Your Form 1099-DIV from ABC Mutual Fund shows total ordinary dividends of $1,000 and qualified dividends of $200. However, you sold the 10,000 shares on August 11, 2016. You have no qualified dividends from ABC Mutual Fund because you held the ABC Mutual Fund stock for less than 61 days.

 Use the Qualified Dividends and Capital Gain Tax Worksheet or the Schedule D Tax Worksheet, whichever applies, to figure your tax. See the instructions for line 44 for details.

Line 10

Taxable Refunds, Credits, or Offsets of State and Local Income Taxes

 None of your refund is taxable if, in the year you paid the tax, you either (a) didn't itemize deductions, or (b) elected to deduct state and local general sales taxes instead of state and local income taxes.

If you received a refund, credit, or offset of state or local income taxes in 2016, you may be required to report this amount. If you didn't receive a Form 1099-G, check with the government agency that made the payments to you. Your 2016 Form 1099-G may have been made available to you only in an electronic format, and you will need to get instructions from the agency to retrieve this document. Report any taxable refund you received even if you didn't receive Form 1099-G.

If you chose to apply part or all of the refund to your 2016 estimated state or local income tax, the amount applied is treated as received in 2016. If the refund was for a tax you paid in 2015 and you deducted state and local income taxes on line 5 of your 2015 Schedule A, use the State and Local Income Tax Refund Worksheet in these instructions to see if any of your refund is taxable.

Exception. See *Itemized Deduction Recoveries* in Pub. 525 instead of using the State and Local Income Tax Refund Worksheet in these instructions if any of the following applies.

1. You received a refund in 2016 that is for a tax year other than 2015.

2. You received a refund other than an income tax refund, such as a general sales tax or real property tax refund, in 2016 of an amount deducted or credit claimed in an earlier year.

3. The amount on your 2015 Form 1040, line 42, was more than the amount on your 2015 Form 1040, line 41.

State and Local Income Tax Refund Worksheet—Line 10

Keep for Your Records

Before you begin: ✓ Be sure you have read the **Exception** in the instructions for this line to see if you can use this worksheet instead of Pub. 525 to figure if any of your refund is taxable.

1. Enter the income tax refund from **Form(s) 1099-G** (or similar statement). But **don't** enter more than the amount of your state and local income taxes shown on your 2015 Schedule A, line 5 .... **1.** _____

2. Enter your total itemized deductions from your 2015 Schedule A, line 29 .... **2.** _____

   Note. If the filing status on your 2015 Form 1040 was married filing separately and your spouse itemized deductions in 2015, skip lines 3 through 5, enter the amount from line 2 on line 6, and go to line 7.

3. Enter the amount shown below for the filing status claimed on your **2015** Form 1040.
   - Single or married filing separately—$6,300
   - Married filing jointly or qualifying widow(er)—$12,600
   - Head of household—$9,250
   } **3.** _____

4. Did you fill in line 39a on your 2015 Form 1040?

   ☐ **No.** Enter -0-.

   ☐ **Yes.** Multiply the number in the box on line 39a of your 2015 Form 1040 by $1,250 ($1,550 if your 2015 filing status was single or head of household). } **4.** _____

5. Add lines 3 and 4 .... **5.** _____

6. Is the amount on line 5 less than the amount on line 2?

   ☐ **No.** (STOP) None of your refund is taxable.

   ☐ **Yes.** Subtract line 5 from line 2 .... **6.** _____

7. **Taxable part of your refund.** Enter the **smaller** of line 1 or line 6 here and on Form 1040, line 10 .... **7.** _____

4. You had taxable income on your 2015 Form 1040, line 43, but no tax on your Form 1040, line 44, because of the 0% tax rate on net capital gain and qualified dividends in certain situations.

5. Your 2015 state and local income tax refund is more than your 2015 state and local income tax deduction minus the amount you could have deducted as your 2015 state and local general sales taxes.

6. You made your last payment of 2015 estimated state or local income tax in 2016.

7. You owed alternative minimum tax in 2015.

8. You couldn't use the full amount of credits you were entitled to in 2015 because the total credits were more than the amount shown on your 2015 Form 1040, line 47.

9. You could be claimed as a dependent by someone else in 2015.

10. You received a refund because of a jointly filed state or local income tax return, but you aren't filing a joint 2016 Form 1040 with the same person.

11. You had to use the Itemized Deductions Worksheet in the 2015 Instructions for Schedule A and both of the following apply.

   a. You couldn't deduct all of the amount on the 2015 Itemized Deductions Worksheet, line 1.

   b. The amount on line 8 of that 2015 worksheet would be more than the amount on line 4 of that worksheet if the amount on line 4 were reduced by 80% of the refund you received in 2016.

Line 11

Alimony Received

Enter amounts received as alimony or separate maintenance. You must let the person who made the payments know your social security number. If you do not, you may have to pay a penalty. For more details, see Pub. 504.

Line 12

Business Income or (Loss)

If you operated a business or practiced your profession as a sole proprietor, report your income and expenses on Schedule C or C-EZ.

Line 13

Capital Gain or (Loss)

If you sold a capital asset, such as a stock or bond, you must complete and attach Form 8949 and Schedule D.

Exception 1. You do not have to file Form 8949 or Schedule D if both of the following apply.

1. You have no capital losses, and your only capital gains are capital gain distributions from Form(s) 1099-DIV, box 2a (or substitute statements).

2. None of the Form(s) 1099-DIV (or substitute statements) have an amount in box 2b (unrecaptured section 1250 gain), box 2c (section 1202 gain), or box 2d (collectibles (28%) gain).

Exception 2. You must file Schedule D, but generally do not have to file Form 8949, if *Exception 1* doesn't apply and your only capital gains and losses are:

• Capital gain distributions,
• A capital loss carryover from 2015,
• A gain from Form 2439 or 6252 or Part I of Form 4797,
• A gain or loss from Form 4684, 6781, or 8824,
• A gain or loss from a partnership, S corporation, estate, or trust, or
• Gains and losses from transactions for which you received a Form 1099-B (or substitute statement) that shows basis was reported to the IRS and for which you do not need to make any adjustments in column (g) of Form 8949 or enter any codes in column (f) of Form 8949.

If *Exception 1* applies, enter your total capital gain distributions (from box 2a of Form(s) 1099-DIV) on line 13 and check the box on that line. If you received capital gain distributions as a nominee (that is, they were paid to you but actually belong to someone else), report on line 13 only the amount that belongs to you. Include a statement showing the full amount you received and the amount you received as a nominee. See the Schedule B instructions for filing requirements for Forms 1099-DIV and 1096.

 If you do not have to file Schedule D, use the Qualified Dividends and Capital Gain Tax Worksheet in the line 44 instructions to figure your tax.

Line 14

Other Gains or (Losses)

If you sold or exchanged assets used in a trade or business, see the Instructions for Form 4797.

Lines 15a and 15b

IRA Distributions

You should receive a Form 1099-R showing the total amount of any distribution from your IRA before income tax or other deductions were withheld. This amount should be shown in box 1 of Form 1099-R. Unless otherwise noted in the line 15a and 15b instructions, an IRA includes a traditional IRA, Roth IRA (including a *my*RA), simplified employee pension (SEP) IRA, and a savings incentive match plan for employees (SIMPLE) IRA. Except as provided next, leave line 15a blank and enter the total distribution (from Form 1099-R, box 1) on line 15b.

Exception 1. Enter the total distribution on line 15a if you rolled over part or all of the distribution from one:
• Roth IRA to another Roth IRA, or
• IRA (other than a Roth IRA) to a qualified plan or another IRA (other than a Roth IRA).

Also, enter "Rollover" next to line 15b. If the total distribution was rolled over in a qualified rollover, enter -0- on line 15b. If the total distribution wasn't rolled over in a qualified rollover, enter the part not rolled over on line 15b unless *Exception 2* applies to the part not rolled over. Generally, a qualified rollover must be made within 60 days after the day you received the distribution. For more details on rollovers, see Pub. 590-A and Pub. 590-B.

If you rolled over the distribution into a qualified plan other than an IRA or you made the rollover in 2017, include a statement explaining what you did.

Exception 2. If any of the following apply, enter the total distribution on line 15a and see Form 8606 and its instructions to figure the amount to enter on line 15b.

1. You received a distribution from an IRA (other than a Roth IRA) and you made nondeductible contributions to any of your traditional or SEP IRAs for 2016 or an earlier year. If you made nondeductible contributions to these IRAs for 2016, also see Pub. 590-A and Pub. 590-B.

2. You received a distribution from a Roth IRA. But if either (a) or (b) below applies, enter -0- on line 15b; you do not have to see Form 8606 or its instructions.

a. Distribution code T is shown in box 7 of Form 1099-R and you made a contribution (including a conversion) to a Roth IRA for 2011 or an earlier year.

b. Distribution code Q is shown in box 7 of Form 1099-R.

3. You converted part or all of a traditional, SEP, or SIMPLE IRA to a Roth IRA in 2016.

4. You had a 2015 or 2016 IRA contribution returned to you, with the related earnings or less any loss, by the due date (including extensions) of your tax return for that year.

5. You made excess contributions to your IRA for an earlier year and had them returned to you in 2016.

6. You recharacterized part or all of a contribution to a Roth IRA as a traditional IRA contribution, or vice versa.

Exception 3. If the distribution is a qualified charitable distribution (QCD), enter the total distribution on line 15a. If the total amount distributed is a QCD, enter -0- on line 15b. If only part of the distribution is a QCD, enter the part that is not a QCD on line 15b unless *Exception 2* applies to that part. Enter "QCD" next to line 15b.

A QCD is a distribution made directly by the trustee of your IRA (other than an ongoing SEP or SIMPLE IRA) to an organization eligible to receive tax-deductible contributions (with certain exceptions). You must have been at least age 70½ when the distribution was made.

Generally, your total QCDs for the year can't be more than $100,000. (On a joint return, your spouse can also have a QCD of up to $100,000.) The amount of the QCD is limited to the amount that

Need more information or forms? Visit IRS.gov.

would otherwise be included in your income. If your IRA includes nondeductible contributions, the distribution is first considered to be paid out of otherwise taxable income. See Pub. 590-A for details.

 You can't claim a charitable contribution deduction for any QCD not included in your income.

Exception 4. If the distribution is a health savings account (HSA) funding distribution (HFD), enter the total distribution on line 15a. If the total amount distributed is an HFD and you elect to exclude it from income, enter -0- on line 15b. If only part of the distribution is an HFD and you elect to exclude that part from income, enter the part that isn't an HFD on line 15b unless *Exception 2* applies to that part. Enter "HFD" next to line 15b.

An HFD is a distribution made directly by the trustee of your IRA (other than an ongoing SEP or SIMPLE IRA) to your HSA. If eligible, you generally can elect to exclude an HFD from your income once in your lifetime. You can't exclude more than the limit on HSA contributions or more than the amount that would otherwise be included in your income. If your IRA includes nondeductible contributions, the HFD is first considered to be paid out of otherwise taxable income. See Pub. 969 for details.

 The amount of an HFD reduces the amount you can contribute to your HSA for the year. If you fail to maintain eligibility for an HSA for the 12 months following the month of the HFD, you may have to report the HFD as income and pay an additional tax. See Form 8889, Part III.

More than one exception applies. If more than one exception applies, include a statement showing the amount of each exception, instead of making an entry next to line 15b. For example: "Line 15b – $1,000 Rollover and $500 HFD." But you do not need to attach a statement if only *Exception 2* and one other exception apply.

More than one distribution. If you (or your spouse if filing jointly) received more than one distribution, figure the taxable amount of each distribution and enter the total of the taxable amounts on

line 15b. Enter the total amount of those distributions on line 15a.

 You may have to pay an additional tax if (a) you received an early distribution from your IRA and the total wasn't rolled over, or (b) you were born before July 1, 1945, and received less than the minimum required distribution from your traditional, SEP, and SIMPLE IRAs. See the instructions for line 59 for details.

More information. For more information about IRAs, see Pub. 590-A and Pub. 590-B.

Lines 16a and 16b
Pensions and Annuities

You should receive a Form 1099-R showing the total amount of your pension and annuity payments before income tax or other deductions were withheld. This amount should be shown in box 1 of Form 1099-R. Pension and annuity payments include distributions from 401(k), 403(b), and governmental 457(b) plans. Rollovers and lump-sum distributions are explained later. Do not include the following payments on lines 16a and 16b. Instead, report them on line 7.

• Disability pensions received before you reach the minimum retirement age set by your employer.

• Corrective distributions (including any earnings) of excess salary deferrals or excess contributions to retirement plans. The plan must advise you of the year(s) the distributions are includible in income.

 Attach Form(s) 1099-R to Form 1040 if any federal income tax was withheld.

Fully Taxable Pensions and Annuities

Your payments are fully taxable if (a) you didn't contribute to the cost (see *Cost,* later) of your pension or annuity, or (b) you got your entire cost back tax free before 2016. But see *Insurance Premiums for Retired Public Safety Officers,* later. If your pension or annuity is fully taxable, enter the total pension or annuity payments (from Form(s) 1099-R, box 1) on line 16b; do not make an entry on line 16a.

Fully taxable pensions and annuities also include military retirement pay shown on Form 1099-R. For details on military disability pensions, see Pub. 525. If you received a Form RRB-1099-R, see Pub. 575 to find out how to report your benefits.

Partially Taxable Pensions and Annuities

Enter the total pension or annuity payments (from Form 1099-R, box 1) on line 16a. If your Form 1099-R doesn't show the taxable amount, you must use the General Rule explained in Pub. 939 to figure the taxable part to enter on line 16b. But if your annuity starting date (defined later) was after July 1, 1986, see *Simplified Method,* later, to find out if you must use that method to figure the taxable part.

You can ask the IRS to figure the taxable part for you for a $1,000 fee. For details, see Pub. 939.

If your Form 1099-R shows a taxable amount, you can report that amount on line 16b. But you may be able to report a lower taxable amount by using the General Rule or the Simplified Method or if the exclusion for retired public safety officers, discussed next, applies.

Insurance Premiums for Retired Public Safety Officers

If you are an eligible retired public safety officer (law enforcement officer, firefighter, chaplain, or member of a rescue squad or ambulance crew), you can elect to exclude from income distributions made from your eligible retirement plan that are used to pay the premiums for coverage by an accident or health plan or a long-term care insurance contract. You can do this only if you retired because of disability or because you reached normal retirement age. The premiums can be for coverage for you, your spouse, or dependents. The distribution must be from a plan maintained by the employer from which you retired as a public safety officer. Also, the distribution must be made directly from the plan to the provider of the accident or health plan or long-term care insurance contract. You can exclude from income the smaller of the amount of the premiums or $3,000. You can make this election only for amounts that would otherwise be included in your income.

An eligible retirement plan is a governmental plan that is a qualified trust or a section 403(a), 403(b), or 457(b) plan.

If you make this election, reduce the otherwise taxable amount of your pension or annuity by the amount excluded. The amount shown in box 2a of Form 1099-R doesn't reflect the exclusion. Report your total distributions on line 16a and the taxable amount on line 16b. Enter "PSO" next to line 16b.

If you are retired on disability and reporting your disability pension on line 7, include only the taxable amount on that line and enter "PSO" and the amount excluded on the dotted line next to line 7.

Simplified Method

You must use the Simplified Method if either of the following applies.

1. Your annuity starting date was after July 1, 1986, and you used this method last year to figure the taxable part.

2. Your annuity starting date was after November 18, 1996, and both of the following apply.

a. The payments are from a qualified employee plan, a qualified employee annuity, or a tax-sheltered annuity.

b. On your annuity starting date, either you were under age 75 or the number of years of guaranteed payments was fewer than 5. See Pub. 575 for the definition of guaranteed payments.

If you must use the Simplified Method, complete the Simplified Method Worksheet in these instructions to figure the taxable part of your pension or annuity. For more details on the Simplified Method, see Pub. 575 (or Pub. 721 for U.S. Civil Service retirement benefits).

 If you received U.S. Civil Service retirement benefits and you chose the alternative annuity option, see Pub. 721 to figure the taxable part of your annuity. Do not use the Simplified Method Worksheet in these instructions.

Annuity Starting Date

Your annuity starting date is the later of the first day of the first period for which you received a payment or the date the plan's obligations became fixed.

Age (or Combined Ages) at Annuity Starting Date

If you are the retiree, use your age on the annuity starting date. If you are the survivor of a retiree, use the retiree's age on his or her annuity starting date. But if your annuity starting date was after 1997 and the payments are for your life and that of your beneficiary, use your combined ages on the annuity starting date.

If you are the beneficiary of an employee who died, see Pub. 575. If there is more than one beneficiary, see Pub. 575 or Pub. 721 to figure each beneficiary's taxable amount.

Cost

Your cost is generally your net investment in the plan as of the annuity starting date. It doesn't include pre-tax contributions. Your net investment should be shown in box 9b of Form 1099-R for the first year you received payments from the plan.

Rollovers

Generally, a qualified rollover is a tax-free distribution of cash or other assets from one retirement plan that is contributed to another plan within 60 days of receiving the distribution. However, a qualified rollover to a Roth IRA or a designated Roth account is generally not a tax-free distribution. Use lines 16a and 16b to report a qualified rollover, including a direct rollover, from one qualified employer's plan to another or to an IRA or SEP.

Enter on line 16a the distribution from Form 1099-R, box 1. From this amount, subtract any contributions (usually shown in box 5) that were taxable to you when made. From that result, subtract the amount of the qualified rollover. Enter the remaining amount on line 16b. If the remaining amount is zero and you have no other distribution to report on line 16b, enter zero on line 16b. Also, enter "Rollover" next to line 16b.

See Pub. 575 for more details on rollovers, including special rules that apply to rollovers from designated Roth accounts, partial rollovers of property, and distributions under qualified domestic relations orders.

Lump-Sum Distributions

If you received a lump-sum distribution from a profit-sharing or retirement plan, your Form 1099-R should have the "Total distribution" box in box 2b checked. You may owe an additional tax if you received an early distribution from a qualified retirement plan and the total amount wasn't rolled over in a qualified rollover. For details, see the instructions for line 59.

Enter the total distribution on line 16a and the taxable part on line 16b. For details, see Pub. 575.

 If you or the plan participant was born before January 2, 1936, you could pay less tax on the distribution. See Form 4972.

Line 19

Unemployment Compensation

You should receive a Form 1099-G showing in box 1 the total unemployment compensation paid to you in 2016. Report this amount on line 19. However, if you made contributions to a governmental unemployment compensation program or to a governmental paid family leave program and you aren't itemizing deductions, reduce the amount you report on line 19 by those contributions. If you are itemizing deductions, see the instructions on Form 1099-G.

If you received an overpayment of unemployment compensation in 2016 and you repaid any of it in 2016, subtract the amount you repaid from the total amount you received. Enter the result on line 19. Also, enter "Repaid" and the amount you repaid on the dotted line next to line 19. If, in 2016, you repaid unemployment compensation that you included in gross income in an earlier year, you can deduct the amount repaid on Schedule A, line 23. But if you repaid more than $3,000, see *Repayments* in Pub. 525 for details on how to report the repayment.

Lines 20a and 20b

Social Security Benefits

You should receive a Form SSA-1099 showing in box 3 the total social security benefits paid to you. Box 4 will show

Simplified Method Worksheet—Lines 16a and 16b

Keep for Your Records

Before you begin: ✓ If you are the beneficiary of a deceased employee or former employee who died **before** August 21, 1996, include any death benefit exclusion that you are entitled to (up to $5,000) in the amount entered on line 2 below.

More than one pension or annuity. If you had more than one partially taxable pension or annuity, figure the taxable part of each separately. Enter the total of the taxable parts on Form 1040, line 16b. Enter the total pension or annuity payments received in 2016 on Form 1040, line 16a.

1. Enter the total pension or annuity payments from Form 1099-R, box 1. Also, enter this amount on Form 1040, line 16a . . . . **1.** _____

2. Enter your cost in the plan at the annuity starting date . . . . **2.** _____

   Note. If you completed this worksheet last year, skip line 3 and enter the amount from line 4 of last year's worksheet on line 4 below (even if the amount of your pension or annuity has changed). Otherwise, go to line 3.

3. Enter the appropriate number from **Table 1** below. **But** if your annuity starting date was **after** 1997 **and** the payments are for your life and that of your beneficiary, enter the appropriate number from **Table 2** below . . . . **3.** _____

4. Divide line 2 by the number on line 3 . . . . **4.** _____

5. Multiply line 4 by the number of months for which this year's payments were made. If your annuity starting date was **before** 1987, skip lines 6 and 7 and enter this amount on line 8. Otherwise, go to line 6 . . . . **5.** _____

6. Enter the amount, if any, recovered tax free in years after 1986. If you completed this worksheet last year, enter the amount from line 10 of last year's worksheet . . . . . . **6.** _____

7. Subtract line 6 from line 2 . . . . **7.** _____

8. Enter the **smaller** of line 5 or line 7 . . . . **8.** _____

9. **Taxable amount.** Subtract line 8 from line 1. Enter the result, but not less than zero. Also, enter this amount on Form 1040, line 16b. If your Form 1099-R shows a larger amount, use the amount on this line instead of the amount from Form 1099-R. If you are a retired public safety officer, see *Insurance Premiums for Retired Public Safety Officers* before entering an amount on line 16b . . . . **9.** _____

10. Was your annuity starting date before 1987?

    ☐ **Yes.** (STOP) Do not complete the rest of this worksheet.

    ☐ **No.** Add lines 6 and 8. This is the **amount you have recovered tax free** through 2016. You will need this number if you need to fill out this worksheet next year . . . . **10.** _____

11. **Balance of cost to be recovered.** Subtract line 10 from line 2. If zero, you won't have to complete this worksheet next year. The payments you receive next year will generally be fully taxable . . . . **11.** _____

Table 1 for Line 3 Above

IF the age at annuity starting date was . . .	AND your annuity starting date was—	
	before November 19, 1996, enter on line 3 . . .	**after** November 18, 1996, enter on line 3 . . .
55 or under	300	360
56–60	260	310
61–65	240	260
66–70	170	210
71 or older	120	160

Table 2 for Line 3 Above

IF the combined ages at annuity starting date were . . .	THEN enter on line 3 . . .
110 or under	410
111–120	360
121–130	310
131–140	260
141 or older	210

Need more information or forms? Visit IRS.gov.

the amount of any benefits you repaid in 2016. If you received railroad retirement benefits treated as social security, you should receive a Form RRB-1099.

Use the Social Security Benefits Worksheet in these instructions to see if any of your benefits are taxable.

Exception. Do not use the Social Security Benefits Worksheet in these instructions if any of the following applies.

• You made contributions to a traditional IRA for 2016 and you or your spouse were covered by a retirement plan at work or through self-employment. Instead, use the worksheets in Pub. 590-A to see if any of your social security benefits are taxable and to figure your IRA deduction.

• You repaid any benefits in 2016 and your total repayments (box 4) were more than your total benefits for 2016 (box 3). None of your benefits are taxable for 2016. Also, you may be able to take an itemized deduction or a credit for part of the excess repayments if they were for benefits you included in gross income in an earlier year. For more details, see Pub. 915.

• You file Form 2555, 2555-EZ, 4563, or 8815, or you exclude employer-provided adoption benefits or income from sources within Puerto Rico. Instead, use the worksheet in Pub. 915.

 Benefits for earlier year received in 2016? *If any of your benefits are taxable for 2016 and they include a lump-sum benefit payment that was for an earlier year, you may be able to reduce the taxable amount. See* Lump-Sum Election *in Pub. 915 for details.*

Social security information. Social security beneficiaries can now get a variety of information from the SSA website with a *my Social Security* account, including getting a replacement Form SSA-1099 if needed. For more information and to set up an account, go to *www.socialsecurity.gov/myaccount*.

Form RRB-1099. If you need a replacement Form RRB-1099, call the Railroad Retirement Board at 1-877-772-5772 or go to *www.rrb.gov*.

Line 21

Other Income

 Do not report on this line any income from self-employment or fees received as a notary public. Instead, you must use Schedule C, C-EZ, or F, even if you do not have any business expenses. Also, do not report on line 21 any nonemployee compensation shown on Form 1099-MISC (unless it isn't self-employment income, such as income from a hobby or a sporadic activity). Instead, see the instructions on Form 1099-MISC to find out where to report that income.

Taxable income. Use line 21 to report any taxable income not reported elsewhere on your return or other schedules. List the type and amount of income. If necessary, include a statement showing the required information. For more details, see *Miscellaneous Income* in Pub. 525.

Examples of income to report on line 21 include the following.

• Most prizes and awards. But see *Olympic and Paralympic medals and USOC prize money*, later.

• Jury duty pay. Also see the instructions for line 36.

• Alaska Permanent Fund dividends.

• Reimbursements or other amounts received for items deducted in an earlier year, such as medical expenses, real estate taxes, general sales taxes, or home mortgage interest. See *Recoveries* in Pub. 525 for details on how to figure the amount to report.

• Income from the rental of personal property if you engaged in the rental for profit but were not in the business of renting such property. Also see the instructions for line 36.

• Income from an activity not engaged in for profit. See Pub. 535.

• Amounts deemed to be income from a health savings account (HSA) because you didn't remain an eligible individual during the testing period. See Form 8889, Part III.

• Gambling winnings, including lotteries, raffles, a lump-sum payment from the sale of a right to receive future lottery payments, etc. For details on gambling losses, see the instructions for Schedule A, line 28.

 Attach Form(s) W-2G to Form 1040 if any federal income tax was withheld.

• Reemployment trade adjustment assistance (RTAA) payments. These payments should be shown in box 5 of Form 1099-G.

• Loss on certain corrective distributions of excess deferrals. See *Retirement Plan Contributions* in Pub. 525.

• Dividends on insurance policies if they exceed the total of all net premiums you paid for the contract.

• Recapture of a charitable contribution deduction relating to the contribution of a fractional interest in tangible personal property. See *Fractional Interest in Tangible Personal Property* in Pub. 526. Interest and an additional 10% tax apply to the amount of the recapture. See the instructions for line 62.

• Recapture of a charitable contribution deduction if the charitable organization disposes of the donated property within 3 years of the contribution. See *Recapture if no exempt use* in Pub. 526.

• Canceled debts. These amounts may be shown in box 2 of Form 1099-C. However, part or all of your income from the cancellation of debt may be nontaxable. See Pub. 4681 or go to IRS.gov and enter "canceled debt" or "foreclosure" in the search box.

• Taxable part of disaster relief payments. See Pub. 525 to figure the taxable part, if any. If any of your disaster relief payment is taxable, attach a statement showing the total payment received and how you figured the taxable part.

• Taxable distributions from a Coverdell education savings account (ESA) or a qualified tuition program (QTP). Distributions from these accounts may be taxable if (a) they are more than the qualified higher education expenses of the designated beneficiary in 2016, and (b) they were not included in a qualified rollover. See Pub. 970. Nontaxable distributions from these accounts, including rollovers, do not have to be reported on Form 1040.

 You may have to pay an additional tax if you received a taxable distribution from a Coverdell ESA or a QTP. See the Instructions for Form 5329.

• Taxable distributions from a health savings account (HSA) or an Archer

Social Security Benefits Worksheet—Lines 20a and 20b

Keep for Your Records

Before you begin:	✓ Complete Form 1040, lines 21 and 23 through 32, if they apply to you.
	✓ Figure any write-in adjustments to be entered on the dotted line next to line 36 (see the instructions for line 36).
	✓ If you are married filing separately and you lived apart from your spouse for all of 2016, enter "D" to the right of the word "benefits" on line 20a. If you do not, you may get a math error notice from the IRS.
	✓ Be sure you have read the **Exception** in the line 20a and 20b instructions to see if you can use this worksheet instead of a publication to find out if any of your benefits are taxable.

1. Enter the total amount from **box 5** of **all** your **Forms SSA-1099** and **Forms RRB-1099.** Also, enter this amount on Form 1040, line 20a . . . .   **1.** _____

2. Multiply line 1 by 50% (0.50) . . . .   **2.** _____

3. Combine the amounts from Form 1040, lines 7, 8a, 9a, 10 through 14, 15b, 16b, 17 through 19, and 21 . . . .   **3.** _____

4. Enter the amount, if any, from Form 1040, line 8b . . . .   **4.** _____

5. Combine lines 2, 3, and 4 . . . .   **5.** _____

6. Enter the total of the amounts from Form 1040, lines 23 through 32, plus any write-in adjustments you entered on the dotted line next to line 36 . . . .   **6.** _____

7. Is the amount on line 6 less than the amount on line 5?

   ☐ **No.** (STOP)   None of your social security benefits are taxable. Enter -0- on Form 1040, line 20b.

   ☐ **Yes.** Subtract line 6 from line 5 . . . .   **7.** _____

8. If you are:
   - Married filing jointly, enter $32,000
   - Single, head of household, qualifying widow(er), or married filing separately and you **lived apart** from your spouse for all of 2016, enter $25,000
   - Married filing separately and you lived with your spouse at any time in 2016, skip lines 8 through 15; multiply line 7 by 85% (0.85) and enter the result on line 16. Then, go to line 17

   . . . .   **8.** _____

9. Is the amount on line 8 less than the amount on line 7?

   ☐ **No.** (STOP)   None of your social security benefits are taxable. Enter -0- on Form 1040, line 20b. If you are married filing separately and you **lived apart** from your spouse for all of 2016, be sure you entered "D" to the right of the word "benefits" on line 20a.

   ☐ **Yes.** Subtract line 8 from line 7 . . . .   **9.** _____

10. Enter: $12,000 if married filing jointly; $9,000 if single, head of household, qualifying widow(er), or married filing separately and you **lived apart** from your spouse for all of 2016 . . . .   **10.** _____

11. Subtract line 10 from line 9. If zero or less, enter -0- . . . .   **11.** _____

12. Enter the **smaller** of line 9 or line 10 . . . .   **12.** _____

13. Enter one-half of line 12 . . . .   **13.** _____

14. Enter the **smaller** of line 2 or line 13 . . . .   **14.** _____

15. Multiply line 11 by 85% (0.85). If line 11 is zero, enter -0- . . . .   **15.** _____

16. Add lines 14 and 15 . . . .   **16.** _____

17. Multiply line 1 by 85% (0.85) . . . .   **17.** _____

18. **Taxable social security benefits.** Enter the **smaller** of line 16 or line 17. Also enter this amount on Form 1040, line 20b . . . .   **18.** _____

TIP   *If any of your benefits are taxable for 2016 **and** they include a lump-sum benefit payment that was for an earlier year, you may be able to reduce the taxable amount. See* Lump-Sum Election *in Pub. 915 for details.*

MSA. Distributions from these accounts may be taxable if (a) they are more than the unreimbursed qualified medical expenses of the account beneficiary or account holder in 2016, and (b) they were not included in a qualified rollover. See Pub. 969.

 You may have to pay an additional tax if you received a taxable distribution from an HSA or an Archer MSA. See the Instructions for Form 8889 for HSAs or the Instructions for Form 8853 for Archer MSAs.

• Taxable distributions from an ABLE account. Distributions from this type of account may be taxable if (a) they are more than the designated beneficiary's qualified disability expenses, and (b) they were not included in a qualified rollover. Enter "ABLE" and the taxable amount on the dotted line next to line 21. See Pub. 907 for more information.

 You may have to pay an additional tax if you received a taxable distribution from an ABLE account. See the Instructions for Form 5329.

Nontaxable income. Do not report any nontaxable income on line 21. Examples of nontaxable income include the following.
 • Child support.
 • Payments you received to help you pay your mortgage loan under the HFA Hardest Hit Fund or the Emergency Homeowners' Loan Program or similar state program.
 • Any Pay-for-Performance Success Payments that reduce the principal balance of your home mortgage under the Home Affordable Modification Program.
 • Life insurance proceeds received because of someone's death (other than from certain employer-owned life insurance contracts).
 • Gifts and bequests. However, if you received a gift or bequest from a foreign person of more than $15,671, you may have to report information about it on Form 3520, Part IV. See the Instructions for Form 3520.

Net operating loss (NOL) deduction. Include on line 21 any NOL deduction from an earlier year. Subtract it from any income on line 21 and enter the result. If the result is less than zero, enter

it in parentheses. On the dotted line next to line 21, enter "NOL" and show the amount of the deduction in parentheses. See Pub. 536 for details.

Medicaid waiver payments to care provider. Certain Medicaid waiver payments you received for caring for someone living in your home with you may be nontaxable. If these payments were incorrectly reported to you in box 1 of Form(s) W-2, and you can't get a corrected Form W-2, include the amount on line 7. On line 21, subtract the nontaxable amount of the payments from any income on line 21 and enter the result. If the result is less than zero, enter it in parentheses. Enter "Notice 2014-7" and the nontaxable amount on the dotted line next to line 21. For more information about these payments, see Pub. 525.

Olympic and Paralympic medals and USOC prize money. The value of Olympic and Paralympic medals and the amount of United States Olympic Committee prize money you receive on account of your participation in the Olympic or Paralympic Games may be nontaxable. These amounts should be reported to you in box 3 of Form 1099-MISC. To see if these amounts are nontaxable, first figure your adjusted gross income including the amount of your medals and prize money. If your adjusted gross income is not more than $1,000,000 ($500,000 if married filing separately), these amounts are nontaxable and you should include the amount in box 3 of Form 1099-MISC on line 21, then subtract it by including it on line 36 along with any other write-in adjustments. On the dotted line next to line 36, enter the nontaxable amount and identify as "USOC."

Adjusted Gross Income

Line 23

Educator Expenses

If you were an eligible educator in 2016, you can deduct on line 23 up to $250 of qualified expenses you paid in 2016. If you and your spouse are filing jointly and both of you were eligible educators,

the maximum deduction is $500. However, neither spouse can deduct more than $250 of his or her qualified expenses on line 23. You may be able to deduct expenses that are more than the $250 (or $500) limit on Schedule A, line 21. An eligible educator is a kindergarten through grade 12 teacher, instructor, counselor, principal, or aide who worked in a school for at least 900 hours during a school year.

Qualified expenses include ordinary and necessary expenses paid:
 • For professional development courses you have taken related to the curriculum you teach or to the students you teach, or
 • In connection with books, supplies, equipment (including computer equipment, software, and services), and other materials used in the classroom.

An ordinary expense is one that is common and accepted in your educational field. A necessary expense is one that is helpful and appropriate for your profession as an educator. An expense does not have to be required to be considered necessary.

Qualified expenses do not include expenses for home schooling or for non-athletic supplies for courses in health or physical education.

You must reduce your qualified expenses by the following amounts.
 • Excludable U.S. series EE and I savings bond interest from Form 8815.
 • Nontaxable qualified tuition program earnings or distributions.
 • Any nontaxable distribution of Coverdell education savings account earnings.
 • Any reimbursements you received for these expenses that were not reported to you in box 1 of your Form W-2.

For more details, use *Tax Topic 458* or see Pub. 529.

Line 24

Certain Business Expenses of Reservists, Performing Artists, and Fee-Basis Government Officials

Include the following deductions on line 24.
 • Certain business expenses of National Guard and reserve members who

Self-Employed Health Insurance Deduction Worksheet—Line 29   *Keep for Your Records*

Before you begin:	✓ If, during 2016, you were an eligible trade adjustment assistance (TAA) recipient, alternative TAA (ATAA) recipient, reemployment TAA (RTAA) recipient, or Pension Benefit Guaranty Corporation pension payee, see the Instructions for Form 8885 to figure the amount to enter on line 1 of this worksheet.
	✓ Be sure you have read the **Exceptions** in the instructions for this line to see if you can use this worksheet instead of Pub. 535 to figure your deduction.

1. Enter the total amount paid in 2016 for health insurance coverage established under your business (or the S corporation in which you were a more-than-2% shareholder) for 2016 for you, your spouse, and your dependents. Your insurance can also cover your child who was under age 27 at the end of 2016, even if the child wasn't your dependent. But do not include amounts for any month you were eligible to participate in an employer-sponsored health plan or amounts paid from retirement plan distributions that were nontaxable because you are a retired public safety officer .... **1.** _____

2. Enter your net profit* and any other earned income** from the business under which the insurance plan is established, minus any deductions on Form 1040, lines 27 and 28. Do not include Conservation Reserve Program payments exempt from self-employment tax .... **2.** _____

3. **Self-employed health insurance deduction.** Enter the **smaller** of line 1 or line 2 here and on Form 1040, line 29. **Do not** include this amount in figuring any medical expense deduction on Schedule A .... **3.** _____

If you used either optional method to figure your net earnings from self-employment, do not enter your net profit. Instead, enter the amount from Schedule SE, Section B, line 4b.

**Earned income *includes net earnings and gains from the sale, transfer, or licensing of property you created. However, it doesn't include capital gain income. If you were a more-than-2% shareholder in the S corporation under which the insurance plan is established, earned income is your Medicare wages (box 5 of Form W-2) from that corporation.*

---

traveled more than 100 miles from home to perform services as a National Guard or reserve member.

- Performing-arts-related expenses as a qualified performing artist.
- Business expenses of fee-basis state or local government officials.

For more details, see Form 2106 or 2106-EZ.

Line 25

Health Savings Account (HSA) Deduction

You may be able to take this deduction if contributions (other than employer contributions, rollovers, and qualified HSA funding distributions from an IRA) were made to your HSA for 2016. See Form 8889.

Line 26

Moving Expenses

If you moved in connection with your job or business or started a new job, you may be able to take this deduction. But your new workplace must be at least 50 miles farther from your old home than your old home was from your old workplace. If you had no former workplace, your new workplace must be at least 50 miles from your old home. Use *Tax Topic 455* or see Form 3903.

Line 27

Deductible Part of Self-Employment Tax

If you were self-employed and owe self-employment tax, fill in Schedule SE to figure the amount of your deduction. If you completed Section A of Schedule SE, the deductible part of your self-employment tax is on line 6. If you completed Section B of Schedule SE, it is on line 13.

Line 28

Self-Employed SEP, SIMPLE, and Qualified Plans

If you were self-employed or a partner, you may be able to take this deduction.

See Pub. 560 or, if you were a minister, Pub. 517.

Line 29

Self-Employed Health Insurance Deduction

You may be able to deduct the amount you paid for health insurance for yourself, your spouse, and your dependents. The insurance can also cover your child who was under age 27 at the end of 2016, even if the child wasn't your dependent. A child includes your son, daughter, stepchild, adopted child, or foster child (defined in the line 6c instructions).

One of the following statements must be true.

- You were self-employed and had a net profit for the year reported on Schedule C, C-EZ, or F.
- You were a partner with net earnings from self-employment.
- You used one of the optional methods to figure your net earnings from self-employment on Schedule SE.

• You received wages in 2016 from an S corporation in which you were a more-than-2% shareholder. Health insurance premiums paid or reimbursed by the S corporation are shown as wages on Form W-2.

The insurance plan must be established under your business. Your personal services must have been a material income-producing factor in the business. If you are filing Schedule C, C-EZ, or F, the policy can be either in your name or in the name of the business.

If you are a partner, the policy can be either in your name or in the name of the partnership. You can either pay the premiums yourself or your partnership can pay them and report them as guaranteed payments. If the policy is in your name and you pay the premiums yourself, the partnership must reimburse you and report the premiums as guaranteed payments.

If you are a more-than-2% shareholder in an S corporation, the policy can be either in your name or in the name of the S corporation. You can either pay the premiums yourself or the S corporation can pay them and report them as wages. If the policy is in your name and you pay the premiums yourself, the S corporation must reimburse you. You can deduct the premiums only if the S corporation reports the premiums paid or reimbursed as wages in box 1 of your Form W-2 in 2016 and you also report the premium payments or reimbursements as wages on Form 1040, line 7.

But if you were also eligible to participate in any subsidized health plan maintained by your or your spouse's employer for any month or part of a month in 2016, amounts paid for health insurance coverage for that month can't be used to figure the deduction. Also, if you were eligible for any month or part of a month to participate in any subsidized health plan maintained by the employer of either your dependent or your child who was under age 27 at the end of 2016, do not use amounts paid for coverage for that month to figure the deduction.

Example. If you were eligible to participate in a subsidized health plan maintained by your spouse's employer from September 30 through December 31, you can't use amounts paid for health insurance coverage for September through December to figure your deduction.

Medicare premiums you voluntarily pay to obtain insurance in your name that is similar to qualifying private health insurance can be used to figure the deduction. Amounts paid for health insurance coverage from retirement plan distributions that were nontaxable because you are a retired public safety officer can't be used to figure the deduction.

For more details, see Pub. 535.

If you qualify to take the deduction, use the Self-Employed Health Insurance Deduction Worksheet to figure the amount you can deduct.

Exceptions. Use Pub. 535 instead of the Self-Employed Health Insurance Deduction Worksheet in these instructions to figure your deduction if any of the following applies.
• You had more than one source of income subject to self-employment tax.
• You file Form 2555 or 2555-EZ.
• You are using amounts paid for qualified long-term care insurance to figure the deduction.

Use Pub. 974 instead of the worksheet in these instructions if the insurance plan was considered to be established under your business and was obtained through the Marketplace, and advance payments of the premium tax credit were made or you are claiming the premium tax credit.

Line 30

Penalty on Early Withdrawal of Savings

The Form 1099-INT or Form 1099-OID you received will show the amount of any penalty you were charged.

Lines 31a and 31b

Alimony Paid

If you made payments to or for your spouse or former spouse under a divorce or separation instrument, you may be able to take this deduction. Use *Tax Topic 452* or see Pub. 504.

Line 32

IRA Deduction

 If you made any nondeductible contributions to a traditional individual retirement arrangement (IRA) for 2016, you must report them on Form 8606.

If you made contributions to a traditional IRA for 2016, you may be able to take an IRA deduction. But you, or your spouse if filing a joint return, must have had earned income to do so. For IRA purposes, earned income includes alimony and separate maintenance payments reported on line 11. If you were a member of the U.S. Armed Forces, earned income includes any nontaxable combat pay you received. If you were self-employed, earned income is generally your net earnings from self-employment if your personal services were a material income-producing factor. For more details, see Pub. 590-A. A statement should be sent to you by May 31, 2017, that shows all contributions to your traditional IRA for 2016.

Use the IRA Deduction Worksheet to figure the amount, if any, of your IRA deduction. But read the following 11-item list before you fill in the worksheet.

1. If you were age 70½ or older at the end of 2016, you can't deduct any contributions made to your traditional IRA for 2016 or treat them as nondeductible contributions.

2. You can't deduct contributions to a Roth IRA. But you may be able to take the retirement savings contributions credit (saver's credit). See the instructions for line 51.

3. If you are filing a joint return and you or your spouse made contributions to both a traditional IRA and a Roth IRA for 2016, do not use the IRA Deduction Worksheet in these instructions. Instead, see Pub. 590-A to figure the amount, if any, of your IRA deduction.

4. You can't deduct elective deferrals to a 401(k) plan, 403(b) plan, section 457 plan, SIMPLE plan, or the federal Thrift Savings Plan. These amounts aren't included as income in box 1 of your Form W-2. But you may be able to take the retirement savings contributions credit. See the instructions for line 51.

Need more information or forms? Visit IRS.gov.

5. If you made contributions to your IRA in 2016 that you deducted for 2015, do not include them in the worksheet.

6. If you received income from a nonqualified deferred compensation plan or nongovernmental section 457 plan that is included in box 1 of your Form W-2, or in box 7 of Form 1099-MISC, do not include that income on line 8 of the worksheet. The income should be shown in (a) box 11 of your Form W-2, (b) box 12 of your Form W-2 with code Z, or (c) box 15b of Form 1099-MISC. If it isn't, contact your employer or the payer for the amount of the income.

7. You must file a joint return to deduct contributions to your spouse's IRA. Enter the total IRA deduction for you and your spouse on line 32.

8. Do not include qualified rollover contributions in figuring your deduction. Instead, see the instructions for lines 15a and 15b.

9. Do not include trustees' fees that were billed separately and paid by you for your IRA. These fees can be deducted only as an itemized deduction on Schedule A.

10. Do not include any repayments of qualified reservist distributions. You can't deduct them. For information on how to report these repayments, see *Qualified reservist repayments* in Pub. 590-A.

11. If the total of your IRA deduction on line 32 plus any nondeductible contribution to your traditional IRAs shown on Form 8606 is less than your total traditional IRA contributions for 2016, see Pub. 590-A for special rules.

 By April 1 of the year after the year in which you turn age 70½, you must start taking minimum required distributions from your traditional IRA. If you do not, you may have to pay a 50% additional tax on the amount that should have been distributed. For details, including how to figure the minimum required distribution, see Pub. 590-B.

Were You Covered by a Retirement Plan?

If you were covered by a retirement plan (qualified pension, profit-sharing (including 401(k)), annuity, SEP, SIMPLE, etc.) at work or through self-employment, your IRA deduction may be reduced or eliminated. But you can still make contributions to an IRA even if you can't deduct them. In any case, the income earned on your IRA contributions isn't taxed until it is paid to you.

The "Retirement plan" box in box 13 of your Form W-2 should be checked if you were covered by a plan at work even if you were not vested in the plan. You are also covered by a plan if you were self-employed and had a SEP, SIMPLE, or qualified retirement plan.

If you were covered by a retirement plan and you file Form 2555, 2555-EZ, or 8815, or you exclude employer-provided adoption benefits, see Pub. 590-A to figure the amount, if any, of your IRA deduction.

Married persons filing separately. If you were not covered by a retirement plan but your spouse was, you are considered covered by a plan unless you lived apart from your spouse for all of 2016.

 You may be able to take the retirement savings contributions credit. See the line 51 instructions.

IRA Deduction Worksheet—Line 32

Keep for Your Records

 CAUTION *If you were age 70½ or older at the end of 2016, you can't deduct any contributions made to your traditional IRA or treat them as nondeductible contributions.* **Do not** *complete this worksheet for anyone age 70½ or older at the end of 2016. If you are married filing jointly and only one spouse was under age 70½ at the end of 2016, complete this worksheet only for that spouse.*

Before you begin: ✓ Be sure you have read the 11-item list in the instructions for this line. You may not be able to use this worksheet.
   ✓ Figure any write-in adjustments to be entered on the dotted line next to line 36 (see the instructions for line 36).
   ✓ If you are married filing separately and you lived apart from your spouse for all of 2016, enter "D" on the dotted line next to Form 1040, line 32. If you do not, you may get a math error notice from the IRS.

		Your IRA	**Spouse's IRA**

1a. Were you covered by a retirement plan (see *Were You Covered by a Retirement Plan?*)? . . . . **1a.** ☐ Yes ☐ No

b. If married filing jointly, was your spouse covered by a retirement plan? . . . . **1b.** ☐ Yes ☐ No

Next. If you checked "No" on line 1a (and "No" on line 1b if married filing jointly), skip lines 2 through 6, enter the applicable amount below on line 7a (and line 7b if applicable), and go to line 8.
  • $5,500, if under age 50 at the end of 2016.
  • $6,500, if age 50 or older but under age 70½ at the end of 2016.
  Otherwise, go to line 2.

2. Enter the amount shown below that applies to you.
  • Single, head of household, or married filing separately and you **lived apart** from your spouse for all of 2016, enter $71,000.
  • Qualifying widow(er), enter $118,000.
  • Married filing jointly, enter $118,000 in both columns. But if you checked "No" on either line 1a or 1b, enter $194,000 for the person who wasn't covered by a plan.
  • Married filing separately and you lived with your spouse at any time in 2016, enter $10,000.

2a. _____ **2b.** _____

3. Enter the amount from Form 1040, line 22 . . . . **3.** _____

4. Enter the total of the amounts from Form 1040, lines 23 through 31a, plus any write-in adjustments you entered on the dotted line next to line 36 . . . . **4.** _____

5. Subtract line 4 from line 3. If married filing jointly, enter the result in both columns . . . . **5a.** _____ **5b.** _____

6. Is the amount on line 5 less than the amount on line 2?

☐ **No.** (STOP) None of your IRA contributions are deductible. For details on nondeductible IRA contributions, see Form 8606.

☐ **Yes.** Subtract line 5 from line 2 in each column. Follow the instruction below that applies to you.
  • If single, head of household, or married filing separately, and the result is $10,000 or more, enter the applicable amount below on line 7 for that column and go to line 8.
    i. $5,500, if under age 50 at the end of 2016.
    ii. $6,500, if age 50 or older but under age 70½ at the end of 2016.
  If the result is less than $10,000, go to line 7.
  • If married filing jointly or qualifying widow(er), and the result is $20,000 or more ($10,000 or more in the column for the IRA of a person who wasn't covered by a retirement plan), enter the applicable amount below on line 7 for that column and go to line 8.
    i. $5,500, if under age 50 at the end of 2016.
    ii. $6,500 if age 50 or older but under age 70½ at the end of 2016.
  Otherwise, go to line 7.

6a. _____ **6b.** _____

Need more information or forms? Visit IRS.gov.

IRA Deduction Worksheet—*Continued*

		Your IRA	Spouse's IRA

7. Multiply lines 6a and 6b by the percentage below that applies to you. If the result isn't a multiple of $10, increase it to the next multiple of $10 (for example, increase $490.30 to $500). If the result is $200 or more, enter the result. But if it is less than $200, enter $200.

   • Single, head of household, or married filing separately, multiply by 55% (0.55) (or by 65% (0.65) in the column for the IRA of a person who is age 50 or older at the end of 2016).

   • Married filing jointly or qualifying widow(er), multiply by 27.5% (0.275) (or by 32.5% (0.325) in the column for the IRA of a person who is age 50 or older at the end of 2016). But if you checked "No" on either line 1a or 1b, then in the column for the IRA of the person who wasn't covered by a retirement plan, multiply by 55% (0.55) (or by 65% (0.65) if age 50 or older at the end of 2016).

      7a. _____   **7b.** _____

8. Enter the total of your (and your spouse's if filing jointly):

   • Wages, salaries, tips, etc. Generally, this is the amount reported in box 1 of Form W-2. Exceptions are explained earlier in these instructions for line 32.

   • Alimony and separate maintenance payments reported on Form 1040, line 11.

   • Nontaxable combat pay. This amount should be reported in box 12 of Form W-2 with code Q.

      8. _____

9. Enter the earned income you (and your spouse if filing jointly) received as a self-employed individual or a partner. Generally, this is your (and your spouse's if filing jointly) net earnings from self-employment if your personal services were a material income-producing factor, minus any deductions on Form 1040, lines 27 and 28. If zero or less, enter -0-. For more details, see Pub. 590-A . . . . **9.** _____

10. Add lines 8 and 9 . . . . **10.** _____

    ⚠ CAUTION   *If married filing jointly and line 10 is less than $11,000 ($12,000 if one spouse is age 50 or older at the end of 2016; $13,000 if both spouses are age 50 or older at the end of 2016), **stop here** and use the worksheet in Pub. 590-A to figure your IRA deduction.*

11. Enter traditional IRA contributions made, or that will be made by April 18, 2017 for 2016 to your IRA on line 11a and to your spouse's IRA on line 11b . . . . **11a.** _____   **11b.** _____

12. On line 12a, enter the **smallest** of line 7a, 10, or 11a. On line 12b, enter the **smallest** of line 7b, 10, or 11b. This is the most you can deduct. Add the amounts on lines 12a and 12b and enter the total on Form 1040, line 32. Or, if you want, you can deduct a smaller amount and treat the rest as a nondeductible contribution (see Form 8606) . . . . **12a.** _____   **12b.** _____

Line 33

Student Loan Interest Deduction

You can take this deduction only if all of the following apply.

• You paid interest in 2016 on a qualified student loan (defined later).

• Your filing status is any status except married filing separately.

• Your modified adjusted gross income (AGI) is less than: $80,000 if single, head of household, or qualifying widow(er); $160,000 if married filing jointly. Use lines 2 through 4 of the worksheet in these instructions to figure your modified AGI.

• You, or your spouse if filing jointly, aren't claimed as a dependent on someone else's (such as your parent's) 2016 tax return.

Use the worksheet in these instructions to figure your student loan interest deduction.

Exception. Use Pub. 970 instead of the worksheet in these instructions to figure your student loan interest deduction if you file Form 2555, 2555-EZ, or 4563, or you exclude income from sources within Puerto Rico.

Qualified student loan. A qualified student loan is any loan you took out to pay the qualified higher education expenses for any of the following individuals who was an eligible student.

1. Yourself or your spouse.

2. Any person who was your dependent when the loan was taken out.

3. Any person you could have claimed as a dependent for the year the loan was taken out except that:

a. The person filed a joint return,

b. The person had gross income that was equal to or more than the exemption amount for that year ($4,050 for 2016), or

c. You, or your spouse if filing jointly, could be claimed as a dependent on someone else's return.

However, a loan isn't a qualified student loan if (a) any of the proceeds were used for other purposes, or (b) the loan was from either a related person or a person who borrowed the proceeds under a qualified employer plan or a contract purchased under such a plan. For details, see Pub. 970.

Qualified higher education expenses. Qualified higher education expenses generally include tuition, fees, room and board, and related expenses such as books and supplies. The expenses must be for education in a degree, certificate, or similar program at an eligible educational institution. An eligible educational institution includes most colleges, universities, and certain vocational schools. For details, see Pub. 970.

Student Loan Interest Deduction Worksheet—Line 33

Keep for Your Records

Before you begin:
✓ Figure any write-in adjustments to be entered on the dotted line next to line 36 (see the instructions for line 36).
✓ Be sure you have read the **Exception** in the instructions for this line to see if you can use this worksheet instead of Pub. 970 to figure your deduction.

1. Enter the total interest you paid in 2016 on qualified student loans (see the instructions for line 33). **Do not** enter more than $2,500 .... **1.** _____

2. Enter the amount from Form 1040, line 22 .... **2.** _____

3. Enter the total of the amounts from Form 1040, lines 23 through 32, plus any write-in adjustments you entered on the dotted line next to line 36 .... **3.** _____

4. Subtract line 3 from line 2 .... **4.** _____

5. Enter the amount shown below for your filing status.
   • Single, head of household, or qualifying widow(er)—$65,000
   • Married filing jointly—$130,000 .... **5.** _____

6. Is the amount on line 4 more than the amount on line 5?

   ☐ **No.** Skip lines 6 and 7, enter -0- on line 8, and go to line 9.

   ☐ **Yes.** Subtract line 5 from line 4 .... **6.** _____

7. Divide line 6 by $15,000 ($30,000 if married filing jointly). Enter the result as a decimal (rounded to at least three places). If the result is 1.000 or more, enter 1.000 .... **7.** ____ . ____

8. Multiply line 1 by line 7 .... **8.** _____

9. **Student loan interest deduction.** Subtract line 8 from line 1. Enter the result here and on Form 1040, line 33. **Do not** include this amount in figuring any other deduction on your return (such as on Schedule A, C, E, etc.) .... **9.** _____

Need more information or forms? Visit IRS.gov.

Line 34

Tuition and Fees

If you paid qualified tuition and fees for yourself, your spouse, or your dependent(s), you may be able to take this deduction. See Form 8917.

 You may be able to take a credit for your educational expenses instead of a deduction. See the instructions for lines 50 and 68 for details.

Line 35

Domestic Production Activities Deduction

You may be able to deduct up to 9% of your qualified production activities income from the following activities.

1. Construction of real property performed in the United States.

2. Engineering or architectural services performed in the United States for construction of real property in the United States.

3. Any lease, rental, license, sale, exchange, or other disposition of:

a. Tangible personal property, computer software, and sound recordings that you manufactured, produced, grew, or extracted in whole or in significant part in the United States,

b. Any qualified film you produced, or

c. Electricity, natural gas, or potable water you produced in the United States.

Your deduction may be reduced if you had oil-related qualified production activities income.

The deduction doesn't apply to income derived from:
- The sale of food and beverages you prepared at a retail establishment;
- Property you leased, licensed, or rented for use by any related person;
- The transmission or distribution of electricity, natural gas, or potable water; or
- The lease, rental, license, sale, exchange, or other disposition of land.

For details, see Form 8903 and its instructions.

Line 36

Include in the total on line 36 any of the following write-in adjustments. To find out if you can take the deduction, see the form or publication indicated. On the dotted line next to line 36, enter the amount of your deduction and identify it as indicated.

- Archer MSA deduction (see Form 8853). Identify as "MSA."
- Jury duty pay if you gave the pay to your employer because your employer paid your salary while you served on the jury. Identify as "Jury Pay."
- Deductible expenses related to income reported on line 21 from the rental of personal property engaged in for profit. Identify as "PPR."
- Nontaxable amount of the value of Olympic and Paralympic medals and USOC prize money reported on line 21. Identify as "USOC."
- Reforestation amortization and expenses (see Pub. 535). Identify as "RFST."
- Repayment of supplemental unemployment benefits under the Trade Act of 1974 (see Pub. 525). Identify as "Sub-Pay TRA."
- Contributions to section 501(c)(18)(D) pension plans (see Pub. 525). Identify as "501(c)(18)(D)."
- Contributions by certain chaplains to section 403(b) plans (see Pub. 517). Identify as "403(b)."
- Attorney fees and court costs for actions involving certain unlawful discrimination claims, but only to the extent of gross income from such actions (see Pub. 525). Identify as "UDC."
- Attorney fees and court costs you paid in connection with an award from the IRS for information you provided that helped the IRS detect tax law violations, up to the amount of the award includible in your gross income. Identify as "WBF."

Line 37

If line 37 is less than zero, you may have a net operating loss that you can carry to another tax year. See the Instructions for Form 1045 for details.

Tax and Credits

Line 39a

If you were born before January 2, 1952, or were blind at the end of 2016, check the appropriate box(es) on line 39a. If you were married and checked the box on Form 1040, line 6b, and your spouse was born before January 2, 1952, or was blind at the end of 2016, also check the appropriate box(es) for your spouse. Be sure to enter the total number of boxes checked. Do not check any box(es) for your spouse if your filing status is head of household.

Death of spouse in 2016. If your spouse was born before January 2, 1952, but died in 2016 before reaching age 65, do not check the box that says "Spouse was born before January 2, 1952."

A person is considered to reach age 65 on the day before his or her 65th birthday.

Example. Your spouse was born on February 14, 1951, and died on February 13, 2016. Your spouse is considered age 65 at the time of death. Check the appropriate box for your spouse on line 39a. However, if your spouse died on February 12, 2016, your spouse isn't considered age 65. Do not check the box.

Death of taxpayer in 2016. If you are preparing a return for someone who died in 2016, see Pub. 501 before completing line 39a.

Blindness

If you were not totally blind as of December 31, 2016, you must get a statement certified by your eye doctor (ophthalmologist or optometrist) that:
- You can't see better than 20/200 in your better eye with glasses or contact lenses, or
- Your field of vision is 20 degrees or less.

If your eye condition isn't likely to improve beyond the conditions listed above, you can get a statement certified by your eye doctor (ophthalmologist or optometrist) to this effect instead.

You must keep the statement for your records.

Line 39b

If your filing status is married filing separately (box 3 is checked), and your spouse itemizes deductions on his or her return, check the box on line 39b. Also check that box if you were a dual-status alien. But if you were a dual-status alien and you file a joint return with your spouse who was a U.S. citizen or resident alien at the end of 2016 and you and your spouse agree to be taxed on your combined worldwide income, do not check the box.

Line 40

Itemized Deductions or Standard Deduction

In most cases, your federal income tax will be less if you take the larger of your itemized deductions or standard deduction.

Itemized Deductions

To figure your itemized deductions, fill in Schedule A.

Standard Deduction

Most people can find their standard deduction by looking at the amounts listed under "All others" to the left of line 40.

Exception 1—dependent. If you, or your spouse if filing jointly, can be claimed as a dependent on someone else's 2016 return, use the Standard Deduction Worksheet for Dependents to figure your standard deduction.

Exception 2—box on line 39a checked. If you checked any box on line 39a, figure your standard deduction using the Standard Deduction Chart for People Who Were Born Before January 2, 1952, or Were Blind.

Exception 3—box on line 39b checked. If you checked the box on line 39b, your standard deduction is zero, even if you were born before January 2, 1952, or were blind.

Line 42

Exemptions

If the amount on line 38 is over $155,650, use the Deduction for Exemptions Worksheet to figure your deduction for exemptions.

Standard Deduction Worksheet for Dependents—Line 40

Keep for Your Records

Use this worksheet **only** if someone can claim you, or your spouse if filing jointly, as a dependent.

1.	Is your **earned income*** more than $700?	
	☐ **Yes.** Add $350 to your earned income. Enter the total	
	☐ **No.** Enter $1,050	**1.** _____
2.	Enter the amount shown below for your filing status.	
	• Single or married filing separately—$6,300	
	• Married filing jointly—$12,600	
	• Head of household—$9,300	**2.** _____
3.	**Standard deduction.**	
	a. Enter the **smaller** of line 1 or line 2. If born after January 1, 1952, and not blind, **stop here** and enter this amount on Form 1040, line 40. Otherwise, go to line 3b	**3a.** _____
	b. If born before January 2, 1952, or blind, multiply the number on Form 1040, line 39a, by $1,250 ($1,550 if single or head of household)	**3b.** _____
	c. Add lines 3a and 3b. Enter the total here and on Form 1040, line 40	**3c.** _____

*****Earned income** *includes wages, salaries, tips, professional fees, and other compensation received for personal services you performed. It also includes any taxable scholarship or fellowship grant. Generally, your earned income is the total of the amount(s) you reported on Form 1040, lines 7, 12, and 18, minus the amount, if any, on line 27.*

Need more information or forms? Visit IRS.gov.

Standard Deduction Chart for People Who Were Born Before January 2, 1952, or Were Blind

Do not use this chart if someone can claim you, or your spouse if filing jointly, as a dependent. Instead, use the worksheet above.

Enter the number from the box on
Form 1040, line 39a . . . . ▶ ☐

⚠ CAUTION   Do not use the number of exemptions from line 6d.

IF your filing status is . . .	AND the number in the box above is . . .	THEN your standard deduction is . . .
Single	1 2	$7,850 9,400
Married filing jointly or Qualifying widow(er)	1 2 3 4	$13,850 15,100 16,350 17,600
Married filing separately	1 2 3 4	$7,550 8,800 10,050 11,300
Head of household	1 2	$10,850 12,400

Deduction for Exemptions Worksheet—Line 42

1. Is the amount on Form 1040, line 38, more than the amount shown on line 4 below for your filing status?

    ☐ **No.** (STOP) Multiply $4,050 by the total number of exemptions claimed on Form 1040, line 6d, and enter the result on line 42.

    ☐ **Yes. Continue.**

2. Multiply $4,050 by the total number of exemptions claimed on Form 1040, line 6d .... **2.** _____

3. Enter the amount from Form 1040, line 38 .... **3.** _____

4. Enter the amount shown below for your filing status.
    - Single —$259,400
    - Married filing jointly or qualifying widow(er)—$311,300 .... **4.**
    - Married filing separately—$155,650
    - Head of household—$285,350

5. Subtract line 4 from line 3. If the result is more than $122,500

    ($61,250 if married filing separately) , (STOP) Enter -0- on line 42 .... **5.** _____

6. Divide line 5 by $2,500 ($1,250 if married filing separately). If the result isn't a whole number, increase it to the next higher whole number (for example, increase .00004 to 1) .... **6.** _____

7. Multiply line 6 by 2% (0.02) and enter the result as a decimal (rounded to at least three places) .... **7.** _____

8. Multiply line 2 by line 7 .... **8.** _____

9. **Deduction for exemptions.** Subtract line 8 from line 2. Enter the result here and on Form 1040, line 42 .... **9.** _____

Line 44

Tax

Include in the total on line 44 all of the following taxes that apply.

- Tax on your taxable income. Figure the tax using one of the methods described here.

- Tax from Form(s) 8814 (relating to the election to report child's interest or dividends). Check the appropriate box.

- Tax from Form 4972 (relating to lump-sum distributions). Check the appropriate box.

- Tax due to making a section 962 election (the election made by a domestic shareholder of a controlled foreign corporation to be taxed at corporate rates). See section 962 for details. Check box c and enter the amount and "962" in the space next to that box. Attach a statement showing how you figured the tax.

- Recapture of an education credit. You may owe this tax if you claimed an education credit in an earlier year, and either tax-free educational assistance or a refund of qualified expenses was received in 2016 for the student. See Form 8863 for more details. Check box c and enter the amount and "ECR" in the space next to that box.

- Any tax from Form 8621, line 16e, relating to a section 1291 fund. Check box c and enter the amount of the tax and "1291TAX" in the space next to that box.

Do you want the IRS to figure the tax on your taxable income for you?

☐ **Yes.** See chapter 30 of Pub. 17 for details, including who is eligible and what to do. If you have paid too much, we will send you a refund. If you didn't pay enough, we will send you a bill.

☐ **No.** Use one of the following methods to figure your tax.

Tax Table or Tax Computation Worksheet. If your taxable income is less than $100,000, you must use the Tax Table, later in these instructions, to figure your tax. Be sure you use the correct column. If your taxable income is $100,000 or more, use the Tax Computation Worksheet right after the Tax Table.

However, do not use the Tax Table or Tax Computation Worksheet to figure your tax if any of the following applies.

Form 8615. Form 8615 generally must be used to figure the tax for any child who had more than $2,100 of unearned income, such as taxable interest, ordinary dividends, or capital gains (including capital gain distributions), and who either:

1. Was under age 18 at the end of 2016,

2. Was age 18 at the end of 2016 and didn't have earned income that was more than half of the child's support, or

3. Was a full-time student at least age 19 but under age 24 at the end of 2016 and didn't have earned income that was more than half of the child's support.

But if the child files a joint return for 2016 or if neither of the child's parents was alive at the end of 2016, do not use Form 8615 to figure the child's tax.

A child born on January 1, 1999, is considered to be age 18 at the end of 2016; a child born on January 1, 1998, is considered to be age 19 at the end of 2016; a child born on January 1, 1993, is considered to be age 24 at the end of 2016.

Schedule D Tax Worksheet. If you have to file Schedule D, and line 18 or 19 of Schedule D is more than zero, use the Schedule D Tax Worksheet in the Instructions for Schedule D to figure the amount to enter on Form 1040, line 44. But if you are filing Form 2555 or 2555-EZ, you must use the Foreign Earned Income Tax Worksheet instead.

Qualified Dividends and Capital Gain Tax Worksheet. Use the Qualified Dividends and Capital Gain Tax Worksheet, later, to figure your tax if you do not have to use the Schedule D Tax Worksheet and if any of the following applies.

• You reported qualified dividends on Form 1040, line 9b.

• You do not have to file Schedule D and you reported capital gain distributions on Form 1040, line 13.

• You are filing Schedule D and Schedule D, lines 15 and 16, are both more than zero.

But if you are filing Form 2555 or 2555-EZ, you must use the Foreign Earned Income Tax Worksheet instead.

Schedule J. If you had income from farming or fishing (including certain amounts received in connection with the Exxon Valdez litigation), your tax may be less if you choose to figure it using income averaging on Schedule J.

Foreign Earned Income Tax Worksheet. If you claimed the foreign earned income exclusion, housing exclusion, or housing deduction on Form 2555 or 2555-EZ, you must figure your tax using the Foreign Earned Income Tax Worksheet.

Foreign Earned Income Tax Worksheet—Line 44

> ⚠ **CAUTION**   If Form 1040, line 43, is zero, do not complete this worksheet.

1. Enter the amount from Form 1040, line 43 .... **1.** _____

2a. Enter the amount from your (and your spouse's, if filing jointly) Form 2555, lines 45 and 50, or Form 2555-EZ, line 18 .... **2a.** _____

  b. Enter the total amount of any itemized deductions or exclusions you couldn't claim because they are related to excluded income .... **b.** _____

  c. Subtract line 2b from line 2a. If zero or less, enter -0- .... **c.** _____

3. Add lines 1 and 2c .... **3.** _____

4. **Figure the tax on the amount on line 3**. Use the Tax Table, Tax Computation Worksheet, Qualified Dividends and Capital Gain Tax Worksheet*, Schedule D Tax Worksheet*, or Form 8615, whichever applies. See the instructions for line 44 to see which tax computation method applies. (Do not use a second Foreign Earned Income Tax Worksheet to figure the tax on this line.) .... **4.** _____

5. **Figure the tax on the amount on line 2c**. If the amount on line 2c is less than $100,000, use the Tax Table to figure this tax. If the amount on line 2c is $100,000 or more, use the Tax Computation Worksheet .... **5.** _____

6. Subtract line 5 from line 4. Enter the result. If zero or less, enter -0-. Also include this amount on Form 1040, line 44 .... **6.** _____

*Enter the amount from line 3 above on line 1 of the Qualified Dividends and Capital Gain Tax Worksheet or Schedule D Tax Worksheet if you use either of those worksheets to figure the tax on line 4 above. Complete the rest of that worksheet through line 6 (line 10 if you use the Schedule D Tax Worksheet). Next, you must determine if you have a capital gain excess. To find out if you have a capital gain excess, subtract Form 1040, line 43, from line 6 of your Qualified Dividends and Capital Gain Tax Worksheet (line 10 of your Schedule D Tax Worksheet). If the result is more than zero, that amount is your capital gain excess.

If you do not have a capital gain excess, complete the rest of either of those worksheets according to the worksheet's instructions. Then complete lines 5 and 6 above.

If you have a capital gain excess, complete a second Qualified Dividends and Capital Gain Tax Worksheet or Schedule D Tax Worksheet (whichever applies) as instructed above but in its entirety and with the following additional modifications. Then complete lines 5 and 6 above. These modifications are to be made only for purposes of filling out the Foreign Earned Income Tax Worksheet above.

1. Reduce (but not below zero) the amount you would otherwise enter on line 3 of your Qualified Dividends and Capital Gain Tax Worksheet or line 9 of your Schedule D Tax Worksheet by your capital gain excess.

2. Reduce (but not below zero) the amount you would otherwise enter on line 2 of your Qualified Dividends and Capital Gain Tax Worksheet or line 6 of your Schedule D Tax Worksheet by any of your capital gain excess not used in (1) above.

3. Reduce (but not below zero) the amount on your Schedule D (Form 1040), line 18, by your capital gain excess.

4. Include your capital gain excess as a loss on line 16 of your Unrecaptured Section 1250 Gain Worksheet in the Instructions for Schedule D (Form 1040).

Need more information or forms? Visit IRS.gov.

Qualified Dividends and Capital Gain Tax Worksheet—Line 44

Keep for Your Records

| **Before you begin:** | ✓ See the earlier instructions for line 44 to see if you can use this worksheet to figure your tax.
✓ Before completing this worksheet, complete Form 1040 through line 43.
✓ If you do not have to file Schedule D and you received capital gain distributions, be sure you checked the box on line 13 of Form 1040. |

1. Enter the amount from Form 1040, line 43. However, if you are filing Form 2555 or 2555-EZ (relating to foreign earned income), enter the amount from line 3 of the Foreign Earned Income Tax Worksheet . . . . **1.** _____

2. Enter the amount from Form 1040, line 9b* . . . . **2.** _____

3. Are you filing Schedule D?*

    ☐ **Yes.** Enter the **smaller** of line 15 or 16 of Schedule D. If either line 15 or line 16 is blank or a loss, enter -0-.

    ☐ **No.** Enter the amount from Form 1040, line 13.   **3.** _____

4. Add lines 2 and 3 . . . . **4.** _____

5. If filing Form 4952 (used to figure investment interest expense deduction), enter any amount from line 4g of that form. Otherwise, enter -0- . . . . **5.** _____

6. Subtract line 5 from line 4. If zero or less, enter -0- . . . . **6.** _____

7. Subtract line 6 from line 1. If zero or less, enter -0- . . . . **7.** _____

8. Enter:

    $37,650 if single or married filing separately,
    $75,300 if married filing jointly or qualifying widow(er),
    $50,400 if head of household.   . . . . **8.** _____

9. Enter the smaller of line 1 or line 8 . . . . **9.** _____

10. Enter the smaller of line 7 or line 9 . . . . **10.** _____

11. Subtract line 10 from line 9. This amount is taxed at 0% . . . . **11.** _____

12. Enter the smaller of line 1 or line 6 . . . . **12.** _____

13. Enter the amount from line 11 . . . . **13.** _____

14. Subtract line 13 from line 12 . . . . **14.** _____

15. Enter:

    $415,050 if single,
    $233,475 if married filing separately,
    $466,950 if married filing jointly or qualifying widow(er),
    $441,000 if head of household.   . . . . **15.** _____

16. Enter the smaller of line 1 or line 15 . . . . **16.** _____

17. Add lines 7 and 11 . . . . **17.** _____

18. Subtract line 17 from line 16. If zero or less, enter -0- . . . . **18.** _____

19. Enter the smaller of line 14 or line 18 . . . . **19.** _____

20. Multiply line 19 by 15% (0.15) . . . . **20.** _____

21. Add lines 11 and 19 . . . . **21.** _____

22. Subtract line 21 from line 12 . . . . **22.** _____

23. Multiply line 22 by 20% (0.20) . . . . **23.** _____

24. Figure the tax on the amount on line 7. If the amount on line 7 is less than $100,000, use the Tax Table to figure the tax. If the amount on line 7 is $100,000 or more, use the Tax Computation Worksheet . . . . **24.** _____

25. Add lines 20, 23, and 24 . . . . **25.** _____

26. Figure the tax on the amount on line 1. If the amount on line 1 is less than $100,000, use the Tax Table to figure the tax. If the amount on line 1 is $100,000 or more, use the Tax Computation Worksheet . . . . **26.** _____

27. **Tax on all taxable income.** Enter the **smaller** of line 25 or line 26. Also include this amount on Form 1040, line 44. If you are filing Form 2555 or 2555-EZ, do not enter this amount on Form 1040, line 44. Instead, enter it on line 4 of the Foreign Earned Income Tax Worksheet . . . . **27.** _____

If you are filing Form 2555 or 2555-EZ, see the footnote in the Foreign Earned Income Tax Worksheet before completing this line.

Line 45

Alternative Minimum Tax (AMT)

If you aren't sure whether you owe the AMT, complete the Worksheet To See if You Should Fill in Form 6251.

Exception. Fill in Form 6251 instead of using the worksheet if you claimed or received any of the following items.

- Accelerated depreciation.
- Tax-exempt interest from private activity bonds.
- Intangible drilling, circulation, research, experimental, or mining costs.
- Amortization of pollution-control facilities or depletion.
- Income or (loss) from tax-shelter farm activities, passive activities, partnerships, S corporations, or activities for which you aren't at risk.
- Income from long-term contracts not figured using the percentage-of-completion method.
- Interest paid on a home mortgage not used to buy, build, or substantially improve your home.
- Investment interest expense reported on Form 4952.
- Net operating loss deduction.
- Alternative minimum tax adjustments from an estate, trust, electing large partnership, or cooperative.
- Section 1202 exclusion.
- Stock by exercising an incentive stock option and you didn't dispose of the stock in the same year.
- Any general business credit claimed on Form 3800 if either line 6 (in Part I) or line 25 of Form 3800 is more than zero.
- Qualified electric vehicle credit.
- Alternative fuel vehicle refueling property tax.
- Credit for prior year minimum tax.
- Foreign tax credit.

 Form 6251 should be filled in for certain children who are under age 24 at the end of 2016. See the Instructions for Form 6251 for more information.

For help with the alternative minimum tax, go to *IRS.gov/AMT*.

Line 46

Excess Advance Premium Tax Credit Repayment

The premium tax credit helps pay premiums for health insurance purchased from the Marketplace. Eligible individuals may have advance payments of the premium tax credit paid on their behalf directly to the insurance company. If you, your spouse with whom you are filing a joint return, or your dependent was enrolled in coverage purchased from the Marketplace and advance payments of the premium tax credit were made for the coverage, complete Form 8962 to reconcile (compare) the advance payments with your premium tax credit. You (or whoever enrolled you) should have received Form 1095-A from the Marketplace with information about your coverage and any advance credit payments. If the advance credit payments were more than the premium tax credit you can claim, the amount you must repay will be shown on Form 8962, line 29. Enter that amount, if any, on Form 1040, line 46.

You may have to repay excess advance payments of the premium tax credit even if someone else enrolled you, your spouse, or your dependent in Marketplace coverage. In that case, another individual may have received the Form 1095-A for the coverage. You may also have to repay excess advance payments of the premium tax credit if you enrolled an individual in coverage through the Marketplace, you do not claim the individual as a dependent on your return, and no one else claims that individual as a dependent. For more information, see the Instructions for Form 8962.

Line 48

Foreign Tax Credit

If you paid income tax to a foreign country or U.S. possession, you may be able to take this credit. Generally, you must complete and attach Form 1116 to do so.

Exception. You do not have to complete Form 1116 to take this credit if all of the following apply.

1. All of your foreign source gross income was from interest and dividends and all of that income and the foreign tax paid on it were reported to you on Form 1099-INT, Form 1099-DIV, or Schedule K-1 (or substitute statement).

2. The total of your foreign taxes wasn't more than $300 (not more than $600 if married filing jointly).

3. You held the stock or bonds on which the dividends or interest were paid for at least 16 days and were not obligated to pay these amounts to someone else.

4. You are not filing Form 4563 or excluding income from sources within Puerto Rico.

5. All of your foreign taxes were:

a. Legally owed and not eligible for a refund or reduced tax rate under a tax treaty, and

b. Paid to countries that are recognized by the United States and do not support terrorism.

For more details on these requirements, see the Instructions for Form 1116.

Do you meet all five requirements just listed?

☐ **Yes.** Enter on line 48 the smaller of (a) your total foreign taxes, or (b) the total of the amounts on Form 1040, lines 44 and 46.

☐ **No.** See Form 1116 to find out if you can take the credit and, if you can, if you have to file Form 1116.

Line 49

Credit for Child and Dependent Care Expenses

You may be able to take this credit if you paid someone to care for:

- Your qualifying child under age 13 whom you claim as your dependent,
- Your disabled spouse or any other disabled person who couldn't care for himself or herself, or
- Your child whom you couldn't claim as a dependent because of the rules for *Children of divorced or separated parents* in the instructions for line 6c.

For details, use *Tax Topic 602* or see Form 2441.

Need more information or forms? Visit IRS.gov.

Before you begin: ✓ Be sure you have read the **Exception** in the instructions for this line to see if you must fill in Form 6251 instead of using this worksheet.

1. Are you filing **Schedule A?**

   ☐ **No.**   Skip lines 1 through 3; enter on line 4 the amount from Form 1040, line 38, and go to line 5.

   ☐ **Yes.**   Enter the amount from Form 1040, line 41 .... 1. _____

2. If you or your spouse was age 65 or older, enter the **smaller** of the amount on Schedule A, line 4, or 2.5% (0.025) of the amount on Form 1040, line 38. If zero or less, enter -0- .... 2. _____

3. Enter the total of the amounts from Schedule A, lines 9 and 27 .... 3. _____

4. Add lines 1 through 3 .... 4. _____

5. Enter any tax refund from Form 1040, lines 10 and 21 .... 5. _____

6. If you completed the Itemized Deductions Worksheet in the Instructions for Schedule A, enter the amount from line 9 of that worksheet .... 6. _____

7. Add lines 5 and 6 .... 7. _____

8. Subtract line 7 from line 4 .... 8. _____

9. Enter the amount shown below for your filing status.

   • Single or head of household—$53,900
   • Married filing jointly or qualifying widow(er)—$83,800   } .... 9. _____
   • Married filing separately—$41,900

10. Is the amount on line 8 more than the amount on line 9?

   ☐ **No.** (STOP) You do not need to fill in Form 6251. Do not complete the rest of this worksheet.

   ☐ **Yes.** Subtract line 9 from line 8 .... 10. _____

11. Enter the amount shown below for your filing status.

   • Single or head of household—$119,700
   • Married filing jointly or qualifying widow(er)—$159,700   } .... 11. _____
   • Married filing separately—$79,850

12. Is the amount on line 8 more than the amount on line 11?

   ☐ **No.**   Enter -0-. Skip line 13. Enter on line 14 the amount from line 10, and go to line 15.

   ☐ **Yes.** Subtract line 11 from line 8 .... 12. _____

13. Multiply line 12 by 25% (0.25) and enter the **smaller** of the result or line 9 .... 13. _____

14. Add lines 10 and 13 .... 14. _____

15. Is the amount on line 14 more than $186,300 ($93,150 if married filing separately)?

   ☐ **Yes.** (STOP) Fill in Form 6251 to see if you owe the alternative minimum tax.

   ☐ **No.**   Multiply line 14 by 26% (0.26) .... 15. _____

16. Add Form 1040, line 44 (minus any tax from Form 4972), and Form 1040, line 46. (If you used Schedule J to figure your tax on Form 1040, line 44, refigure that tax without using Schedule J before including it in this calculation) .... 16. _____

Next. Is the amount on line 15 more than the amount on line 16?

   ☐ **Yes.** Fill in Form 6251 to see if you owe the alternative minimum tax.

   ☐ **No.**   You do not owe alternative minimum tax and do not need to fill out Form 6251. Leave line 45 blank.

Line 50

Education Credits

If you (or your dependent) paid qualified expenses in 2016 for yourself, your spouse, or your dependent to enroll in or attend an eligible educational institution, you may be able to take an education credit. See Form 8863 for details. However, you can't take an education credit if any of the following applies.

• You, or your spouse if filing jointly, are claimed as a dependent on someone else's (such as your parent's) 2016 tax return.

• Your filing status is married filing separately.

• The amount on Form 1040, line 38, is $90,000 or more ($180,000 or more if married filing jointly).

• You are taking a deduction for tuition and fees on Form 1040, line 34, for the same student.

• You, or your spouse, were a nonresident alien for any part of 2016 unless your filing status is married filing jointly.

You may be able to increase an education credit if the student chooses to include all or part of a Pell grant or certain other scholarships or fellowships in income.

For more information, see Pub. 970, the instructions for line 68, and *IRS.gov/ EdCredit*.

Line 51

Retirement Savings Contributions Credit (Saver's Credit)

You may be able to take this credit if you, or your spouse if filing jointly, made (a) contributions, other than rollover contributions, to a traditional or Roth IRA (including a *my*RA); (b) elective deferrals to a 401(k) or 403(b) plan (including designated Roth contributions) or to a governmental 457, SEP, or SIMPLE plan; (c) voluntary employee contributions to a qualified retirement plan (including the federal Thrift Savings Plan); or (d) contributions to a 501(c)(18)(D) plan.

However, you can't take the credit if either of the following applies.

1. The amount on Form 1040, line 38, is more than $30,750 ($46,125 if head of household; $61,500 if married filing jointly).

2. The person(s) who made the qualified contribution or elective deferral (a) was born after January 1, 1999, (b) is claimed as a dependent on someone else's 2016 tax return, or (c) was a student (defined next).

You were a student if during any part of 5 calendar months of 2016 you:

• Were enrolled as a full-time student at a school, or

• Took a full-time, on-farm training course given by a school or a state, county, or local government agency.

A school includes a technical, trade, or mechanical school. It doesn't include an on-the-job training course, correspondence school, or school offering courses only through the Internet.

For more details, use *Tax Topic 610* or see Form 8880.

Need more information or forms? Visit IRS.gov.

2016 Child Tax Credit Worksheet—Line 52

 Keep for Your Records

1. To be a qualifying child for the child tax credit, the child must be your dependent, **under age 17** at the end of 2016, and meet all the conditions in Steps 1 through 3 in the instructions for line 6c. Make sure you checked the box on Form 1040, line 6c, column (4), for each qualifying child.

2. If you do not have a qualifying child, you cannot claim the child tax credit.

3. Be sure to see "Social security number" in the instructions for line 6c. If your qualifying child has an ITIN instead of an SSN, file Schedule 8812.

4. Do **not** use this worksheet, but use Pub. 972 instead, if:

   a. You are claiming the adoption credit, mortgage interest credit, District of Columbia first-time homebuyer credit, or residential energy efficient property credit;

   b. You are excluding income from Puerto Rico; or

   c. You are filing Form 2555, 2555-EZ, or 4563.

Part 1

1. Number of qualifying children: _____ × $1,000. Enter the result. | **1**

2. Enter the amount from Form 1040, line 38. | **2**

3. Enter the amount shown below for your filing status.

   ● Married filing jointly — $110,000

   ● Single, head of household, or qualifying widow(er) — $75,000

   ● Married filing separately — $55,000

   } | **3**

4. Is the amount on line 2 more than the amount on line 3?

   ☐ **No.** Leave line 4 blank. Enter -0- on line 5, and go to line 6.

   ☐ **Yes.** Subtract line 3 from line 2.
   If the result is not a multiple of $1,000, increase it to the next multiple of $1,000. For example, increase $425 to $1,000, increase $1,025 to $2,000, etc. | **4**

5. Multiply the amount on line 4 by 5% (0.05). Enter the result. | **5**

6. Is the amount on line 1 more than the amount on line 5?

   ☐ **No.** (STOP)
   You cannot take the child tax credit on Form 1040, line 52. You also cannot take the additional child tax credit on Form 1040, line 67. Complete the rest of your Form 1040.

   ☐ **Yes.** Subtract line 5 from line 1. Enter the result.
   Go to Part 2. | **6**

2016 Child Tax Credit Worksheet—*Continued*

Keep for Your Records

Before you begin Part 2: ✓ Figure the amount of any credits you are claiming on Form 5695, Part II; Form 8910; Form 8936; or Schedule R.

Part 2

7. Enter the amount from Form 1040, line 47.

| **7** | |

8. Add any amounts from:

Form 1040, line 48 _____

Form 1040, line 49 + _____

Form 1040, line 50 + _____

Form 1040, line 51 + _____

Form 5695, line 30 + _____

Form 8910, line 15 + _____

Form 8936, line 23 + _____

Schedule R, line 22 + _____

Enter the total. | **8** | |

9. Are the amounts on lines 7 and 8 the same?

☐ **Yes.** (STOP)
You cannot take this credit because there is no tax to reduce. However, you may be able to take the **additional child tax credit.** See the **TIP** below.

☐ **No.** Subtract line 8 from line 7.

| **9** | |

10. Is the amount on line 6 more than the amount on line 9?

☐ **Yes.** Enter the amount from line 9.
Also, you may be able to take the **additional child tax credit.** See the **TIP** below.

☐ **No.** Enter the amount from line 6.

} **This is your child tax credit.**

| **10** | |

Enter this amount on Form 1040, line 52.

TIP

*You may be able to take the **additional child tax credit** on Form 1040, line 67, if you answered "Yes" on line 9 **or** line 10 above.*

● *First, complete your Form 1040 through lines 66a and 66b.*

● *Then, use Schedule 8812 to figure any additional child tax credit.*

Need more information or forms? Visit IRS.gov.

Line 53

Residential Energy Credits

Residential energy efficient property credit. You may be able to take this credit by completing and attaching Form 5695 if you paid for any of the following during 2016.

- Qualified solar electric property for use in your home located in the United States.
- Qualified solar water heating property for use in your home located in the United States.
- Qualified fuel cell property installed on or in connection with your main home located in the United States.
- Qualified small wind energy property for use in connection with your home located in the United States.
- Qualified geothermal heat pump property installed on or in connection with your home located in the United States.

Nonbusiness energy property credit. You may be able to take this credit by completing and attaching Form 5695 for any of the following improvements to your main home located in the United States in 2016 if they are new and meet certain requirements for energy efficiency.

- Any insulation material or system primarily designed to reduce heat gain or loss in your home.
- Exterior windows (including skylights).
- Exterior doors.
- A metal roof or asphalt roof with pigmented coatings or cooling granules primarily designed to reduce the heat gain in your home.

You may also be able to take this credit for the cost of the following items if the items meet certain performance and quality standards.

- Certain electric heat pump water heaters, electric heat pumps, central air conditioners, and natural gas, propane, or oil water heaters.
- A qualified furnace or hot water boiler that uses natural gas, propane, or oil.
- A stove that burns biomass fuel to heat your home or to heat water for use in your home.
- An advanced main air circulating fan used in a natural gas, propane, or oil furnace.

Condos and co-ops. If you are a member of a condominium management association for a condominium you own or a tenant-stockholder in a cooperative housing corporation, you are treated as having paid your proportionate share of any costs of such association or corporation for purposes of these credits.

More details. For details, see Form 5695.

Line 54

Other Credits

Enter the total of the following credits on line 54 and check the appropriate box(es). Check all boxes that apply. If box c is checked, also enter the applicable form number. To find out if you can take the credit, see the form or publication indicated.

- General business credit. This credit consists of a number of credits that usually apply only to individuals who are partners, shareholders in an S corporation, self-employed, or who have rental property. See Form 3800 or Pub. 334.
- Credit for prior year minimum tax. If you paid alternative minimum tax in a prior year, see Form 8801.
- Mortgage interest credit. If a state or local government gave you a mortgage credit certificate, see Form 8396.
- Credit for the elderly or the disabled. See Schedule R.
- Adoption credit. You may be able to take this credit if you paid expenses to adopt a child or you adopted a child with special needs and the adoption became final in 2016. See the Instructions for Form 8839.
- District of Columbia first-time homebuyer credit. You can't claim this credit for a home you bought after 2011. You can claim it only if you have a credit carryforward from 2015. See Form 8859.
- Qualified plug-in electric drive motor vehicle credit. See Form 8936.
- Qualified electric vehicle credit. You can't claim this credit for a vehicle placed in service after 2006. You can claim this credit only if you have an electric vehicle passive activity credit carried forward from a prior year. See Form 8834.

- Alternative motor vehicle credit. See Form 8910 if you placed a new fuel cell motor vehicle in service during 2016.
- Alternative fuel vehicle refueling property credit. See Form 8911.
- Credit to holders of tax credit bonds. See Form 8912.

Other Taxes

Line 58

Unreported Social Security and Medicare Tax from Forms 4137 and 8919

Enter the total of any taxes from Form 4137 and Form 8919. Check the appropriate box(es).

Form 4137. If you received tips of $20 or more in any month and you didn't report the full amount to your employer, you must pay the social security and Medicare or railroad retirement (RRTA) tax on the unreported tips.

Do not include the value of any noncash tips, such as tickets or passes. You do not pay social security and Medicare taxes or RRTA tax on these noncash tips.

To figure the social security and Medicare tax, use Form 4137. If you owe RRTA tax, contact your employer. Your employer will figure and collect the RRTA tax.

 You may be charged a penalty equal to 50% of the social security and Medicare or RRTA tax due on tips you received but didn't report to your employer.

Form 8919. If you are an employee who received wages from an employer who didn't withhold social security and Medicare tax from your wages, use Form 8919 to figure your share of the unreported tax. Include on line 58 the amount from line 13 of Form 8919. Include the amount from line 6 of Form 8919 on Form 1040, line 7.

Line 59

Additional Tax on IRAs, Other Qualified Retirement Plans, etc.

If any of the following apply, see Form 5329 and its instructions to find out if you owe this tax and if you must file Form 5329. Also see Form 5329 and its instructions for definitions of the terms used here.

1. You received an early distribution from (a) an IRA or other qualified retirement plan, (b) an annuity, or (c) a modified endowment contract entered into after June 20, 1988, and the total distribution wasn't rolled over in a qualified rollover contribution.

2. Excess contributions were made to your IRA, Coverdell education savings account (ESA), Archer MSA, health savings account (HSA), or ABLE account.

3. You received a taxable distribution from a Coverdell ESA, qualified tuition program, or ABLE account.

4. You were born before July 1, 1945, and didn't take the minimum required distribution from your IRA or other qualified retirement plan.

Exception. If only item (1) applies and distribution code 1 is correctly shown in box 7 of all your Forms 1099-R, you do not have to file Form 5329. Instead, multiply the taxable amount of the distribution by 10% (0.10) and enter the result on line 59. The taxable amount of the distribution is the part of the distribution you reported on Form 1040, line 15b or line 16b, or on Form 4972. Also, enter "No" under the heading *Other Taxes* to the left of line 59 to indicate that you do not have to file Form 5329. But you must file Form 5329 if distribution code 1 is incorrectly shown in box 7 of Form 1099-R or you qualify for an exception, such as the exceptions for qualified medical expenses, qualified higher education expenses, qualified first-time homebuyer distributions, or a qualified reservist distribution.

Line 60a

Household Employment Taxes

Enter the household employment taxes you owe for having a household employee. If any of the following apply, see Schedule H and its instructions to find out if you owe these taxes.

1. You paid any one household employee (defined below) cash wages of $2,000 or more in 2016. Cash wages include wages paid by check, money order, etc. But do not count amounts paid to an employee who was under age 18 at any time in 2016 and was a student.

2. You withheld federal income tax during 2016 at the request of any household employee.

3. You paid total cash wages of $1,000 or more in any calendar quarter of 2015 or 2016 to household employees.

Any person who does household work is a household employee if you can control what will be done and how it will be done. Household work includes work done in or around your home by babysitters, nannies, health aides, housekeepers, yard workers, and similar domestic workers.

Line 60b

First-time Homebuyer Credit Repayment

Enter the first-time homebuyer credit you have to repay if:
- You bought the home in 2008, or
- The home you bought was destroyed, condemned, or sold under threat of condemnation in 2014 and that event occurred during the 36-month period that began on the date you bought the home.

If you bought the home in 2008 and owned and used it as your main home for all of 2016, you can enter your 2016 repayment on this line without attaching Form 5405.

See the Form 5405 instructions for details and for exceptions to the repayment rule.

Line 61

Health Care: Individual Responsibility

For each month of 2016, you must either:
- Have qualifying health care coverage for yourself, your spouse (if filing jointly), and anyone you can or do claim as a dependent (you are treated as having coverage for any month in which you have coverage for at least 1 day of the month),
- Qualify for an exemption from the requirement to have health care coverage, or
- Make a shared responsibility payment with your return and enter the amount on this line.

If you had qualifying health care coverage (called minimum essential coverage) for every month of 2016 for yourself, your spouse (if filing jointly), and anyone you can or do claim as a dependent, check the box on this line and leave the entry space blank.

You can check the box even if:
- A dependent child who was born or adopted during the year was not covered by your insurance during the month of or months before birth or adoption (but the child must have had minimum essential coverage every month of 2016 following the birth or adoption), or
- A spouse or dependent who died during the year was not covered by your insurance during the month of death and months after death (but he or she must have had minimum essential coverage every month of 2016 he or she was alive).

If you cannot check the box on this line, you must generally either claim a coverage exemption on Form 8965 or report a shared responsibility payment on line 61 for each month that you, your spouse (if filing jointly), or someone you can or do claim as a dependent didn't have coverage. See the Instructions for Form 8965 for information on coverage exemptions and figuring the shared responsibility payment. However, if you can be claimed as a dependent, you do not need to check the box, claim a coverage exemption or report a payment. Leave the entry space blank. You do not need to attach Form 8965 or see its instructions.

Need more information or forms? Visit IRS.gov.

If you or someone in your household had minimum essential coverage in 2016, the provider of that coverage is required to send you a Form 1095-A, 1095-B, or 1095-C (with Part III completed) that lists individuals in your family who were enrolled in the coverage and shows their months of coverage.

- Individuals enrolled in health insurance coverage through the Marketplace generally receive this information on Form 1095-A, Health Insurance Marketplace Statement.

- Individuals enrolled in health insurance coverage provided by their employer generally receive this information on either Form 1095-B, Health Coverage, or on Form 1095-C, Employer-Provided Health Insurance Offer and Coverage.

- Individuals enrolled in a government-sponsored health program or in other types of coverage generally receive this information on Form 1095-B, Health Coverage.

You should receive the Form 1095-A by early February 2017 and Form 1095-B or 1095-C by early March 2017, if applicable. You do not need to wait to receive your Form 1095-B or 1095-C to file your return. You may rely on other information about your coverage to complete line 61. Do not include Form 1095-A, Form 1095-B, or Form 1095-C with your tax return.

Your health care coverage provider may have asked for your social security number. To understand why, go to *IRS.gov/ACASSN*.

Minimum essential coverage. Most health care coverage that people have is minimum essential coverage.

Minimum essential coverage includes:
- Most types of health care coverage provided by your employer,
- Many types of government-sponsored health care coverage including Medicare, most Medicaid coverage, and most health care coverage provided to veterans and active duty service members,
- Health care coverage you buy through the Marketplace, and
- Certain types of health care coverage you buy directly from an insurance company.

See the Instructions for Form 8965 for more information on what qualifies as minimum essential coverage.

Reminder—health care coverage. If you need health care coverage, go to *www.HealthCare.gov* to learn about health insurance options for you and your family, how to buy health insurance, and how you might qualify to get financial assistance to buy health insurance.

Premium tax credit. If you, your spouse, or a dependent enrolled in health insurance through the Marketplace, you may be able to claim the premium tax credit. See the instructions for line 69 and Form 8962.

Line 62

Other Taxes

Use line 62 to report any taxes not reported elsewhere on your return or other schedules. To find out if you owe the tax, see the form or publication indicated. Enter on line 62 the total of all the following taxes you owe.

Additional Medicare Tax. See Form 8959 and its instructions if the total of your 2016 wages and any self-employment income was more than:
- $125,000 if married filing separately,
- $250,000 if married filing jointly, or
- $200,000 if single, head of household, or qualifying widow(er).

Also see Form 8959 if you had railroad retirement (RRTA) compensation that was more than the amount just listed that applies to you.

If you are married filing jointly and either you or your spouse had wages or RRTA compensation of more than $200,000, your employer may have withheld Additional Medicare Tax even if you do not owe the tax. In that case, you may be able to get a refund of the tax withheld. See the Instructions for Form 8959 to find out how to report the withheld tax on Form 8959.

Check box a if you owe the tax.

Net Investment Income Tax. See Form 8960 and its instructions if the amount on Form 1040, line 38, is more than:

- $125,000 if married filing separately,
- $250,000 if married filing jointly or qualifying widow(er), or
- $200,000 if single or head of household.

If you file Form 2555 or 2555-EZ, see Form 8960 and its instructions if the amount on Form 1040, line 38, is more than:
- $23,700 if married filing separately,
- $148,700 if married filing jointly or qualifying widow(er), or
- $98,700 if single or head of household.

Check box b if you owe the tax.

Other taxes. For the following taxes, check box c and, in the space next to that box, enter the amount of the tax and the code that identifies it. If you need more room, attach a statement listing the amount of each tax and the code.

1. Additional tax on health savings account (HSA) distributions (see Form 8889, Part II). Identify as "HSA."

2. Additional tax on an HSA because you didn't remain an eligible individual during the testing period (see Form 8889, Part III). Identify as "HDHP."

3. Additional tax on Archer MSA distributions (see Form 8853). Identify as "MSA."

4. Additional tax on Medicare Advantage MSA distributions (see Form 8853). Identify as "Med MSA."

5. Recapture of the following credits.

a. Investment credit (see Form 4255). Identify as "ICR."

b. Low-income housing credit (see Form 8611). Identify as "LIHCR."

c. Indian employment credit (see Form 8845). Identify as "IECR."

d. New markets credit (see Form 8874). Identify as "NMCR."

e. Credit for employer-provided child care facilities (see Form 8882). Identify as "ECCFR."

f. Alternative motor vehicle credit (see Form 8910). Identify as "AMVCR."

g. Alternative fuel vehicle refueling property credit (see Form 8911). Identify as "ARPCR."

h. Qualified plug-in electric drive motor vehicle credit (see Form 8936). Identify as "8936R."

6. Recapture of federal mortgage subsidy. If you sold your home in 2016 and it was financed (in whole or in part) from the proceeds of any tax-exempt qualified mortgage bond or you claimed the mortgage interest credit, see Form 8828. Identify as "FMSR."

7. Section 72(m)(5) excess benefits tax (see Pub. 560). Identify as "Sec. 72(m)(5)."

8. Uncollected social security and Medicare or RRTA tax on tips or group-term life insurance. This tax should be shown in box 12 of Form W-2 with codes A and B or M and N. Identify as "UT."

9. Golden parachute payments. If you received an excess parachute payment (EPP), you must pay a 20% tax on it. This tax should be shown in box 12 of Form W-2 with code K. If you received a Form 1099-MISC, the tax is 20% of the EPP shown in box 13. Identify as "EPP."

10. Tax on accumulation distribution of trusts (see Form 4970). Identify as "ADT."

11. Excise tax on insider stock compensation from an expatriated corporation. See section 4985. Identify as "ISC."

12. Interest on the tax due on installment income from the sale of certain residential lots and timeshares. Identify as "453(l)(3)."

13. Interest on the deferred tax on gain from certain installment sales with a sales price over $150,000. Identify as "453A(c)."

14. Additional tax on recapture of a charitable contribution deduction relating to a fractional interest in tangible personal property. See Pub. 526. Identify as "FITPP."

15. Look-back interest under section 167(g) or 460(b). See Form 8697 or 8866. Identify as "8697" or "8866."

16. Additional tax on income you received from a nonqualified deferred compensation plan that fails to meet the requirements of section 409A. This income should be shown in box 12 of Form W-2 with code Z, or in box 15b of Form 1099-MISC. The tax is 20% of the amount required to be included in income plus an interest amount determined under section 409A(a)(1)(B)(ii). See section 409A(a)(1)(B) for details. Identify as "NQDC."

17. Additional tax on compensation you received from a nonqualified deferred compensation plan described in section 457A if the compensation would have been includible in your income in an earlier year except that the amount wasn't determinable until 2016. The tax is 20% of the amount required to be included in income plus an interest amount determined under section 457A(c)(2). See section 457A for details. Identify as "457A."

18. Tax on noneffectively connected income for any part of the year you were a nonresident alien (see the Instructions for Form 1040NR). Identify as "1040NR."

19. Any interest amount from Form 8621, line 16f, relating to distributions from, and dispositions of, stock of a section 1291 fund. Identify as "1291INT."

20. Any interest amount from Form 8621, line 24. Identify as "1294INT."

Payments

Line 64

Federal Income Tax Withheld

Add the amounts shown as federal income tax withheld on your Forms W-2, W-2G, and 1099-R. Enter the total on line 64. The amount withheld should be shown in box 2 of Form W-2 and in box 4 of Form W-2G or 1099-R. Attach your Form(s) W-2 to the front of your return. Attach Forms W-2G and 1099-R to the front of your return if federal income tax was withheld.

If you received a 2016 Form 1099 showing federal income tax withheld on dividends, taxable or tax-exempt interest income, unemployment compensation, social security benefits, railroad retirement benefits, or other income you received, include the amount withheld in the total on line 64. This should be shown in box 4 of Form 1099, box 6 of Form SSA-1099, or box 10 of Form RRB-1099.

If you had Additional Medicare Tax withheld, include the amount shown on Form 8959, line 24, in the total on line 64. Attach Form 8959.

Also include on line 64 any federal income tax withheld that is shown on a Schedule K-1.

Line 65

2016 Estimated Tax Payments

Enter any estimated federal income tax payments you made for 2016. Include any overpayment that you applied to your 2016 estimated tax from:
- Your 2015 return, or
- An amended return (Form 1040X).

If you and your spouse paid joint estimated tax but are now filing separate income tax returns, you can divide the amount paid in any way you choose as long as you both agree. If you can't agree, you must divide the payments in proportion to each spouse's individual tax as shown on your separate returns for 2016. For an example and more information, see Pub. 505. Be sure to show both social security numbers (SSNs) in the space provided on the separate returns. If you or your spouse paid separate estimated tax but you are now filing a joint return, add the amounts you each paid. Follow these instructions even if your spouse died in 2016 or in 2017 before filing a 2016 return.

Divorced taxpayers. If you got divorced in 2016 and you made joint estimated tax payments with your former spouse, enter your former spouse's SSN in the space provided on the front of Form 1040. If you were divorced and remarried in 2016, enter your present spouse's SSN in the space provided on the front of Form 1040. Also, under the heading *Payments* to the left of line 65, enter your former spouse's SSN, followed by "DIV."

Name change. If you changed your name and you made estimated tax payments using your former name, attach a statement to the front of Form 1040 that explains all the payments you and your spouse made in 2016 and the name(s) and SSN(s) under which you made them.

Need more information or forms? Visit IRS.gov.

Lines 66a and 66b—
Earned Income Credit (EIC)

What Is the EIC?

The EIC is a credit for certain people who work. The credit may give you a refund even if you do not owe any tax or did not have any tax withheld.

To Take the EIC:

- Follow the steps below.
- Complete the worksheet that applies to you or let the IRS figure the credit for you.
- If you have a qualifying child, complete and attach Schedule EIC.

For help in determining if you are eligible for the EIC, go to *IRS.gov/eitc* and click on "EITC Assistant." This service is available in English and Spanish.

 If you take the EIC even though you aren't eligible and it is determined that your error is due to reckless or intentional disregard of the EIC rules, you won't be allowed to take the credit for 2 years even if you are otherwise eligible to do so. If you fraudulently take the EIC, you won't be allowed to take the credit for 10 years. See Form 8862, who must file, *later. You may also have to pay penalties.*

Step 1 All Filers

1. If, in 2016:
   - 3 or more children lived with you, is the amount on Form 1040, line 38, less than $47,955 ($53,505 if married filing jointly)?
   - 2 children lived with you, is the amount on Form 1040, line 38, less than $44,648 ($50,198 if married filing jointly)?
   - 1 child lived with you, is the amount on Form 1040, line 38, less than $39,296 ($44,846 if married filing jointly)?
   - No children lived with you, is the amount on Form 1040, line 38, less than $14,880 ($20,430 if married filing jointly)?

   ☐ **Yes.** Continue ☐ **No.**
   You can't take the credit.

2. Do you, and your spouse if filing a joint return, have a social security number that allows you to work and is valid for EIC purposes (explained later under *Definitions and Special Rules*)?

   ☐ **Yes.** Continue ☐ **No.**
   You can't take the credit. Enter "No" on the dotted line next to line 66a.

3. Is your filing status married filing separately?

   ☐ **Yes.** (STOP) ☐ **No.** Continue
   You can't take the credit.

4. Are you filing Form 2555 or 2555-EZ (relating to foreign earned income)?

   ☐ **Yes.** (STOP) ☐ **No.** Continue
   You can't take the credit.

5. Were you or your spouse a nonresident alien for any part of 2016?

   ☐ **Yes.** See *Nonresident aliens,* later, under *Definitions and Special Rules.* ☐ **No.** Go to Step 2.

Step 2 Investment Income

1. Add the amounts from Form 1040:

Line 8a		_____
Line 8b	+	_____
Line 9a	+	_____
Line 13*	+	_____
Investment Income	=	[_____]

   *If line 13 is a loss, enter -0-.

2. Is your investment income more than $3,400?

   ☐ **Yes.** Continue ☐ **No.** Skip question 3; go to question 4.

3. Are you filing Form 4797 (relating to sales of business property)?

   ☐ **Yes.** See *Form 4797 filers,* later, under *Definitions and Special Rules.* ☐ **No.** (STOP)
   You can't take the credit.

4. Do any of the following apply for 2016?
   - You are filing Schedule E.
   - You are reporting income from the rental of personal property not used in a trade or business.
   - You are filing Form 8814 (relating to election to report child's interest and dividends on your return).
   - You have income or loss from a passive activity.

   ☐ **Yes.** Use Worksheet 1 in Pub. 596 to see if you can take the credit. ☐ **No.** Go to Step 3.

Step 3 Qualifying Child

A qualifying child for the EIC is a child who is your...

Son, daughter, stepchild, foster child, brother, sister, stepbrother, stepsister, half brother, half sister, or a descendant of any of them (for example, your grandchild, niece, or nephew)

was ...

Under age 19 at the end of 2016 and younger than you
(or your spouse, if filing jointly)

or

Under age 24 at the end of 2016, a student (defined later), and younger than you
(or your spouse, if filing jointly)

or

Any age and permanently and totally disabled (defined later)

Who isn't filing a joint return for 2016
or is filing a joint return for 2016 only to claim a refund of withheld income tax or estimated tax paid (see Pub. 596 for examples)

Who lived with you in the United States for more than half of 2016.

> **⚠ CAUTION** *You can't take the credit for a child who didn't live with you for more than half the year, even if you paid most of the child's living expenses. The IRS may ask you for documents to show you lived with each qualifying child. Documents you might want to keep for this purpose include school and child care records and other records that show your child's address.*

> **TIP** *If the child didn't live with you for more than half of 2016 because of a temporary absence, birth, death, or kidnapping, see* Exception to time lived with you, *later.*

> **⚠ CAUTION** *If the child meets the conditions to be a qualifying child of any other person (other than your spouse if filing a joint return) for 2016, see* Qualifying child of more than one person, *later. If the child was married, see* Married child, *later.*

---

1. Do you have at least one child who meets the conditions to be your qualifying child?

   ☐ **Yes.** The child must have a valid social security number (SSN) as defined later, unless the child was born and died in 2016. If at least one qualifying child has a valid SSN (or was born or died in 2016), go to question 2. Otherwise, you can't take the credit.

   ☐ **No.** Skip questions 2 and 3; go to Step 4.

2. Are you filing a joint return for 2016?

   ☐ **Yes.** Skip question 3 and Step 4; go to Step 5.

   ☐ **No.** Continue ⬎

3. Could you be a qualifying child of another person for 2016? (Check "No" if the other person isn't required to file, and isn't filing, a 2016 tax return or is filing a 2016 return only to claim a refund of withheld income tax or estimated tax paid (see Pub. 596 for examples).)

   ☐ **Yes.** (STOP) You can't take the credit. Enter "No" on the dotted line next to line 66a.

   ☐ **No.** Skip Step 4; go to Step 5.

Step 4 Filers Without a Qualifying Child

1. Is the amount on Form 1040, line 38, less than $14,880 ($20,430 if married filing jointly)?

   ☐ **Yes.** Continue ⬎

   ☐ **No.** (STOP) You can't take the credit.

2. Were you, or your spouse if filing a joint return, at least age 25 but under age 65 at the end of 2016? (Check "Yes" if you, or your spouse if filing a joint return, were born after December 31, 1951, and before January 2, 1992.) If your spouse died in 2016 or if you are preparing a return for someone who died in 2016, see Pub. 596 before you answer.

   ☐ **Yes.** Continue ⬎

   ☐ **No.** (STOP) You can't take the credit.

3. Was your main home, and your spouse's if filing a joint return, in the United States for more than half of 2016? Members of the military stationed outside the United States, see *Members of the military,* later, before you answer.

   ☐ **Yes.** Continue ⬎

   ☐ **No.** (STOP) You can't take the credit. Enter "No" on the dotted line next to line 66a.

Need more information or forms? Visit IRS.gov.

4. Are you filing a joint return for 2016?

☐ **Yes.** Skip questions 5 and 6; go to Step 5. ☐ **No.** Continue ➘

5. Could you be a qualifying child of another person for 2016? (Check "No" if the other person isn't required to file, and isn't filing, a 2016 tax return or is filing a 2016 return only to claim a refund of withheld income tax or estimated tax paid (see Pub. 596 for examples).)

☐ **Yes.** (STOP) ☐ **No.** Continue ➘

You can't take the credit. Enter "No" on the dotted line next to line 66a.

6. Can you be claimed as a dependent on someone else's 2016 tax return?

☐ **Yes.** (STOP) ☐ **No.** Go to Step 5.

You can't take the credit.

Step 5 Earned Income

1. Are you filing Schedule SE because you were a member of the clergy or you had church employee income of $108.28 or more?

☐ **Yes.** See *Clergy* or *Church employees*, whichever applies. ☐ **No.** Complete the following worksheet.

1. Enter the amount from Form 1040, line 7 . . . . 1._____

2. Enter any amount included on Form 1040, line 7, that is a taxable scholarship or fellowship grant not reported on a Form W-2 . . . . 2._____

3. Enter any amount included on Form 1040, line 7, that you received for work performed while an inmate in a penal institution. (Enter "PRI" and the same amount on the dotted line next to Form 1040, line 7) . . . . 3._____

4. Enter any amount included on Form 1040, line 7, that you received as a pension or annuity from a nonqualified deferred compensation plan or a nongovernmental section 457 plan. (Enter "DFC" and the same amount on the dotted line next to Form 1040, line 7.) This amount may be shown in box 11 of Form W-2. If you received such an amount but box 11 is blank, contact your employer for the amount received . . . . . . 4._____

5. Enter any amount included on Form 1040, line 7, that is a Medicaid waiver payment you exclude from income. (See the instructions for line 21) . . . . 5._____

6. Add lines 2, 3, 4, and 5 . . . . 6._____

7. Subtract line 6 from line 1 . . . . 7._____

8. Enter all of your nontaxable combat pay if you elect to include it in earned income. Also enter this amount on Form 1040, line 66b. See *Combat pay, nontaxable*, later . . . . 8._____

⚠ CAUTION *Electing to include nontaxable combat pay may increase or decrease your EIC. Figure the credit with and without your nontaxable combat pay before making the election.*

9. Add lines 7 and 8. **This is your earned income** . . . . 9._____

2. Were you self-employed at any time in 2016, or are you filing Schedule SE because you were a member of the clergy or you had church employee income, or are you filing Schedule C or C-EZ as a statutory employee?

☐ **Yes.** Skip question 3 and Step 6; go to Worksheet B. ☐ **No.** Continue ➘

3. If you have:
   - 3 or more qualifying children, is your earned income less than $47,955 ($53,505 if married filing jointly)?
   - 2 qualifying children, is your earned income less than $44,648 ($50,198 if married filing jointly)?
   - 1 qualifying child, is your earned income less than $39,296 ($44,846 if married filing jointly)?
   - No qualifying children, is your earned income less than $14,880 ($20,430 if married filing jointly)?

☐ **Yes.** Go to Step 6. ☐ **No.** (STOP)

You can't take the credit.

Step 6 How To Figure the Credit

1. Do you want the IRS to figure the credit for you?

☐ **Yes.** See *Credit figured by the IRS*, later. ☐ **No.** Go to Worksheet A.

Definitions and Special Rules

Adopted child. An adopted child is always treated as your own child. An adopted child includes a child lawfully placed with you for legal adoption.

Church employees. Determine how much of the amount on Form 1040, line 7, was also reported on Schedule SE, Section B, line 5a. Subtract that amount from the amount on Form 1040, line 7, and enter the result on line 1 of the worksheet in Step 5 (instead of entering the actual amount from Form 1040, line 7). Be sure to answer "Yes" to question 2 in Step 5.

Clergy. The following instructions apply to ministers, members of religious orders who have not taken a vow of poverty, and Christian Science practitioners. If you are filing Schedule SE and the amount on line 2 of that schedule includes an amount that was also reported on Form 1040, line 7:

1. Enter "Clergy" on the dotted line next to Form 1040, line 66a.

2. Determine how much of the amount on Form 1040, line 7, was also reported on Schedule SE, Section A, line 2, or Section B, line 2.

3. Subtract that amount from the amount on Form 1040, line 7. Enter the result on line 1 of the worksheet in Step 5 (instead of entering the actual amount from Form 1040, line 7).

4. Be sure to answer "Yes" to question 2 in Step 5.

Combat pay, nontaxable. If you were a member of the U.S. Armed Forces who served in a combat zone, certain pay is excluded from your income. See *Combat Zone Exclusion* in Pub. 3. You can elect to include this pay in your earned income when figuring the EIC. The amount of your nontaxable combat pay should be shown in box 12 of Form(s) W-2 with code Q. If you are filing a joint return and both you and your spouse received nontaxable combat pay, you can each make your own election. In other words, if one of you makes the election, the other one can also make it but doesn't have to.

Credit figured by the IRS. To have the IRS figure your EIC:

1. Enter "EIC" on the dotted line next to Form 1040, line 66a.

2. Be sure you enter the nontaxable combat pay you elect to include in earned income on Form 1040, line 66b. See *Combat pay, nontaxable*, earlier.

3. If you have a qualifying child, complete and attach Schedule EIC. If your EIC for a year after 1996 was reduced or disallowed, see *Form 8862, who must file*, later.

Exception to time lived with you. Temporary absences by you or the child for special circumstances, such as school, vacation, business, medical care, military service, or detention in a juvenile facility, count as time the child lived with you. Also see *Kidnapped child* in the instructions for line 6c and *Members of the military*, later. A child is considered to have lived with you for more than half of 2016 if the child was born or died in 2016 and your home was this child's home for more than half the time he or she was alive in 2016.

Form 4797 filers. If the amount on Form 1040, line 13, includes an amount from Form 4797, you must use Worksheet 1 in Pub. 596 to see if you can take the EIC. Otherwise, stop; you can't take the EIC.

Form 8862, who must file. You must file Form 8862 if your EIC for a year after 1996 was reduced or disallowed for any reason other than a math or clerical error. But do not file Form 8862 if either of the following applies.

• You filed Form 8862 for another year, the EIC was allowed for that year, and your EIC hasn't been reduced or disallowed again for any reason other than a math or clerical error.

• You are taking the EIC without a qualifying child and the only reason your EIC was reduced or disallowed in the other year was because it was determined that a child listed on Schedule EIC wasn't your qualifying child.

Also, do not file Form 8862 or take the credit for the:

• 2 years after the most recent tax year for which there was a final determination that your EIC claim was due to reckless or intentional disregard of the EIC rules, or

• 10 years after the most recent tax year for which there was a final determination that your EIC claim was due to fraud.

Foster child. A foster child is any child placed with you by an authorized placement agency or by judgment, decree, or other order of any court of competent jurisdiction. For more details on authorized placement agencies, see Pub. 596.

Married child. A child who was married at the end of 2016 is a qualifying child only if (a) you can claim him or her as your dependent on Form 1040, line 6c, or (b) you could have claimed him or her as your dependent except for the special rule for *Children of divorced or separated parents* in the instructions for line 6c.

Members of the military. If you were on extended active duty outside the United States, your main home is considered to be in the United States during that duty period. Extended active duty is military duty ordered for an indefinite period or for a period of more than 90 days. Once you begin serving extended active duty, you are considered to be on extended active duty even if you do not serve more than 90 days.

Nonresident aliens. If your filing status is married filing jointly, go to Step 2. Otherwise, stop; you can't take the EIC. Enter "No" on the dotted line next to line 66a.

Permanently and totally disabled. A person is permanently and totally disabled if, at any time in 2016, the person couldn't engage in any substantial gainful activity because of a physical or mental condition and a doctor has determined that this condition (a) has lasted or can be expected to last continuously for at least a year, or (b) can be expected to lead to death.

Qualifying child of more than one person. Even if a child meets the conditions to be the qualifying child of more than one person, only one person can claim the child as a qualifying child for all of the following tax benefits, unless the special rule for *Children of divorced or separated parents* in the instructions for line 6c applies.

1. Dependency exemption (line 6c).

2. Child tax credits (lines 52 and 67).

3. Head of household filing status (line 4).

4. Credit for child and dependent care expenses (line 49).

5. Exclusion for dependent care benefits (Form 2441, Part III).

6. Earned income credit (lines 66a and 66b).

No other person can take any of the six tax benefits just listed unless he or she has a different qualifying child. If you and any other person can claim the child as a qualifying child, the following rules apply.

• If only one of the persons is the child's parent, the child is treated as the qualifying child of the parent.

• If the parents file a joint return together and can claim the child as a qualifying child, the child is treated as the qualifying child of the parents.

• If the parents do not file a joint return together but both parents claim the child as a qualifying child, the IRS will treat the child as the qualifying child of the parent with whom the child lived for the longer period of time in 2016. If the child lived with each parent for the same amount of time, the IRS will

Need more information or forms? Visit IRS.gov.

treat the child as the qualifying child of the parent who had the higher adjusted gross income (AGI) for 2016.

- If no parent can claim the child as a qualifying child, the child is treated as the qualifying child of the person who had the highest AGI for 2016.

- If a parent can claim the child as a qualifying child but no parent does so claim the child, the child is treated as the qualifying child of the person who had the highest AGI for 2016, but only if that person's AGI is higher than the highest AGI of any parent of the child who can claim the child.

Example. Your daughter meets the conditions to be a qualifying child for both you and your mother. Your daughter doesn't meet the conditions to be a qualifying child of any other person, including her other parent. Under the rules just described, you can claim your daughter as a qualifying child for all of the six tax benefits listed here for which you otherwise qualify. Your mother can't claim any of the six tax benefits listed here unless she has a different qualifying child. However, if your mother's AGI is higher than yours and you do not claim your daughter as a qualifying child, your daughter is the qualifying child of your mother.

For more details and examples, see Pub. 596.

If you won't be taking the EIC with a qualifying child, enter "No" on the dotted line next to line 66a. Otherwise, go to Step 3, question 1.

Social security number (SSN). For the EIC, a valid SSN is a number issued by the Social Security Administration unless "Not Valid for Employment" is printed on the social security card and the number was issued solely to allow the recipient of the SSN to apply for or receive a federally funded benefit. However, if "Valid for Work Only With DHS Authorization" is printed on your social security card, your SSN is valid for EIC purposes only as long as the DHS authorization is still valid.

To find out how to get an SSN, see *Social Security Number (SSN)* near the beginning of these instructions. If you won't have an SSN by the date your return is due, see *What if You Can't File on Time?*

If you didn't have an SSN by the due date of your 2016 return (including extensions), you can't claim the EIC on either your original or an amended 2016 return, even if you later get an SSN. Also, if a child didn't have an SSN by the due date of your return (including extensions), you can't count that child as a qualifying child in figuring the EIC on either your original or an amended 2016 return, even if that child later gets an SSN.

Student. A student is a child who during any part of 5 calendar months of 2016 was enrolled as a full-time student at a school, or took a full-time, on-farm training course given by a school or a state, county, or local government agency. A school includes a technical, trade, or mechanical school. It doesn't include an on-the-job training course, correspondence school, or school offering courses only through the Internet.

Welfare benefits, effect of credit on. Any refund you receive as a result of taking the EIC can't be counted as income when determining if you or anyone else is eligible for benefits or assistance, or how much you or anyone else can receive, under any federal program or under any state or local program financed in whole or in part with federal funds. These programs include Temporary Assistance for Needy Families (TANF), Medicaid, Supplemental Security Income (SSI), and Supplemental Nutrition Assistance Program (food stamps). In addition, when determining eligibility, the refund can't be counted as a resource for at least 12 months after you receive it. Check with your local benefit coordinator to find out if your refund will affect your benefits.

Worksheet A—2016 EIC—Lines 66a and 66b

Keep for Your Records

Before you begin: √ Be sure you are using the correct worksheet. Use this worksheet only if you answered "No" to Step 5, question 2. Otherwise, use Worksheet B.

Part 1

All Filers Using Worksheet A

1. Enter your earned income from Step 5.

   1 [ ]

2. Look up the amount on line 1 above in the EIC Table (right after Worksheet B) to find the credit. Be sure you use the correct column for your filing status and the number of children you have. Enter the credit here.

   If line 2 is zero, (STOP) You cannot take the credit.
   Enter "No" on the dotted line next to line 66a.

   2 [ ]

3. Enter the amount from Form 1040, line 38.

   3 [ ]

4. Are the amounts on lines 3 and 1 the same?

   [ ] **Yes.** Skip line 5; enter the amount from line 2 on line 6.

   [ ] **No.** Go to line 5.

Part 2

Filers Who Answered "No" on Line 4

5. If you have:

   ● No qualifying children, is the amount on line 3 less than $8,300 ($13,850 if married filing jointly)?

   ● 1 or more qualifying children, is the amount on line 3 less than $18,200 ($23,750 if married filing jointly)?

   [ ] **Yes.** Leave line 5 blank; enter the amount from line 2 on line 6.

   [ ] **No.** Look up the amount on line 3 in the EIC Table to find the credit. Be sure you use the correct column for your filing status and the number of children you have. Enter the credit here.
   Look at the amounts on lines 5 and 2.
   Then, enter the **smaller** amount on line 6.

   5 [ ]

Part 3

Your Earned Income Credit

6. **This is your earned income credit.**

   6 [ ]

   Enter this amount on Form 1040, line 66a.

Reminder—

√ If you have a qualifying child, complete and attach Schedule EIC.

⚠ **CAUTION** *If your EIC for a year after 1996 was reduced or disallowed, see Form 8862, who must file, earlier, to find out if you must file Form 8862 to take the credit for 2016.*

Need more information or forms? Visit IRS.gov.

Worksheet B—2016 EIC—Lines 66a and 66b

Keep for Your Records

Use this worksheet if you answered "Yes" to Step 5, question 2.

√ Complete the parts below (Parts 1 through 3) that apply to you. Then, continue to Part 4.

√ If you are married filing a joint return, include your spouse's amounts, if any, with yours to figure the amounts to enter in Parts 1 through 3.

Part 1

Self-Employed, Members of the Clergy, and People With Church Employee Income Filing Schedule SE

1a. Enter the amount from Schedule SE, Section A, line 3, or Section B, line 3, whichever applies. | **1a** |
  b. Enter any amount from Schedule SE, Section B, line 4b, and line 5a. | + **1b** |
  c. Combine lines 1a and 1b. | = **1c** |
  d. Enter the amount from Schedule SE, Section A, line 6, or Section B, line 13, whichever applies. | − **1d** |
  e. Subtract line 1d from 1c. | = **1e** |

Part 2

Self-Employed NOT Required To File Schedule SE

For example, your net earnings from self-employment were less than $400.

2. Do not include on these lines any statutory employee income, any net profit from services performed as a notary public, any amount exempt from self-employment tax as the result of the filing and approval of Form 4029 or Form 4361, or any other amounts exempt from self-employment tax.

  a. Enter any net farm profit or (loss) from Schedule F, line 34, and from farm partnerships, Schedule K-1 (Form 1065), box 14, code A*. | **2a** |
  b. Enter any net profit or (loss) from Schedule C, line 31; Schedule C-EZ, line 3; Schedule K-1 (Form 1065), box 14, code A (other than farming); and Schedule K-1 (Form 1065-B), box 9, code J1*. | + **2b** |
  c. Combine lines 2a and 2b. | = **2c** |

  *If you have any Schedule K-1 amounts, complete the appropriate line(s) of Schedule SE, Section A. Reduce the Schedule K-1 amounts as described in the Partner's Instructions for Schedule K-1. Enter your name and social security number on Schedule SE and attach it to your return.

Part 3

Statutory Employees Filing Schedule C or C-EZ

3. Enter the amount from Schedule C, line 1, or Schedule C-EZ, line 1, that you are filing as a statutory employee. | **3** |

Part 4

All Filers Using Worksheet B

Note. If line 4b includes income on which you should have paid self-employment tax but didn't, we may reduce your credit by the amount of self-employment tax not paid.

4a. Enter your earned income from Step 5. | **4a** |

  b. Combine lines 1e, 2c, 3, and 4a. **This is your total earned income.** | **4b** |

If line 4b is zero or less, ⬣STOP You cannot take the credit. Enter "No" on the dotted line next to line 66a.

5. If you have:
  • 3 or more qualifying children, is line 4b less than $47,955 ($53,505 if married filing jointly)?
  • 2 qualifying children, is line 4b less than $44,648 ($50,198 if married filing jointly)?
  • 1 qualifying child, is line 4b less than $39,296 ($44,846 if married filing jointly)?
  • No qualifying children, is line 4b less than $14,880 ($20,430 if married filing jointly)?

  ☐ **Yes.** If you want the IRS to figure your credit, see *Credit figured by the IRS*, earlier. If you want to figure the credit yourself, enter the amount from line 4b on line 6 of this worksheet.

  ☐ **No.** ⬣STOP You cannot take the credit. Enter "No" on the dotted line next to line 66a.

Worksheet **B**—2016 EIC—Lines 66a and 66b—*Continued*   *Keep for Your Records*

Part 5

All Filers Using Worksheet B

6. Enter your total earned income from Part 4, line 4b. **6** [ ]

7. Look up the amount on line 6 above in the EIC Table to find the credit. Be sure you use the correct column for your filing status and the number of children you have. Enter the credit here. **7** [ ]

   If line 7 is zero, (STOP) You cannot take the credit.
   Enter "No" on the dotted line next to line 66a.

8. Enter the amount from Form 1040, line 38. **8** [ ]

9. Are the amounts on lines 8 and 6 the same?

   ☐ **Yes.** Skip line 10; enter the amount from line 7 on line 11.

   ☐ **No.** Go to line 10.

Part 6

Filers Who Answered "No" on Line 9

10. If you have:
    ● No qualifying children, is the amount on line 8 less than $8,300 ($13,850 if married filing jointly)?
    ● 1 or more qualifying children, is the amount on line 8 less than $18,200 ($23,750 if married filing jointly)?

    ☐ **Yes.** Leave line 10 blank; enter the amount from line 7 on line 11.

    ☐ **No.** Look up the amount on line 8 in the EIC Table to find the credit. Be sure you use the correct column for your filing status and the number of children you have. Enter the credit here. **10** [ ]
    Look at the amounts on lines 10 and 7.
    Then, enter the **smaller** amount on line 11.

Part 7

Your Earned Income Credit

11. **This is your earned income credit.** **11** [ ]

    Enter this amount on Form 1040, line 66a.

    Reminder—

    √ If you have a qualifying child, complete and attach Schedule EIC.

 If your EIC for a year after 1996 was reduced or disallowed, see Form 8862, who must file, earlier, to find out if you must file Form 8862 to take the credit for 2016.

2016 Earned Income Credit (EIC) Table
Caution. This is **not** a tax table.

1. To find your credit, read down the "At least - But less than" columns and find the line that includes the amount you were told to look up from your EIC Worksheet.

2. Then, go to the column that includes your filing status and the number of qualifying children you have. Enter the credit from that column on your EIC Worksheet.

Example. If your filing status is single, you have one qualifying child, and the amount you are looking up from your EIC Worksheet is $2,455, you would enter $842.

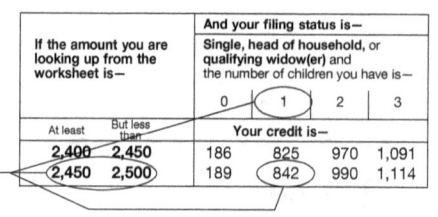

If the amount you are looking up from the worksheet is—		And your filing status is—			
		Single, head of household, or qualifying widow(er) and the number of children you have is—			
At least	But less than	0	1	2	3
		Your credit is—			
2,400	2,450	186	825	970	1,091
2,450	2,500	189	842	990	1,114

If the amount you are looking up from the worksheet is—		Single, head of household, or qualifying widow(er) and the number of children you have is—				Married filing jointly and the number of children you have is—			
At least	But less than	0	1	2	3	0	1	2	3
		Your credit is—				Your credit is—			
$1	$50	$2	$9	$10	$11	$2	$9	$10	$11
50	100	6	26	30	34	6	26	30	34
100	150	10	43	50	56	10	43	50	56
150	200	13	60	70	79	13	60	70	79
200	250	17	77	90	101	17	77	90	101
250	300	21	94	110	124	21	94	110	124
300	350	25	111	130	146	25	111	130	146
350	400	29	128	150	169	29	128	150	169
400	450	33	145	170	191	33	145	170	191
450	500	36	162	190	214	36	162	190	214
500	550	40	179	210	236	40	179	210	236
550	600	44	196	230	259	44	196	230	259
600	650	48	213	250	281	48	213	250	281
650	700	52	230	270	304	52	230	270	304
700	750	55	247	290	326	55	247	290	326
750	800	59	264	310	349	59	264	310	349
800	850	63	281	330	371	63	281	330	371
850	900	67	298	350	394	67	298	350	394
900	950	71	315	370	416	71	315	370	416
950	1,000	75	332	390	439	75	332	390	439
1,000	1,050	78	349	410	461	78	349	410	461
1,050	1,100	82	366	430	484	82	366	430	484
1,100	1,150	86	383	450	506	86	383	450	506
1,150	1,200	90	400	470	529	90	400	470	529
1,200	1,250	94	417	490	551	94	417	490	551
1,250	1,300	98	434	510	574	98	434	510	574
1,300	1,350	101	451	530	596	101	451	530	596
1,350	1,400	105	468	550	619	105	468	550	619
1,400	1,450	109	485	570	641	109	485	570	641
1,450	1,500	113	502	590	664	113	502	590	664
1,500	1,550	117	519	610	686	117	519	610	686
1,550	1,600	120	536	630	709	120	536	630	709
1,600	1,650	124	553	650	731	124	553	650	731
1,650	1,700	128	570	670	754	128	570	670	754
1,700	1,750	132	587	690	776	132	587	690	776
1,750	1,800	136	604	710	799	136	604	710	799
1,800	1,850	140	621	730	821	140	621	730	821
1,850	1,900	143	638	750	844	143	638	750	844
1,900	1,950	147	655	770	866	147	655	770	866
1,950	2,000	151	672	790	889	151	672	790	889
2,000	2,050	155	689	810	911	155	689	810	911
2,050	2,100	159	706	830	934	159	706	830	934
2,100	2,150	163	723	850	956	163	723	850	956
2,150	2,200	166	740	870	979	166	740	870	979
2,200	2,250	170	757	890	1,001	170	757	890	1,001
2,250	2,300	174	774	910	1,024	174	774	910	1,024
2,300	2,350	178	791	930	1,046	178	791	930	1,046
2,350	2,400	182	808	950	1,069	182	808	950	1,069
2,400	2,450	186	825	970	1,091	186	825	970	1,091
2,450	2,500	189	842	990	1,114	189	842	990	1,114
2,500	2,550	193	859	1,010	1,136	193	859	1,010	1,136
2,550	2,600	197	876	1,030	1,159	197	876	1,030	1,159
2,600	2,650	201	893	1,050	1,181	201	893	1,050	1,181
2,650	2,700	205	910	1,070	1,204	205	910	1,070	1,204
2,700	2,750	208	927	1,090	1,226	208	927	1,090	1,226
2,750	2,800	212	944	1,110	1,249	212	944	1,110	1,249

If the amount you are looking up from the worksheet is—		Single, head of household, or qualifying widow(er) and the number of children you have is—				Married filing jointly and the number of children you have is—			
At least	But less than	0	1	2	3	0	1	2	3
		Your credit is—				Your credit is—			
2,800	2,850	216	961	1,130	1,271	216	961	1,130	1,271
2,850	2,900	220	978	1,150	1,294	220	978	1,150	1,294
2,900	2,950	224	995	1,170	1,316	224	995	1,170	1,316
2,950	3,000	228	1,012	1,190	1,339	228	1,012	1,190	1,339
3,000	3,050	231	1,029	1,210	1,361	231	1,029	1,210	1,361
3,050	3,100	235	1,046	1,230	1,384	235	1,046	1,230	1,384
3,100	3,150	239	1,063	1,250	1,406	239	1,063	1,250	1,406
3,150	3,200	243	1,080	1,270	1,429	243	1,080	1,270	1,429
3,200	3,250	247	1,097	1,290	1,451	247	1,097	1,290	1,451
3,250	3,300	251	1,114	1,310	1,474	251	1,114	1,310	1,474
3,300	3,350	254	1,131	1,330	1,496	254	1,131	1,330	1,496
3,350	3,400	258	1,148	1,350	1,519	258	1,148	1,350	1,519
3,400	3,450	262	1,165	1,370	1,541	262	1,165	1,370	1,541
3,450	3,500	266	1,182	1,390	1,564	266	1,182	1,390	1,564
3,500	3,550	270	1,199	1,410	1,586	270	1,199	1,410	1,586
3,550	3,600	273	1,216	1,430	1,609	273	1,216	1,430	1,609
3,600	3,650	277	1,233	1,450	1,631	277	1,233	1,450	1,631
3,650	3,700	281	1,250	1,470	1,654	281	1,250	1,470	1,654
3,700	3,750	285	1,267	1,490	1,676	285	1,267	1,490	1,676
3,750	3,800	289	1,284	1,510	1,699	289	1,284	1,510	1,699
3,800	3,850	293	1,301	1,530	1,721	293	1,301	1,530	1,721
3,850	3,900	296	1,318	1,550	1,744	296	1,318	1,550	1,744
3,900	3,950	300	1,335	1,570	1,766	300	1,335	1,570	1,766
3,950	4,000	304	1,352	1,590	1,789	304	1,352	1,590	1,789
4,000	4,050	308	1,369	1,610	1,811	308	1,369	1,610	1,811
4,050	4,100	312	1,386	1,630	1,834	312	1,386	1,630	1,834
4,100	4,150	316	1,403	1,650	1,856	316	1,403	1,650	1,856
4,150	4,200	319	1,420	1,670	1,879	319	1,420	1,670	1,879
4,200	4,250	323	1,437	1,690	1,901	323	1,437	1,690	1,901
4,250	4,300	327	1,454	1,710	1,924	327	1,454	1,710	1,924
4,300	4,350	331	1,471	1,730	1,946	331	1,471	1,730	1,946
4,350	4,400	335	1,488	1,750	1,969	335	1,488	1,750	1,969
4,400	4,450	339	1,505	1,770	1,991	339	1,505	1,770	1,991
4,450	4,500	342	1,522	1,790	2,014	342	1,522	1,790	2,014
4,500	4,550	346	1,539	1,810	2,036	346	1,539	1,810	2,036
4,550	4,600	350	1,556	1,830	2,059	350	1,556	1,830	2,059
4,600	4,650	354	1,573	1,850	2,081	354	1,573	1,850	2,081
4,650	4,700	358	1,590	1,870	2,104	358	1,590	1,870	2,104
4,700	4,750	361	1,607	1,890	2,126	361	1,607	1,890	2,126
4,750	4,800	365	1,624	1,910	2,149	365	1,624	1,910	2,149
4,800	4,850	369	1,641	1,930	2,171	369	1,641	1,930	2,171
4,850	4,900	373	1,658	1,950	2,194	373	1,658	1,950	2,194
4,900	4,950	377	1,675	1,970	2,216	377	1,675	1,970	2,216
4,950	5,000	381	1,692	1,990	2,239	381	1,692	1,990	2,239
5,000	5,050	384	1,709	2,010	2,261	384	1,709	2,010	2,261
5,050	5,100	388	1,726	2,030	2,284	388	1,726	2,030	2,284
5,100	5,150	392	1,743	2,050	2,306	392	1,743	2,050	2,306
5,150	5,200	396	1,760	2,070	2,329	396	1,760	2,070	2,329
5,200	5,250	400	1,777	2,090	2,351	400	1,777	2,090	2,351
5,250	5,300	404	1,794	2,110	2,374	404	1,794	2,110	2,374
5,300	5,350	407	1,811	2,130	2,396	407	1,811	2,130	2,396
5,350	5,400	411	1,828	2,150	2,419	411	1,828	2,150	2,419
5,400	5,450	415	1,845	2,170	2,441	415	1,845	2,170	2,441
5,450	5,500	419	1,862	2,190	2,464	419	1,862	2,190	2,464
5,500	5,550	423	1,879	2,210	2,486	423	1,879	2,210	2,486
5,550	5,600	426	1,896	2,230	2,509	426	1,896	2,230	2,509

(Continued)

Need more information or forms? Visit IRS.gov.

Earned Income Credit (EIC) Table - Continued (Caution. This is not a tax table.)

If the amount you are looking up from the worksheet is–		Single, head of household, or qualifying widow(er) and the number of children you have is–				Married filing jointly and the number of children you have is–			
At least	But less than	0	1	2	3	0	1	2	3
		Your credit is–				Your credit is–			
5,600	5,650	430	1,913	2,250	2,531	430	1,913	2,250	2,531
5,650	5,700	434	1,930	2,270	2,554	434	1,930	2,270	2,554
5,700	5,750	438	1,947	2,290	2,576	438	1,947	2,290	2,576
5,750	5,800	442	1,964	2,310	2,599	442	1,964	2,310	2,599
5,800	5,850	446	1,981	2,330	2,621	446	1,981	2,330	2,621
5,850	5,900	449	1,998	2,350	2,644	449	1,998	2,350	2,644
5,900	5,950	453	2,015	2,370	2,666	453	2,015	2,370	2,666
5,950	6,000	457	2,032	2,390	2,689	457	2,032	2,390	2,689
6,000	6,050	461	2,049	2,410	2,711	461	2,049	2,410	2,711
6,050	6,100	465	2,066	2,430	2,734	465	2,066	2,430	2,734
6,100	6,150	469	2,083	2,450	2,756	469	2,083	2,450	2,756
6,150	6,200	472	2,100	2,470	2,779	472	2,100	2,470	2,779
6,200	6,250	476	2,117	2,490	2,801	476	2,117	2,490	2,801
6,250	6,300	480	2,134	2,510	2,824	480	2,134	2,510	2,824
6,300	6,350	484	2,151	2,530	2,846	484	2,151	2,530	2,846
6,350	6,400	488	2,168	2,550	2,869	488	2,168	2,550	2,869
6,400	6,450	492	2,185	2,570	2,891	492	2,185	2,570	2,891
6,450	6,500	495	2,202	2,590	2,914	495	2,202	2,590	2,914
6,500	6,550	499	2,219	2,610	2,936	499	2,219	2,610	2,936
6,550	6,600	503	2,236	2,630	2,959	503	2,236	2,630	2,959
6,600	6,650	506	2,253	2,650	2,981	506	2,253	2,650	2,981
6,650	6,700	506	2,270	2,670	3,004	506	2,270	2,670	3,004
6,700	6,750	506	2,287	2,690	3,026	506	2,287	2,690	3,026
6,750	6,800	506	2,304	2,710	3,049	506	2,304	2,710	3,049
6,800	6,850	506	2,321	2,730	3,071	506	2,321	2,730	3,071
6,850	6,900	506	2,338	2,750	3,094	506	2,338	2,750	3,094
6,900	6,950	506	2,355	2,770	3,116	506	2,355	2,770	3,116
6,950	7,000	506	2,372	2,790	3,139	506	2,372	2,790	3,139
7,000	7,050	506	2,389	2,810	3,161	506	2,389	2,810	3,161
7,050	7,100	506	2,406	2,830	3,184	506	2,406	2,830	3,184
7,100	7,150	506	2,423	2,850	3,206	506	2,423	2,850	3,206
7,150	7,200	506	2,440	2,870	3,229	506	2,440	2,870	3,229
7,200	7,250	506	2,457	2,890	3,251	506	2,457	2,890	3,251
7,250	7,300	506	2,474	2,910	3,274	506	2,474	2,910	3,274
7,300	7,350	506	2,491	2,930	3,296	506	2,491	2,930	3,296
7,350	7,400	506	2,508	2,950	3,319	506	2,508	2,950	3,319
7,400	7,450	506	2,525	2,970	3,341	506	2,525	2,970	3,341
7,450	7,500	506	2,542	2,990	3,364	506	2,542	2,990	3,364
7,500	7,550	506	2,559	3,010	3,386	506	2,559	3,010	3,386
7,550	7,600	506	2,576	3,030	3,409	506	2,576	3,030	3,409
7,600	7,650	506	2,593	3,050	3,431	506	2,593	3,050	3,431
7,650	7,700	506	2,610	3,070	3,454	506	2,610	3,070	3,454
7,700	7,750	506	2,627	3,090	3,476	506	2,627	3,090	3,476
7,750	7,800	506	2,644	3,110	3,499	506	2,644	3,110	3,499
7,800	7,850	506	2,661	3,130	3,521	506	2,661	3,130	3,521
7,850	7,900	506	2,678	3,150	3,544	506	2,678	3,150	3,544
7,900	7,950	506	2,695	3,170	3,566	506	2,695	3,170	3,566
7,950	8,000	506	2,712	3,190	3,589	506	2,712	3,190	3,589
8,000	8,050	506	2,729	3,210	3,611	506	2,729	3,210	3,611
8,050	8,100	506	2,746	3,230	3,634	506	2,746	3,230	3,634
8,100	8,150	506	2,763	3,250	3,656	506	2,763	3,250	3,656
8,150	8,200	506	2,780	3,270	3,679	506	2,780	3,270	3,679
8,200	8,250	506	2,797	3,290	3,701	506	2,797	3,290	3,701
8,250	8,300	506	2,814	3,310	3,724	506	2,814	3,310	3,724
8,300	8,350	501	2,831	3,330	3,746	506	2,831	3,330	3,746
8,350	8,400	498	2,848	3,350	3,769	506	2,848	3,350	3,769
8,400	8,450	494	2,865	3,370	3,791	506	2,865	3,370	3,791
8,450	8,500	490	2,882	3,390	3,814	506	2,882	3,390	3,814
8,500	8,550	486	2,899	3,410	3,836	506	2,899	3,410	3,836
8,550	8,600	482	2,916	3,430	3,859	506	2,916	3,430	3,859
8,600	8,650	479	2,933	3,450	3,881	506	2,933	3,450	3,881
8,650	8,700	475	2,950	3,470	3,904	506	2,950	3,470	3,904
8,700	8,750	471	2,967	3,490	3,926	506	2,967	3,490	3,926
8,750	8,800	467	2,984	3,510	3,949	506	2,984	3,510	3,949
8,800	8,850	463	3,001	3,530	3,971	506	3,001	3,530	3,971
8,850	8,900	459	3,018	3,550	3,994	506	3,018	3,550	3,994
8,900	8,950	456	3,035	3,570	4,016	506	3,035	3,570	4,016
8,950	9,000	452	3,052	3,590	4,039	506	3,052	3,590	4,039
9,000	9,050	448	3,069	3,610	4,061	506	3,069	3,610	4,061
9,050	9,100	444	3,086	3,630	4,084	506	3,086	3,630	4,084
9,100	9,150	440	3,103	3,650	4,106	506	3,103	3,650	4,106
9,150	9,200	436	3,120	3,670	4,129	506	3,120	3,670	4,129
9,200	9,250	433	3,137	3,690	4,151	506	3,137	3,690	4,151
9,250	9,300	429	3,154	3,710	4,174	506	3,154	3,710	4,174
9,300	9,350	425	3,171	3,730	4,196	506	3,171	3,730	4,196
9,350	9,400	421	3,188	3,750	4,219	506	3,188	3,750	4,219
9,400	9,450	417	3,205	3,770	4,241	506	3,205	3,770	4,241
9,450	9,500	413	3,222	3,790	4,264	506	3,222	3,790	4,264
9,500	9,550	410	3,239	3,810	4,286	506	3,239	3,810	4,286
9,550	9,600	406	3,256	3,830	4,309	506	3,256	3,830	4,309
9,600	9,650	402	3,273	3,850	4,331	506	3,273	3,850	4,331
9,650	9,700	398	3,290	3,870	4,354	506	3,290	3,870	4,354
9,700	9,750	394	3,307	3,890	4,376	506	3,307	3,890	4,376
9,750	9,800	391	3,324	3,910	4,399	506	3,324	3,910	4,399
9,800	9,850	387	3,341	3,930	4,421	506	3,341	3,930	4,421
9,850	9,900	383	3,358	3,950	4,444	506	3,358	3,950	4,444
9,900	9,950	379	3,373	3,970	4,466	506	3,373	3,970	4,466
9,950	10,000	375	3,373	3,990	4,489	506	3,373	3,990	4,489
10,000	10,050	371	3,373	4,010	4,511	506	3,373	4,010	4,511
10,050	10,100	368	3,373	4,030	4,534	506	3,373	4,030	4,534
10,100	10,150	364	3,373	4,050	4,556	506	3,373	4,050	4,556
10,150	10,200	360	3,373	4,070	4,579	506	3,373	4,070	4,579
10,200	10,250	356	3,373	4,090	4,601	506	3,373	4,090	4,601
10,250	10,300	352	3,373	4,110	4,624	506	3,373	4,110	4,624
10,300	10,350	348	3,373	4,130	4,646	506	3,373	4,130	4,646
10,350	10,400	345	3,373	4,150	4,669	506	3,373	4,150	4,669
10,400	10,450	341	3,373	4,170	4,691	506	3,373	4,170	4,691
10,450	10,500	337	3,373	4,190	4,714	506	3,373	4,190	4,714
10,500	10,550	333	3,373	4,210	4,736	506	3,373	4,210	4,736
10,550	10,600	329	3,373	4,230	4,759	506	3,373	4,230	4,759
10,600	10,650	326	3,373	4,250	4,781	506	3,373	4,250	4,781
10,650	10,700	322	3,373	4,270	4,804	506	3,373	4,270	4,804
10,700	10,750	318	3,373	4,290	4,826	506	3,373	4,290	4,826
10,750	10,800	314	3,373	4,310	4,849	506	3,373	4,310	4,849
10,800	10,850	310	3,373	4,330	4,871	506	3,373	4,330	4,871
10,850	10,900	306	3,373	4,350	4,894	506	3,373	4,350	4,894
10,900	10,950	303	3,373	4,370	4,916	506	3,373	4,370	4,916
10,950	11,000	299	3,373	4,390	4,939	506	3,373	4,390	4,939
11,000	11,050	295	3,373	4,410	4,961	506	3,373	4,410	4,961
11,050	11,100	291	3,373	4,430	4,984	506	3,373	4,430	4,984
11,100	11,150	287	3,373	4,450	5,006	506	3,373	4,450	5,006
11,150	11,200	283	3,373	4,470	5,029	506	3,373	4,470	5,029
11,200	11,250	280	3,373	4,490	5,051	506	3,373	4,490	5,051
11,250	11,300	276	3,373	4,510	5,074	506	3,373	4,510	5,074
11,300	11,350	272	3,373	4,530	5,096	506	3,373	4,530	5,096
11,350	11,400	268	3,373	4,550	5,119	506	3,373	4,550	5,119
11,400	11,450	264	3,373	4,570	5,141	506	3,373	4,570	5,141
11,450	11,500	260	3,373	4,590	5,164	506	3,373	4,590	5,164
11,500	11,550	257	3,373	4,610	5,186	506	3,373	4,610	5,186
11,550	11,600	253	3,373	4,630	5,209	506	3,373	4,630	5,209
11,600	11,650	249	3,373	4,650	5,231	506	3,373	4,650	5,231
11,650	11,700	245	3,373	4,670	5,254	506	3,373	4,670	5,254
11,700	11,750	241	3,373	4,690	5,276	506	3,373	4,690	5,276
11,750	11,800	238	3,373	4,710	5,299	506	3,373	4,710	5,299
11,800	11,850	234	3,373	4,730	5,321	506	3,373	4,730	5,321
11,850	11,900	230	3,373	4,750	5,344	506	3,373	4,750	5,344
11,900	11,950	226	3,373	4,770	5,366	506	3,373	4,770	5,366
11,950	12,000	222	3,373	4,790	5,389	506	3,373	4,790	5,389
12,000	12,050	218	3,373	4,810	5,411	506	3,373	4,810	5,411
12,050	12,100	215	3,373	4,830	5,434	506	3,373	4,830	5,434
12,100	12,150	211	3,373	4,850	5,456	506	3,373	4,850	5,456
12,150	12,200	207	3,373	4,870	5,479	506	3,373	4,870	5,479
12,200	12,250	203	3,373	4,890	5,501	506	3,373	4,890	5,501
12,250	12,300	199	3,373	4,910	5,524	506	3,373	4,910	5,524
12,300	12,350	195	3,373	4,930	5,546	506	3,373	4,930	5,546
12,350	12,400	192	3,373	4,950	5,569	506	3,373	4,950	5,569
12,400	12,450	188	3,373	4,970	5,591	506	3,373	4,970	5,591
12,450	12,500	184	3,373	4,990	5,614	506	3,373	4,990	5,614
12,500	12,550	180	3,373	5,010	5,636	506	3,373	5,010	5,636
12,550	12,600	176	3,373	5,030	5,659	506	3,373	5,030	5,659
12,600	12,650	173	3,373	5,050	5,681	506	3,373	5,050	5,681
12,650	12,700	169	3,373	5,070	5,704	506	3,373	5,070	5,704
12,700	12,750	165	3,373	5,090	5,726	506	3,373	5,090	5,726
12,750	12,800	161	3,373	5,110	5,749	506	3,373	5,110	5,749

(Continued)

Earned Income Credit (EIC) Table - Continued
(**Caution.** This is **not** a tax table.)

If the amount you are looking up from the worksheet is–		Single, head of household, or qualifying widow(er) and the number of children you have is–				Married filing jointly and the number of children you have is–				If the amount you are looking up from the worksheet is–		Single, head of household, or qualifying widow(er) and the number of children you have is–				Married filing jointly and the number of children you have is–			
At least	But less than	0	1	2	3	0	1	2	3	At least	But less than	0	1	2	3	0	1	2	3
		Your credit is–				Your credit is–						Your credit is–				Your credit is–			
12,800	12,850	157	3,373	5,130	5,771	506	3,373	5,130	5,771	16,000	16,050	0	3,373	5,572	6,269	337	3,373	5,572	6,269
12,850	12,900	153	3,373	5,150	5,794	506	3,373	5,150	5,794	16,050	16,100	0	3,373	5,572	6,269	333	3,373	5,572	6,269
12,900	12,950	150	3,373	5,170	5,816	506	3,373	5,170	5,816	16,100	16,150	0	3,373	5,572	6,269	329	3,373	5,572	6,269
12,950	13,000	146	3,373	5,190	5,839	506	3,373	5,190	5,839	16,150	16,200	0	3,373	5,572	6,269	326	3,373	5,572	6,269
13,000	13,050	142	3,373	5,210	5,861	506	3,373	5,210	5,861	16,200	16,250	0	3,373	5,572	6,269	322	3,373	5,572	6,269
13,050	13,100	138	3,373	5,230	5,884	506	3,373	5,230	5,884	16,250	16,300	0	3,373	5,572	6,269	318	3,373	5,572	6,269
13,100	13,150	134	3,373	5,250	5,906	506	3,373	5,250	5,906	16,300	16,350	0	3,373	5,572	6,269	314	3,373	5,572	6,269
13,150	13,200	130	3,373	5,270	5,929	506	3,373	5,270	5,929	16,350	16,400	0	3,373	5,572	6,269	310	3,373	5,572	6,269
13,200	13,250	127	3,373	5,290	5,951	506	3,373	5,290	5,951	16,400	16,450	0	3,373	5,572	6,269	306	3,373	5,572	6,269
13,250	13,300	123	3,373	5,310	5,974	506	3,373	5,310	5,974	16,450	16,500	0	3,373	5,572	6,269	303	3,373	5,572	6,269
13,300	13,350	119	3,373	5,330	5,996	506	3,373	5,330	5,996	16,500	16,550	0	3,373	5,572	6,269	299	3,373	5,572	6,269
13,350	13,400	115	3,373	5,350	6,019	506	3,373	5,350	6,019	16,550	16,600	0	3,373	5,572	6,269	295	3,373	5,572	6,269
13,400	13,450	111	3,373	5,370	6,041	506	3,373	5,370	6,041	16,600	16,650	0	3,373	5,572	6,269	291	3,373	5,572	6,269
13,450	13,500	107	3,373	5,390	6,064	506	3,373	5,390	6,064	16,650	16,700	0	3,373	5,572	6,269	287	3,373	5,572	6,269
13,500	13,550	104	3,373	5,410	6,086	506	3,373	5,410	6,086	16,700	16,750	0	3,373	5,572	6,269	283	3,373	5,572	6,269
13,550	13,600	100	3,373	5,430	6,109	506	3,373	5,430	6,109	16,750	16,800	0	3,373	5,572	6,269	280	3,373	5,572	6,269
13,600	13,650	96	3,373	5,450	6,131	506	3,373	5,450	6,131	16,800	16,850	0	3,373	5,572	6,269	276	3,373	5,572	6,269
13,650	13,700	92	3,373	5,470	6,154	506	3,373	5,470	6,154	16,850	16,900	0	3,373	5,572	6,269	272	3,373	5,572	6,269
13,700	13,750	88	3,373	5,490	6,176	506	3,373	5,490	6,176	16,900	16,950	0	3,373	5,572	6,269	268	3,373	5,572	6,269
13,750	13,800	85	3,373	5,510	6,199	506	3,373	5,510	6,199	16,950	17,000	0	3,373	5,572	6,269	264	3,373	5,572	6,269
13,800	13,850	81	3,373	5,530	6,221	506	3,373	5,530	6,221	17,000	17,050	0	3,373	5,572	6,269	260	3,373	5,572	6,269
13,850	13,900	77	3,373	5,550	6,244	501	3,373	5,550	6,244	17,050	17,100	0	3,373	5,572	6,269	257	3,373	5,572	6,269
13,900	13,950	73	3,373	5,572	6,269	498	3,373	5,572	6,269	17,100	17,150	0	3,373	5,572	6,269	253	3,373	5,572	6,269
13,950	14,000	69	3,373	5,572	6,269	494	3,373	5,572	6,269	17,150	17,200	0	3,373	5,572	6,269	249	3,373	5,572	6,269
14,000	14,050	65	3,373	5,572	6,269	490	3,373	5,572	6,269	17,200	17,250	0	3,373	5,572	6,269	245	3,373	5,572	6,269
14,050	14,100	62	3,373	5,572	6,269	486	3,373	5,572	6,269	17,250	17,300	0	3,373	5,572	6,269	241	3,373	5,572	6,269
14,100	14,150	58	3,373	5,572	6,269	482	3,373	5,572	6,269	17,300	17,350	0	3,373	5,572	6,269	238	3,373	5,572	6,269
14,150	14,200	54	3,373	5,572	6,269	479	3,373	5,572	6,269	17,350	17,400	0	3,373	5,572	6,269	234	3,373	5,572	6,269
14,200	14,250	50	3,373	5,572	6,269	475	3,373	5,572	6,269	17,400	17,450	0	3,373	5,572	6,269	230	3,373	5,572	6,269
14,250	14,300	46	3,373	5,572	6,269	471	3,373	5,572	6,269	17,450	17,500	0	3,373	5,572	6,269	226	3,373	5,572	6,269
14,300	14,350	42	3,373	5,572	6,269	467	3,373	5,572	6,269	17,500	17,550	0	3,373	5,572	6,269	222	3,373	5,572	6,269
14,350	14,400	39	3,373	5,572	6,269	463	3,373	5,572	6,269	17,550	17,600	0	3,373	5,572	6,269	218	3,373	5,572	6,269
14,400	14,450	35	3,373	5,572	6,269	459	3,373	5,572	6,269	17,600	17,650	0	3,373	5,572	6,269	215	3,373	5,572	6,269
14,450	14,500	31	3,373	5,572	6,269	456	3,373	5,572	6,269	17,650	17,700	0	3,373	5,572	6,269	211	3,373	5,572	6,269
14,500	14,550	27	3,373	5,572	6,269	452	3,373	5,572	6,269	17,700	17,750	0	3,373	5,572	6,269	207	3,373	5,572	6,269
14,550	14,600	23	3,373	5,572	6,269	448	3,373	5,572	6,269	17,750	17,800	0	3,373	5,572	6,269	203	3,373	5,572	6,269
14,600	14,650	20	3,373	5,572	6,269	444	3,373	5,572	6,269	17,800	17,850	0	3,373	5,572	6,269	199	3,373	5,572	6,269
14,650	14,700	16	3,373	5,572	6,269	440	3,373	5,572	6,269	17,850	17,900	0	3,373	5,572	6,269	195	3,373	5,572	6,269
14,700	14,750	12	3,373	5,572	6,269	436	3,373	5,572	6,269	17,900	17,950	0	3,373	5,572	6,269	192	3,373	5,572	6,269
14,750	14,800	8	3,373	5,572	6,269	433	3,373	5,572	6,269	17,950	18,000	0	3,373	5,572	6,269	188	3,373	5,572	6,269
14,800	14,850	4	3,373	5,572	6,269	429	3,373	5,572	6,269	18,000	18,050	0	3,373	5,572	6,269	184	3,373	5,572	6,269
14,850	14,900	*	3,373	5,572	6,269	425	3,373	5,572	6,269	18,050	18,100	0	3,373	5,572	6,269	180	3,373	5,572	6,269
14,900	14,950	0	3,373	5,572	6,269	421	3,373	5,572	6,269	18,100	18,150	0	3,373	5,572	6,269	176	3,373	5,572	6,269
14,950	15,000	0	3,373	5,572	6,269	417	3,373	5,572	6,269	18,150	18,200	0	3,373	5,572	6,269	173	3,373	5,572	6,269
15,000	15,050	0	3,373	5,572	6,269	413	3,373	5,572	6,269	18,200	18,250	0	3,367	5,565	6,261	169	3,373	5,572	6,269
15,050	15,100	0	3,373	5,572	6,269	410	3,373	5,572	6,269	18,250	18,300	0	3,359	5,554	6,251	165	3,373	5,572	6,269
15,100	15,150	0	3,373	5,572	6,269	406	3,373	5,572	6,269	18,300	18,350	0	3,351	5,544	6,240	161	3,373	5,572	6,269
15,150	15,200	0	3,373	5,572	6,269	402	3,373	5,572	6,269	18,350	18,400	0	3,343	5,533	6,230	157	3,373	5,572	6,269
15,200	15,250	0	3,373	5,572	6,269	398	3,373	5,572	6,269	18,400	18,450	0	3,335	5,523	6,219	153	3,373	5,572	6,269
15,250	15,300	0	3,373	5,572	6,269	394	3,373	5,572	6,269	18,450	18,500	0	3,327	5,512	6,208	150	3,373	5,572	6,269
15,300	15,350	0	3,373	5,572	6,269	391	3,373	5,572	6,269	18,500	18,550	0	3,319	5,501	6,198	146	3,373	5,572	6,269
15,350	15,400	0	3,373	5,572	6,269	387	3,373	5,572	6,269	18,550	18,600	0	3,311	5,491	6,187	142	3,373	5,572	6,269
15,400	15,450	0	3,373	5,572	6,269	383	3,373	5,572	6,269	18,600	18,650	0	3,303	5,480	6,177	138	3,373	5,572	6,269
15,450	15,500	0	3,373	5,572	6,269	379	3,373	5,572	6,269	18,650	18,700	0	3,295	5,470	6,166	134	3,373	5,572	6,269
15,500	15,550	0	3,373	5,572	6,269	375	3,373	5,572	6,269	18,700	18,750	0	3,287	5,459	6,156	130	3,373	5,572	6,269
15,550	15,600	0	3,373	5,572	6,269	371	3,373	5,572	6,269	18,750	18,800	0	3,279	5,449	6,145	127	3,373	5,572	6,269
15,600	15,650	0	3,373	5,572	6,269	368	3,373	5,572	6,269	18,800	18,850	0	3,271	5,438	6,135	123	3,373	5,572	6,269
15,650	15,700	0	3,373	5,572	6,269	364	3,373	5,572	6,269	18,850	18,900	0	3,263	5,428	6,124	119	3,373	5,572	6,269
15,700	15,750	0	3,373	5,572	6,269	360	3,373	5,572	6,269	18,900	18,950	0	3,255	5,417	6,114	115	3,373	5,572	6,269
15,750	15,800	0	3,373	5,572	6,269	356	3,373	5,572	6,269	18,950	19,000	0	3,247	5,407	6,103	111	3,373	5,572	6,269
15,800	15,850	0	3,373	5,572	6,269	352	3,373	5,572	6,269	19,000	19,050	0	3,239	5,396	6,093	107	3,373	5,572	6,269
15,850	15,900	0	3,373	5,572	6,269	348	3,373	5,572	6,269	19,050	19,100	0	3,231	5,386	6,082	104	3,373	5,572	6,269
15,900	15,950	0	3,373	5,572	6,269	345	3,373	5,572	6,269	19,100	19,150	0	3,223	5,375	6,072	100	3,373	5,572	6,269
15,950	16,000	0	3,373	5,572	6,269	341	3,373	5,572	6,269	19,150	19,200	0	3,215	5,365	6,061	96	3,373	5,572	6,269

* If the amount you are looking up from the worksheet is at least $14,850 but less than $14,880, and you have no qualifying children, your credit is $1.
If the amount you are looking up from the worksheet is $14,880 or more, and you have no qualifying children, you can't take the credit.

(Continued)

Need more information or forms? Visit IRS.gov.

Earned Income Credit (EIC) Table - *Continued*

(Caution. This is not a tax table.)

If the amount you are looking up from the worksheet is—		Single, head of household, or qualifying widow(er) and the number of children you have is—				Married filing jointly and the number of children you have is—			
At least	But less than	0	1	2	3	0	1	2	3
		Your credit is—				Your credit is—			
19,200	19,250	0	3,207	5,354	6,051	92	3,373	5,572	6,269
19,250	19,300	0	3,199	5,343	6,040	88	3,373	5,572	6,269
19,300	19,350	0	3,191	5,333	6,029	85	3,373	5,572	6,269
19,350	19,400	0	3,183	5,322	6,019	81	3,373	5,572	6,269
19,400	19,450	0	3,175	5,312	6,008	77	3,373	5,572	6,269
19,450	19,500	0	3,167	5,301	5,998	73	3,373	5,572	6,269
19,500	19,550	0	3,159	5,291	5,987	69	3,373	5,572	6,269
19,550	19,600	0	3,151	5,280	5,977	65	3,373	5,572	6,269
19,600	19,650	0	3,143	5,270	5,966	62	3,373	5,572	6,269
19,650	19,700	0	3,135	5,259	5,956	58	3,373	5,572	6,269
19,700	19,750	0	3,128	5,249	5,945	54	3,373	5,572	6,269
19,750	19,800	0	3,120	5,238	5,935	50	3,373	5,572	6,269
19,800	19,850	0	3,112	5,228	5,924	46	3,373	5,572	6,269
19,850	19,900	0	3,104	5,217	5,914	42	3,373	5,572	6,269
19,900	19,950	0	3,096	5,207	5,903	39	3,373	5,572	6,269
19,950	20,000	0	3,088	5,196	5,893	35	3,373	5,572	6,269
20,000	20,050	0	3,080	5,186	5,882	31	3,373	5,572	6,269
20,050	20,100	0	3,072	5,175	5,872	27	3,373	5,572	6,269
20,100	20,150	0	3,064	5,164	5,861	23	3,373	5,572	6,269
20,150	20,200	0	3,056	5,154	5,850	20	3,373	5,572	6,269
20,200	20,250	0	3,048	5,143	5,840	16	3,373	5,572	6,269
20,250	20,300	0	3,040	5,133	5,829	12	3,373	5,572	6,269
20,300	20,350	0	3,032	5,122	5,819	8	3,373	5,572	6,269
20,350	20,400	0	3,024	5,112	5,808	4	3,373	5,572	6,269
20,400	20,450	0	3,016	5,101	5,798	*	3,373	5,572	6,269
20,450	20,500	0	3,008	5,091	5,787	0	3,373	5,572	6,269
20,500	20,550	0	3,000	5,080	5,777	0	3,373	5,572	6,269
20,550	20,600	0	2,992	5,070	5,766	0	3,373	5,572	6,269
20,600	20,650	0	2,984	5,059	5,756	0	3,373	5,572	6,269
20,650	20,700	0	2,976	5,049	5,745	0	3,373	5,572	6,269
20,700	20,750	0	2,968	5,038	5,735	0	3,373	5,572	6,269
20,750	20,800	0	2,960	5,028	5,724	0	3,373	5,572	6,269
20,800	20,850	0	2,952	5,017	5,714	0	3,373	5,572	6,269
20,850	20,900	0	2,944	5,007	5,703	0	3,373	5,572	6,269
20,900	20,950	0	2,936	4,996	5,693	0	3,373	5,572	6,269
20,950	21,000	0	2,928	4,985	5,682	0	3,373	5,572	6,269
21,000	21,050	0	2,920	4,975	5,671	0	3,373	5,572	6,269
21,050	21,100	0	2,912	4,964	5,661	0	3,373	5,572	6,269
21,100	21,150	0	2,904	4,954	5,650	0	3,373	5,572	6,269
21,150	21,200	0	2,896	4,943	5,640	0	3,373	5,572	6,269
21,200	21,250	0	2,888	4,933	5,629	0	3,373	5,572	6,269
21,250	21,300	0	2,880	4,922	5,619	0	3,373	5,572	6,269
21,300	21,350	0	2,872	4,912	5,608	0	3,373	5,572	6,269
21,350	21,400	0	2,864	4,901	5,598	0	3,373	5,572	6,269
21,400	21,450	0	2,856	4,891	5,587	0	3,373	5,572	6,269
21,450	21,500	0	2,848	4,880	5,577	0	3,373	5,572	6,269
21,500	21,550	0	2,840	4,870	5,566	0	3,373	5,572	6,269
21,550	21,600	0	2,832	4,859	5,556	0	3,373	5,572	6,269
21,600	21,650	0	2,824	4,849	5,545	0	3,373	5,572	6,269
21,650	21,700	0	2,816	4,838	5,535	0	3,373	5,572	6,269
21,700	21,750	0	2,808	4,828	5,524	0	3,373	5,572	6,269
21,750	21,800	0	2,800	4,817	5,513	0	3,373	5,572	6,269
21,800	21,850	0	2,792	4,806	5,503	0	3,373	5,572	6,269
21,850	21,900	0	2,784	4,796	5,492	0	3,373	5,572	6,269
21,900	21,950	0	2,776	4,785	5,482	0	3,373	5,572	6,269
21,950	22,000	0	2,768	4,775	5,471	0	3,373	5,572	6,269
22,000	22,050	0	2,760	4,764	5,461	0	3,373	5,572	6,269
22,050	22,100	0	2,752	4,754	5,450	0	3,373	5,572	6,269
22,100	22,150	0	2,744	4,743	5,440	0	3,373	5,572	6,269
22,150	22,200	0	2,736	4,733	5,429	0	3,373	5,572	6,269
22,200	22,250	0	2,728	4,722	5,419	0	3,373	5,572	6,269
22,250	22,300	0	2,720	4,712	5,408	0	3,373	5,572	6,269
22,300	22,350	0	2,712	4,701	5,398	0	3,373	5,572	6,269
22,350	22,400	0	2,704	4,691	5,387	0	3,373	5,572	6,269

If the amount you are looking up from the worksheet is—		Single, head of household, or qualifying widow(er) and the number of children you have is—				Married filing jointly and the number of children you have is—			
At least	But less than	0	1	2	3	0	1	2	3
		Your credit is—				Your credit is—			
22,400	22,450	0	2,696	4,680	5,377	0	3,373	5,572	6,269
22,450	22,500	0	2,688	4,670	5,366	0	3,373	5,572	6,269
22,500	22,550	0	2,680	4,659	5,356	0	3,373	5,572	6,269
22,550	22,600	0	2,672	4,649	5,345	0	3,373	5,572	6,269
22,600	22,650	0	2,664	4,638	5,334	0	3,373	5,572	6,269
22,650	22,700	0	2,656	4,627	5,324	0	3,373	5,572	6,269
22,700	22,750	0	2,648	4,617	5,313	0	3,373	5,572	6,269
22,750	22,800	0	2,640	4,606	5,303	0	3,373	5,572	6,269
22,800	22,850	0	2,632	4,596	5,292	0	3,373	5,572	6,269
22,850	22,900	0	2,624	4,585	5,282	0	3,373	5,572	6,269
22,900	22,950	0	2,616	4,575	5,271	0	3,373	5,572	6,269
22,950	23,000	0	2,608	4,564	5,261	0	3,373	5,572	6,269
23,000	23,050	0	2,600	4,554	5,250	0	3,373	5,572	6,269
23,050	23,100	0	2,592	4,543	5,240	0	3,373	5,572	6,269
23,100	23,150	0	2,584	4,533	5,229	0	3,373	5,572	6,269
23,150	23,200	0	2,576	4,522	5,219	0	3,373	5,572	6,269
23,200	23,250	0	2,568	4,512	5,208	0	3,373	5,572	6,269
23,250	23,300	0	2,560	4,501	5,198	0	3,373	5,572	6,269
23,300	23,350	0	2,552	4,491	5,187	0	3,373	5,572	6,269
23,350	23,400	0	2,544	4,480	5,177	0	3,373	5,572	6,269
23,400	23,450	0	2,536	4,470	5,166	0	3,373	5,572	6,269
23,450	23,500	0	2,528	4,459	5,155	0	3,373	5,572	6,269
23,500	23,550	0	2,520	4,448	5,145	0	3,373	5,572	6,269
23,550	23,600	0	2,512	4,438	5,134	0	3,373	5,572	6,269
23,600	23,650	0	2,504	4,427	5,124	0	3,373	5,572	6,269
23,650	23,700	0	2,496	4,417	5,113	0	3,373	5,572	6,269
23,700	23,750	0	2,488	4,406	5,103	0	3,373	5,572	6,269
23,750	23,800	0	2,480	4,396	5,092	0	3,367	5,565	6,261
23,800	23,850	0	2,472	4,385	5,082	0	3,359	5,554	6,251
23,850	23,900	0	2,464	4,375	5,071	0	3,351	5,544	6,240
23,900	23,950	0	2,456	4,364	5,061	0	3,343	5,533	6,230
23,950	24,000	0	2,448	4,354	5,050	0	3,335	5,523	6,219
24,000	24,050	0	2,440	4,343	5,040	0	3,327	5,512	6,208
24,050	24,100	0	2,432	4,333	5,029	0	3,319	5,501	6,198
24,100	24,150	0	2,424	4,322	5,019	0	3,311	5,491	6,187
24,150	24,200	0	2,416	4,312	5,008	0	3,303	5,480	6,177
24,200	24,250	0	2,408	4,301	4,998	0	3,295	5,470	6,166
24,250	24,300	0	2,400	4,290	4,987	0	3,287	5,459	6,156
24,300	24,350	0	2,392	4,280	4,976	0	3,279	5,449	6,145
24,350	24,400	0	2,384	4,269	4,966	0	3,271	5,438	6,135
24,400	24,450	0	2,376	4,259	4,955	0	3,263	5,428	6,124
24,450	24,500	0	2,368	4,248	4,945	0	3,255	5,417	6,114
24,500	24,550	0	2,360	4,238	4,934	0	3,247	5,407	6,103
24,550	24,600	0	2,352	4,227	4,924	0	3,239	5,396	6,093
24,600	24,650	0	2,344	4,217	4,913	0	3,231	5,386	6,082
24,650	24,700	0	2,336	4,206	4,903	0	3,223	5,375	6,072
24,700	24,750	0	2,329	4,196	4,892	0	3,215	5,365	6,061
24,750	24,800	0	2,321	4,185	4,882	0	3,207	5,354	6,051
24,800	24,850	0	2,313	4,175	4,871	0	3,199	5,343	6,040
24,850	24,900	0	2,305	4,164	4,861	0	3,191	5,333	6,029
24,900	24,950	0	2,297	4,154	4,850	0	3,183	5,322	6,019
24,950	25,000	0	2,289	4,143	4,840	0	3,175	5,312	6,008
25,000	25,050	0	2,281	4,133	4,829	0	3,167	5,301	5,998
25,050	25,100	0	2,273	4,122	4,819	0	3,159	5,291	5,987
25,100	25,150	0	2,265	4,111	4,808	0	3,151	5,280	5,977
25,150	25,200	0	2,257	4,101	4,797	0	3,143	5,270	5,966
25,200	25,250	0	2,249	4,090	4,787	0	3,135	5,259	5,956
25,250	25,300	0	2,241	4,080	4,776	0	3,128	5,249	5,945
25,300	25,350	0	2,233	4,069	4,766	0	3,120	5,238	5,935
25,350	25,400	0	2,225	4,059	4,755	0	3,112	5,228	5,924
25,400	25,450	0	2,217	4,048	4,745	0	3,104	5,217	5,914
25,450	25,500	0	2,209	4,038	4,734	0	3,096	5,207	5,903
25,500	25,550	0	2,201	4,027	4,724	0	3,088	5,196	5,893
25,550	25,600	0	2,193	4,017	4,713	0	3,080	5,186	5,882

* If the amount you are looking up from the worksheet is at least $20,400 but less than $20,430, and you have no qualifying children, your credit is $1. If the amount you are looking up from the worksheet is $20,430 or more, and you have no qualifying children, you can't take the credit.

(Continued)

At least	But less than	Single, head of household, or qualifying widow(er) 0	1	2	3	Married filing jointly 0	1	2	3
25,600	25,650	0	2,185	4,006	4,703	0	3,072	5,175	5,872
25,650	25,700	0	2,177	3,996	4,692	0	3,064	5,164	5,861
25,700	25,750	0	2,169	3,985	4,682	0	3,056	5,154	5,850
25,750	25,800	0	2,161	3,975	4,671	0	3,048	5,143	5,840
25,800	25,850	0	2,153	3,964	4,661	0	3,040	5,133	5,829
25,850	25,900	0	2,145	3,954	4,650	0	3,032	5,122	5,819
25,900	25,950	0	2,137	3,943	4,640	0	3,024	5,112	5,808
25,950	26,000	0	2,129	3,932	4,629	0	3,016	5,101	5,798
26,000	26,050	0	2,121	3,922	4,618	0	3,008	5,091	5,787
26,050	26,100	0	2,113	3,911	4,608	0	3,000	5,080	5,777
26,100	26,150	0	2,105	3,901	4,597	0	2,992	5,070	5,766
26,150	26,200	0	2,097	3,890	4,587	0	2,984	5,059	5,756
26,200	26,250	0	2,089	3,880	4,576	0	2,976	5,049	5,745
26,250	26,300	0	2,081	3,869	4,566	0	2,968	5,038	5,735
26,300	26,350	0	2,073	3,859	4,555	0	2,960	5,028	5,724
26,350	26,400	0	2,065	3,848	4,545	0	2,952	5,017	5,714
26,400	26,450	0	2,057	3,838	4,534	0	2,944	5,007	5,703
26,450	26,500	0	2,049	3,827	4,524	0	2,936	4,996	5,693
26,500	26,550	0	2,041	3,817	4,513	0	2,928	4,985	5,682
26,550	26,600	0	2,033	3,806	4,503	0	2,920	4,975	5,671
26,600	26,650	0	2,025	3,796	4,492	0	2,912	4,964	5,661
26,650	26,700	0	2,017	3,785	4,482	0	2,904	4,954	5,650
26,700	26,750	0	2,009	3,775	4,471	0	2,896	4,943	5,640
26,750	26,800	0	2,001	3,764	4,460	0	2,888	4,933	5,629
26,800	26,850	0	1,993	3,753	4,450	0	2,880	4,922	5,619
26,850	26,900	0	1,985	3,743	4,439	0	2,872	4,912	5,608
26,900	26,950	0	1,977	3,732	4,429	0	2,864	4,901	5,598
26,950	27,000	0	1,969	3,722	4,418	0	2,856	4,891	5,587
27,000	27,050	0	1,961	3,711	4,408	0	2,848	4,880	5,577
27,050	27,100	0	1,953	3,701	4,397	0	2,840	4,870	5,566
27,100	27,150	0	1,945	3,690	4,387	0	2,832	4,859	5,556
27,150	27,200	0	1,937	3,680	4,376	0	2,824	4,849	5,545
27,200	27,250	0	1,929	3,669	4,366	0	2,816	4,838	5,535
27,250	27,300	0	1,921	3,659	4,355	0	2,808	4,828	5,524
27,300	27,350	0	1,913	3,648	4,345	0	2,800	4,817	5,513
27,350	27,400	0	1,905	3,638	4,334	0	2,792	4,806	5,503
27,400	27,450	0	1,897	3,627	4,324	0	2,784	4,796	5,492
27,450	27,500	0	1,889	3,617	4,313	0	2,776	4,785	5,482
27,500	27,550	0	1,881	3,606	4,303	0	2,768	4,775	5,471
27,550	27,600	0	1,873	3,596	4,292	0	2,760	4,764	5,461
27,600	27,650	0	1,865	3,585	4,281	0	2,752	4,754	5,450
27,650	27,700	0	1,857	3,574	4,271	0	2,744	4,743	5,440
27,700	27,750	0	1,849	3,564	4,260	0	2,736	4,733	5,429
27,750	27,800	0	1,841	3,553	4,250	0	2,728	4,722	5,419
27,800	27,850	0	1,833	3,543	4,239	0	2,720	4,712	5,408
27,850	27,900	0	1,825	3,532	4,229	0	2,712	4,701	5,398
27,900	27,950	0	1,817	3,522	4,218	0	2,704	4,691	5,387
27,950	28,000	0	1,809	3,511	4,208	0	2,696	4,680	5,377
28,000	28,050	0	1,801	3,501	4,197	0	2,688	4,670	5,366
28,050	28,100	0	1,793	3,490	4,187	0	2,680	4,659	5,356
28,100	28,150	0	1,785	3,480	4,176	0	2,672	4,649	5,345
28,150	28,200	0	1,777	3,469	4,166	0	2,664	4,638	5,334
28,200	28,250	0	1,769	3,459	4,155	0	2,656	4,627	5,324
28,250	28,300	0	1,761	3,448	4,145	0	2,648	4,617	5,313
28,300	28,350	0	1,753	3,438	4,134	0	2,640	4,606	5,303
28,350	28,400	0	1,745	3,427	4,124	0	2,632	4,596	5,292
28,400	28,450	0	1,737	3,417	4,113	0	2,624	4,585	5,282
28,450	28,500	0	1,729	3,406	4,102	0	2,616	4,575	5,271
28,500	28,550	0	1,721	3,395	4,092	0	2,608	4,564	5,261
28,550	28,600	0	1,713	3,385	4,081	0	2,600	4,554	5,250
28,600	28,650	0	1,705	3,374	4,071	0	2,592	4,543	5,240
28,650	28,700	0	1,697	3,364	4,060	0	2,584	4,533	5,229
28,700	28,750	0	1,689	3,353	4,050	0	2,576	4,522	5,219
28,750	28,800	0	1,681	3,343	4,039	0	2,568	4,512	5,208
28,800	28,850	0	1,673	3,332	4,029	0	2,560	4,501	5,198
28,850	28,900	0	1,665	3,322	4,018	0	2,552	4,491	5,187
28,900	28,950	0	1,657	3,311	4,008	0	2,544	4,480	5,177
28,950	29,000	0	1,649	3,301	3,997	0	2,536	4,470	5,166
29,000	29,050	0	1,641	3,290	3,987	0	2,528	4,459	5,155
29,050	29,100	0	1,633	3,280	3,976	0	2,520	4,448	5,145
29,100	29,150	0	1,625	3,269	3,966	0	2,512	4,438	5,134
29,150	29,200	0	1,617	3,259	3,955	0	2,504	4,427	5,124

At least	But less than	Single, head of household, or qualifying widow(er) 0	1	2	3	Married filing jointly 0	1	2	3
29,200	29,250	0	1,609	3,248	3,945	0	2,496	4,417	5,113
29,250	29,300	0	1,601	3,237	3,934	0	2,488	4,406	5,103
29,300	29,350	0	1,593	3,227	3,923	0	2,480	4,396	5,092
29,350	29,400	0	1,585	3,216	3,913	0	2,472	4,385	5,082
29,400	29,450	0	1,577	3,206	3,902	0	2,464	4,375	5,071
29,450	29,500	0	1,569	3,195	3,892	0	2,456	4,364	5,061
29,500	29,550	0	1,561	3,185	3,881	0	2,448	4,354	5,050
29,550	29,600	0	1,553	3,174	3,871	0	2,440	4,343	5,040
29,600	29,650	0	1,545	3,164	3,860	0	2,432	4,333	5,029
29,650	29,700	0	1,537	3,153	3,850	0	2,424	4,322	5,019
29,700	29,750	0	1,530	3,143	3,839	0	2,416	4,312	5,008
29,750	29,800	0	1,522	3,132	3,829	0	2,408	4,301	4,998
29,800	29,850	0	1,514	3,122	3,818	0	2,400	4,290	4,987
29,850	29,900	0	1,506	3,111	3,808	0	2,392	4,280	4,976
29,900	29,950	0	1,498	3,101	3,797	0	2,384	4,269	4,966
29,950	30,000	0	1,490	3,090	3,787	0	2,376	4,259	4,955
30,000	30,050	0	1,482	3,080	3,776	0	2,368	4,248	4,945
30,050	30,100	0	1,474	3,069	3,766	0	2,360	4,238	4,934
30,100	30,150	0	1,466	3,058	3,755	0	2,352	4,227	4,924
30,150	30,200	0	1,458	3,048	3,744	0	2,344	4,217	4,913
30,200	30,250	0	1,450	3,037	3,734	0	2,336	4,206	4,903
30,250	30,300	0	1,442	3,027	3,723	0	2,329	4,196	4,892
30,300	30,350	0	1,434	3,016	3,713	0	2,321	4,185	4,882
30,350	30,400	0	1,426	3,006	3,702	0	2,313	4,175	4,871
30,400	30,450	0	1,418	2,995	3,692	0	2,305	4,164	4,861
30,450	30,500	0	1,410	2,985	3,681	0	2,297	4,154	4,850
30,500	30,550	0	1,402	2,974	3,671	0	2,289	4,143	4,840
30,550	30,600	0	1,394	2,964	3,660	0	2,281	4,133	4,829
30,600	30,650	0	1,386	2,953	3,650	0	2,273	4,122	4,819
30,650	30,700	0	1,378	2,943	3,639	0	2,265	4,111	4,808
30,700	30,750	0	1,370	2,932	3,629	0	2,257	4,101	4,797
30,750	30,800	0	1,362	2,922	3,618	0	2,249	4,090	4,787
30,800	30,850	0	1,354	2,911	3,608	0	2,241	4,080	4,776
30,850	30,900	0	1,346	2,901	3,597	0	2,233	4,069	4,766
30,900	30,950	0	1,338	2,890	3,587	0	2,225	4,059	4,755
30,950	31,000	0	1,330	2,879	3,576	0	2,217	4,048	4,745
31,000	31,050	0	1,322	2,869	3,565	0	2,209	4,038	4,734
31,050	31,100	0	1,314	2,858	3,555	0	2,201	4,027	4,724
31,100	31,150	0	1,306	2,848	3,544	0	2,193	4,017	4,713
31,150	31,200	0	1,298	2,837	3,534	0	2,185	4,006	4,703
31,200	31,250	0	1,290	2,827	3,523	0	2,177	3,996	4,692
31,250	31,300	0	1,282	2,816	3,513	0	2,169	3,985	4,682
31,300	31,350	0	1,274	2,806	3,502	0	2,161	3,975	4,671
31,350	31,400	0	1,266	2,795	3,492	0	2,153	3,964	4,661
31,400	31,450	0	1,258	2,785	3,481	0	2,145	3,954	4,650
31,450	31,500	0	1,250	2,774	3,471	0	2,137	3,943	4,640
31,500	31,550	0	1,242	2,764	3,460	0	2,129	3,932	4,629
31,550	31,600	0	1,234	2,753	3,450	0	2,121	3,922	4,618
31,600	31,650	0	1,226	2,743	3,439	0	2,113	3,911	4,608
31,650	31,700	0	1,218	2,732	3,429	0	2,105	3,901	4,597
31,700	31,750	0	1,210	2,722	3,418	0	2,097	3,890	4,587
31,750	31,800	0	1,202	2,711	3,407	0	2,089	3,880	4,576
31,800	31,850	0	1,194	2,700	3,397	0	2,081	3,869	4,566
31,850	31,900	0	1,186	2,690	3,386	0	2,073	3,859	4,555
31,900	31,950	0	1,178	2,679	3,376	0	2,065	3,848	4,545
31,950	32,000	0	1,170	2,669	3,365	0	2,057	3,838	4,534
32,000	32,050	0	1,162	2,658	3,355	0	2,049	3,827	4,524
32,050	32,100	0	1,154	2,648	3,344	0	2,041	3,817	4,513
32,100	32,150	0	1,146	2,637	3,334	0	2,033	3,806	4,503
32,150	32,200	0	1,138	2,627	3,323	0	2,025	3,796	4,492
32,200	32,250	0	1,130	2,616	3,313	0	2,017	3,785	4,482
32,250	32,300	0	1,122	2,606	3,302	0	2,009	3,775	4,471
32,300	32,350	0	1,114	2,595	3,292	0	2,001	3,764	4,460
32,350	32,400	0	1,106	2,585	3,281	0	1,993	3,753	4,450
32,400	32,450	0	1,098	2,574	3,271	0	1,985	3,743	4,439
32,450	32,500	0	1,090	2,564	3,260	0	1,977	3,732	4,429
32,500	32,550	0	1,082	2,553	3,250	0	1,969	3,722	4,418
32,550	32,600	0	1,074	2,543	3,239	0	1,961	3,711	4,408
32,600	32,650	0	1,066	2,532	3,228	0	1,953	3,701	4,397
32,650	32,700	0	1,058	2,521	3,218	0	1,945	3,690	4,387
32,700	32,750	0	1,050	2,511	3,207	0	1,937	3,680	4,376
32,750	32,800	0	1,042	2,500	3,197	0	1,929	3,669	4,366

(Continued)

    Need more information or forms? Visit IRS.gov.

Earned Income Credit (EIC) Table - *Continued*

(Caution. This is not a tax table.)

If the amount you are looking up from the worksheet is—		Single, head of household, or qualifying widow(er) and the number of children you have is—				Married filing jointly and the number of children you have is—			
At least	But less than	0	1	2	3	0	1	2	3
		Your credit is—				Your credit is—			
32,800	32,850	0	1,034	2,490	3,186	0	1,921	3,659	4,355
32,850	32,900	0	1,026	2,479	3,176	0	1,913	3,648	4,345
32,900	32,950	0	1,018	2,469	3,165	0	1,905	3,638	4,334
32,950	33,000	0	1,010	2,458	3,155	0	1,897	3,627	4,324
33,000	33,050	0	1,002	2,448	3,144	0	1,889	3,617	4,313
33,050	33,100	0	994	2,437	3,134	0	1,881	3,606	4,303
33,100	33,150	0	986	2,427	3,123	0	1,873	3,596	4,292
33,150	33,200	0	978	2,416	3,113	0	1,865	3,585	4,281
33,200	33,250	0	970	2,406	3,102	0	1,857	3,574	4,271
33,250	33,300	0	962	2,395	3,092	0	1,849	3,564	4,260
33,300	33,350	0	954	2,385	3,081	0	1,841	3,553	4,250
33,350	33,400	0	946	2,374	3,071	0	1,833	3,543	4,239
33,400	33,450	0	938	2,364	3,060	0	1,825	3,532	4,229
33,450	33,500	0	930	2,353	3,049	0	1,817	3,522	4,218
33,500	33,550	0	922	2,342	3,039	0	1,809	3,511	4,208
33,550	33,600	0	914	2,332	3,028	0	1,801	3,501	4,197
33,600	33,650	0	906	2,321	3,018	0	1,793	3,490	4,187
33,650	33,700	0	898	2,311	3,007	0	1,785	3,480	4,176
33,700	33,750	0	890	2,300	2,997	0	1,777	3,469	4,166
33,750	33,800	0	882	2,290	2,986	0	1,769	3,459	4,155
33,800	33,850	0	874	2,279	2,976	0	1,761	3,448	4,145
33,850	33,900	0	866	2,269	2,965	0	1,753	3,438	4,134
33,900	33,950	0	858	2,258	2,955	0	1,745	3,427	4,124
33,950	34,000	0	850	2,248	2,944	0	1,737	3,417	4,113
34,000	34,050	0	842	2,237	2,934	0	1,729	3,406	4,102
34,050	34,100	0	834	2,227	2,923	0	1,721	3,395	4,092
34,100	34,150	0	826	2,216	2,913	0	1,713	3,385	4,081
34,150	34,200	0	818	2,206	2,902	0	1,705	3,374	4,071
34,200	34,250	0	810	2,195	2,892	0	1,697	3,364	4,060
34,250	34,300	0	802	2,184	2,881	0	1,689	3,353	4,050
34,300	34,350	0	794	2,174	2,870	0	1,681	3,343	4,039
34,350	34,400	0	786	2,163	2,860	0	1,673	3,332	4,029
34,400	34,450	0	778	2,153	2,849	0	1,665	3,322	4,018
34,450	34,500	0	770	2,142	2,839	0	1,657	3,311	4,008
34,500	34,550	0	762	2,132	2,828	0	1,649	3,301	3,997
34,550	34,600	0	754	2,121	2,818	0	1,641	3,290	3,987
34,600	34,650	0	746	2,111	2,807	0	1,633	3,280	3,976
34,650	34,700	0	738	2,100	2,797	0	1,625	3,269	3,966
34,700	34,750	0	731	2,090	2,786	0	1,617	3,259	3,955
34,750	34,800	0	723	2,079	2,776	0	1,609	3,248	3,945
34,800	34,850	0	715	2,069	2,765	0	1,601	3,237	3,934
34,850	34,900	0	707	2,058	2,755	0	1,593	3,227	3,923
34,900	34,950	0	699	2,048	2,744	0	1,585	3,216	3,913
34,950	35,000	0	691	2,037	2,734	0	1,577	3,206	3,902
35,000	35,050	0	683	2,027	2,723	0	1,569	3,195	3,892
35,050	35,100	0	675	2,016	2,713	0	1,561	3,185	3,881
35,100	35,150	0	667	2,005	2,702	0	1,553	3,174	3,871
35,150	35,200	0	659	1,995	2,691	0	1,545	3,164	3,860
35,200	35,250	0	651	1,984	2,681	0	1,537	3,153	3,850
35,250	35,300	0	643	1,974	2,670	0	1,530	3,143	3,839
35,300	35,350	0	635	1,963	2,660	0	1,522	3,132	3,829
35,350	35,400	0	627	1,953	2,649	0	1,514	3,122	3,818
35,400	35,450	0	619	1,942	2,639	0	1,506	3,111	3,808
35,450	35,500	0	611	1,932	2,628	0	1,498	3,101	3,797
35,500	35,550	0	603	1,921	2,618	0	1,490	3,090	3,787
35,550	35,600	0	595	1,911	2,607	0	1,482	3,080	3,776
35,600	35,650	0	587	1,900	2,597	0	1,474	3,069	3,766
35,650	35,700	0	579	1,890	2,586	0	1,466	3,058	3,755
35,700	35,750	0	571	1,879	2,576	0	1,458	3,048	3,744
35,750	35,800	0	563	1,869	2,565	0	1,450	3,037	3,734
35,800	35,850	0	555	1,858	2,555	0	1,442	3,027	3,723
35,850	35,900	0	547	1,848	2,544	0	1,434	3,016	3,713
35,900	35,950	0	539	1,837	2,534	0	1,426	3,006	3,702
35,950	36,000	0	531	1,826	2,523	0	1,418	2,995	3,692

If the amount you are looking up from the worksheet is—		Single, head of household, or qualifying widow(er) and the number of children you have is—				Married filing jointly and the number of children you have is—			
At least	But less than	0	1	2	3	0	1	2	3
		Your credit is—				Your credit is—			
36,000	36,050	0	523	1,816	2,512	0	1,410	2,985	3,681
36,050	36,100	0	515	1,805	2,502	0	1,402	2,974	3,671
36,100	36,150	0	507	1,795	2,491	0	1,394	2,964	3,660
36,150	36,200	0	499	1,784	2,481	0	1,386	2,953	3,650
36,200	36,250	0	491	1,774	2,470	0	1,378	2,943	3,639
36,250	36,300	0	483	1,763	2,460	0	1,370	2,932	3,629
36,300	36,350	0	475	1,753	2,449	0	1,362	2,922	3,618
36,350	36,400	0	467	1,742	2,439	0	1,354	2,911	3,608
36,400	36,450	0	459	1,732	2,428	0	1,346	2,901	3,597
36,450	36,500	0	451	1,721	2,418	0	1,338	2,890	3,587
36,500	36,550	0	443	1,711	2,407	0	1,330	2,879	3,576
36,550	36,600	0	435	1,700	2,397	0	1,322	2,869	3,565
36,600	36,650	0	427	1,690	2,386	0	1,314	2,858	3,555
36,650	36,700	0	419	1,679	2,376	0	1,306	2,848	3,544
36,700	36,750	0	411	1,669	2,365	0	1,298	2,837	3,534
36,750	36,800	0	403	1,658	2,354	0	1,290	2,827	3,523
36,800	36,850	0	395	1,647	2,344	0	1,282	2,816	3,513
36,850	36,900	0	387	1,637	2,333	0	1,274	2,806	3,502
36,900	36,950	0	379	1,626	2,323	0	1,266	2,795	3,492
36,950	37,000	0	371	1,616	2,312	0	1,258	2,785	3,481
37,000	37,050	0	363	1,605	2,302	0	1,250	2,774	3,471
37,050	37,100	0	355	1,595	2,291	0	1,242	2,764	3,460
37,100	37,150	0	347	1,584	2,281	0	1,234	2,753	3,450
37,150	37,200	0	339	1,574	2,270	0	1,226	2,743	3,439
37,200	37,250	0	331	1,563	2,260	0	1,218	2,732	3,429
37,250	37,300	0	323	1,553	2,249	0	1,210	2,722	3,418
37,300	37,350	0	315	1,542	2,239	0	1,202	2,711	3,407
37,350	37,400	0	307	1,532	2,228	0	1,194	2,700	3,397
37,400	37,450	0	299	1,521	2,218	0	1,186	2,690	3,386
37,450	37,500	0	291	1,511	2,207	0	1,178	2,679	3,376
37,500	37,550	0	283	1,500	2,197	0	1,170	2,669	3,365
37,550	37,600	0	275	1,490	2,186	0	1,162	2,658	3,355
37,600	37,650	0	267	1,479	2,175	0	1,154	2,648	3,344
37,650	37,700	0	259	1,468	2,165	0	1,146	2,637	3,334
37,700	37,750	0	251	1,458	2,154	0	1,138	2,627	3,323
37,750	37,800	0	243	1,447	2,144	0	1,130	2,616	3,313
37,800	37,850	0	235	1,437	2,133	0	1,122	2,606	3,302
37,850	37,900	0	227	1,426	2,123	0	1,114	2,595	3,292
37,900	37,950	0	219	1,416	2,112	0	1,106	2,585	3,281
37,950	38,000	0	211	1,405	2,102	0	1,098	2,574	3,271
38,000	38,050	0	203	1,395	2,091	0	1,090	2,564	3,260
38,050	38,100	0	195	1,384	2,081	0	1,082	2,553	3,250
38,100	38,150	0	187	1,374	2,070	0	1,074	2,543	3,239
38,150	38,200	0	179	1,363	2,060	0	1,066	2,532	3,228
38,200	38,250	0	171	1,353	2,049	0	1,058	2,521	3,218
38,250	38,300	0	163	1,342	2,039	0	1,050	2,511	3,207
38,300	38,350	0	155	1,332	2,028	0	1,042	2,500	3,197
38,350	38,400	0	147	1,321	2,018	0	1,034	2,490	3,186
38,400	38,450	0	139	1,311	2,007	0	1,026	2,479	3,176
38,450	38,500	0	131	1,300	1,996	0	1,018	2,469	3,165
38,500	38,550	0	123	1,289	1,986	0	1,010	2,458	3,155
38,550	38,600	0	115	1,279	1,975	0	1,002	2,448	3,144
38,600	38,650	0	107	1,268	1,965	0	994	2,437	3,134
38,650	38,700	0	99	1,258	1,954	0	986	2,427	3,123
38,700	38,750	0	91	1,247	1,944	0	978	2,416	3,113
38,750	38,800	0	83	1,237	1,933	0	970	2,406	3,102
38,800	38,850	0	75	1,226	1,923	0	962	2,395	3,092
38,850	38,900	0	67	1,216	1,912	0	954	2,385	3,081
38,900	38,950	0	59	1,205	1,902	0	946	2,374	3,071
38,950	39,000	0	51	1,195	1,891	0	938	2,364	3,060
39,000	39,050	0	43	1,184	1,881	0	930	2,353	3,049
39,050	39,100	0	35	1,174	1,870	0	922	2,342	3,039
39,100	39,150	0	27	1,163	1,860	0	914	2,332	3,028
39,150	39,200	0	19	1,153	1,849	0	906	2,321	3,018

(Continued)

Earned Income Credit (EIC) Table - Continued

(Caution. This is not a tax table.)

If the amount you are looking up from the worksheet is–		Single, head of household, or qualifying widow(er) and the number of children you have is–				Married filing jointly and the number of children you have is–			
At least	But less than	0	1	2	3	0	1	2	3
		Your credit is–				Your credit is–			
39,200	39,250	0	11	1,142	1,839	0	898	2,311	3,007
39,250	39,300	0	*	1,131	1,828	0	890	2,300	2,997
39,300	39,350	0	0	1,121	1,817	0	882	2,290	2,986
39,350	39,400	0	0	1,110	1,807	0	874	2,279	2,976
39,400	39,450	0	0	1,100	1,796	0	866	2,269	2,965
39,450	39,500	0	0	1,089	1,786	0	858	2,258	2,955
39,500	39,550	0	0	1,079	1,775	0	850	2,248	2,944
39,550	39,600	0	0	1,068	1,765	0	842	2,237	2,934
39,600	39,650	0	0	1,058	1,754	0	834	2,227	2,923
39,650	39,700	0	0	1,047	1,744	0	826	2,216	2,913
39,700	39,750	0	0	1,037	1,733	0	818	2,206	2,902
39,750	39,800	0	0	1,026	1,723	0	810	2,195	2,892
39,800	39,850	0	0	1,016	1,712	0	802	2,184	2,881
39,850	39,900	0	0	1,005	1,702	0	794	2,174	2,870
39,900	39,950	0	0	995	1,691	0	786	2,163	2,860
39,950	40,000	0	0	984	1,681	0	778	2,153	2,849
40,000	40,050	0	0	974	1,670	0	770	2,142	2,839
40,050	40,100	0	0	963	1,660	0	762	2,132	2,828
40,100	40,150	0	0	952	1,649	0	754	2,121	2,818
40,150	40,200	0	0	942	1,638	0	746	2,111	2,807
40,200	40,250	0	0	931	1,628	0	738	2,100	2,797
40,250	40,300	0	0	921	1,617	0	731	2,090	2,786
40,300	40,350	0	0	910	1,607	0	723	2,079	2,776
40,350	40,400	0	0	900	1,596	0	715	2,069	2,765
40,400	40,450	0	0	889	1,586	0	707	2,058	2,755
40,450	40,500	0	0	879	1,575	0	699	2,048	2,744
40,500	40,550	0	0	868	1,565	0	691	2,037	2,734
40,550	40,600	0	0	858	1,554	0	683	2,027	2,723
40,600	40,650	0	0	847	1,544	0	675	2,016	2,713
40,650	40,700	0	0	837	1,533	0	667	2,005	2,702
40,700	40,750	0	0	826	1,523	0	659	1,995	2,691
40,750	40,800	0	0	816	1,512	0	651	1,984	2,681
40,800	40,850	0	0	805	1,502	0	643	1,974	2,670
40,850	40,900	0	0	795	1,491	0	635	1,963	2,660
40,900	40,950	0	0	784	1,481	0	627	1,953	2,649
40,950	41,000	0	0	773	1,470	0	619	1,942	2,639
41,000	41,050	0	0	763	1,459	0	611	1,932	2,628
41,050	41,100	0	0	752	1,449	0	603	1,921	2,618
41,100	41,150	0	0	742	1,438	0	595	1,911	2,607
41,150	41,200	0	0	731	1,428	0	587	1,900	2,597
41,200	41,250	0	0	721	1,417	0	579	1,890	2,586
41,250	41,300	0	0	710	1,407	0	571	1,879	2,576
41,300	41,350	0	0	700	1,396	0	563	1,869	2,565
41,350	41,400	0	0	689	1,386	0	555	1,858	2,555
41,400	41,450	0	0	679	1,375	0	547	1,848	2,544
41,450	41,500	0	0	668	1,365	0	539	1,837	2,534
41,500	41,550	0	0	658	1,354	0	531	1,826	2,523
41,550	41,600	0	0	647	1,344	0	523	1,816	2,512
41,600	41,650	0	0	637	1,333	0	515	1,805	2,502
41,650	41,700	0	0	626	1,323	0	507	1,795	2,491
41,700	41,750	0	0	616	1,312	0	499	1,784	2,481
41,750	41,800	0	0	605	1,301	0	491	1,774	2,470
41,800	41,850	0	0	594	1,291	0	483	1,763	2,460
41,850	41,900	0	0	584	1,280	0	475	1,753	2,449
41,900	41,950	0	0	573	1,270	0	467	1,742	2,439
41,950	42,000	0	0	563	1,259	0	459	1,732	2,428
42,000	42,050	0	0	552	1,249	0	451	1,721	2,418
42,050	42,100	0	0	542	1,238	0	443	1,711	2,407
42,100	42,150	0	0	531	1,228	0	435	1,700	2,397
42,150	42,200	0	0	521	1,217	0	427	1,690	2,386
42,200	42,250	0	0	510	1,207	0	419	1,679	2,376
42,250	42,300	0	0	500	1,196	0	411	1,669	2,365
42,300	42,350	0	0	489	1,186	0	403	1,658	2,354
42,350	42,400	0	0	479	1,175	0	395	1,647	2,344

If the amount you are looking up from the worksheet is–		Single, head of household, or qualifying widow(er) and the number of children you have is–				Married filing jointly and the number of children you have is–			
At least	But less than	0	1	2	3	0	1	2	3
		Your credit is–				Your credit is–			
42,400	42,450	0	0	468	1,165	0	387	1,637	2,333
42,450	42,500	0	0	458	1,154	0	379	1,626	2,323
42,500	42,550	0	0	447	1,144	0	371	1,616	2,312
42,550	42,600	0	0	437	1,133	0	363	1,605	2,302
42,600	42,650	0	0	426	1,122	0	355	1,595	2,291
42,650	42,700	0	0	415	1,112	0	347	1,584	2,281
42,700	42,750	0	0	405	1,101	0	339	1,574	2,270
42,750	42,800	0	0	394	1,091	0	331	1,563	2,260
42,800	42,850	0	0	384	1,080	0	323	1,553	2,249
42,850	42,900	0	0	373	1,070	0	315	1,542	2,239
42,900	42,950	0	0	363	1,059	0	307	1,532	2,228
42,950	43,000	0	0	352	1,049	0	299	1,521	2,218
43,000	43,050	0	0	342	1,038	0	291	1,511	2,207
43,050	43,100	0	0	331	1,028	0	283	1,500	2,197
43,100	43,150	0	0	321	1,017	0	275	1,490	2,186
43,150	43,200	0	0	310	1,007	0	267	1,479	2,175
43,200	43,250	0	0	300	996	0	259	1,468	2,165
43,250	43,300	0	0	289	986	0	251	1,458	2,154
43,300	43,350	0	0	279	975	0	243	1,447	2,144
43,350	43,400	0	0	268	965	0	235	1,437	2,133
43,400	43,450	0	0	258	954	0	227	1,426	2,123
43,450	43,500	0	0	247	943	0	219	1,416	2,112
43,500	43,550	0	0	236	933	0	211	1,405	2,102
43,550	43,600	0	0	226	922	0	203	1,395	2,091
43,600	43,650	0	0	215	912	0	195	1,384	2,081
43,650	43,700	0	0	205	901	0	187	1,374	2,070
43,700	43,750	0	0	194	891	0	179	1,363	2,060
43,750	43,800	0	0	184	880	0	171	1,353	2,049
43,800	43,850	0	0	173	870	0	163	1,342	2,039
43,850	43,900	0	0	163	859	0	155	1,332	2,028
43,900	43,950	0	0	152	849	0	147	1,321	2,018
43,950	44,000	0	0	142	838	0	139	1,311	2,007
44,000	44,050	0	0	131	828	0	131	1,300	1,996
44,050	44,100	0	0	121	817	0	123	1,289	1,986
44,100	44,150	0	0	110	807	0	115	1,279	1,975
44,150	44,200	0	0	100	796	0	107	1,268	1,965
44,200	44,250	0	0	89	786	0	99	1,258	1,954
44,250	44,300	0	0	78	775	0	91	1,247	1,944
44,300	44,350	0	0	68	764	0	83	1,237	1,933
44,350	44,400	0	0	57	754	0	75	1,226	1,923
44,400	44,450	0	0	47	743	0	67	1,216	1,912
44,450	44,500	0	0	36	733	0	59	1,205	1,902
44,500	44,550	0	0	26	722	0	51	1,195	1,891
44,550	44,600	0	0	15	712	0	43	1,184	1,881
44,600	44,650	0	0	**	701	0	35	1,174	1,870
44,650	44,700	0	0	0	691	0	27	1,163	1,860
44,700	44,750	0	0	0	680	0	19	1,153	1,849
44,750	44,800	0	0	0	670	0	11	1,142	1,839
44,800	44,850	0	0	0	659	0	***	1,131	1,828
44,850	44,900	0	0	0	649	0	0	1,121	1,817
44,900	44,950	0	0	0	638	0	0	1,110	1,807
44,950	45,000	0	0	0	628	0	0	1,100	1,796
45,000	45,050	0	0	0	617	0	0	1,089	1,786
45,050	45,100	0	0	0	607	0	0	1,079	1,775
45,100	45,150	0	0	0	596	0	0	1,068	1,765
45,150	45,200	0	0	0	585	0	0	1,058	1,754
45,200	45,250	0	0	0	575	0	0	1,047	1,744
45,250	45,300	0	0	0	564	0	0	1,037	1,733
45,300	45,350	0	0	0	554	0	0	1,026	1,723
45,350	45,400	0	0	0	543	0	0	1,016	1,712
45,400	45,450	0	0	0	533	0	0	1,005	1,702
45,450	45,500	0	0	0	522	0	0	995	1,691
45,500	45,550	0	0	0	512	0	0	984	1,681
45,550	45,600	0	0	0	501	0	0	974	1,670

* If the amount you are looking up from the worksheet is at least $39,250 but less than $39,296, and you have one qualifying child, your credit is $4. If the amount you are looking up from the worksheet is $39,296 or more, and you have one qualifying child, you can't take the credit.

** If the amount you are looking up from the worksheet is at least $44,600 but less than $44,648, and you have two qualifying children, your credit is $5. If the amount you are looking up from the worksheet is $44,648 or more, and you have two qualifying children, you can't take the credit.

*** If the amount you are looking up from the worksheet is at least $44,800 but less than $44,846, and you have one qualifying child, your credit is $4. If the amount you are looking up from the worksheet is $44,846 or more, and you have one qualifying child, you can't take the credit.

(Continued)

Need more information or forms? Visit IRS.gov.

Earned Income Credit (EIC) Table - Continued

(Caution. This is not a tax table.)

At least	But less than	Single/HoH: 0	1	2	3	MFJ: 0	1	2	3
45,600	45,650	0	0	0	491	0	0	963	1,660
45,650	45,700	0	0	0	480	0	0	952	1,649
45,700	45,750	0	0	0	470	0	0	942	1,638
45,750	45,800	0	0	0	459	0	0	931	1,628
45,800	45,850	0	0	0	449	0	0	921	1,617
45,850	45,900	0	0	0	438	0	0	910	1,607
45,900	45,950	0	0	0	428	0	0	900	1,596
45,950	46,000	0	0	0	417	0	0	889	1,586
46,000	46,050	0	0	0	406	0	0	879	1,575
46,050	46,100	0	0	0	396	0	0	868	1,565
46,100	46,150	0	0	0	385	0	0	858	1,554
46,150	46,200	0	0	0	375	0	0	847	1,544
46,200	46,250	0	0	0	364	0	0	837	1,533
46,250	46,300	0	0	0	354	0	0	826	1,523
46,300	46,350	0	0	0	343	0	0	816	1,512
46,350	46,400	0	0	0	333	0	0	805	1,502
46,400	46,450	0	0	0	322	0	0	795	1,491
46,450	46,500	0	0	0	312	0	0	784	1,481
46,500	46,550	0	0	0	301	0	0	773	1,470
46,550	46,600	0	0	0	291	0	0	763	1,459
46,600	46,650	0	0	0	280	0	0	752	1,449
46,650	46,700	0	0	0	270	0	0	742	1,438
46,700	46,750	0	0	0	259	0	0	731	1,428
46,750	46,800	0	0	0	248	0	0	721	1,417
46,800	46,850	0	0	0	238	0	0	710	1,407
46,850	46,900	0	0	0	227	0	0	700	1,396
46,900	46,950	0	0	0	217	0	0	689	1,386
46,950	47,000	0	0	0	206	0	0	679	1,375
47,000	47,050	0	0	0	196	0	0	668	1,365
47,050	47,100	0	0	0	185	0	0	658	1,354
47,100	47,150	0	0	0	175	0	0	647	1,344
47,150	47,200	0	0	0	164	0	0	637	1,333
47,200	47,250	0	0	0	154	0	0	626	1,323
47,250	47,300	0	0	0	143	0	0	616	1,312
47,300	47,350	0	0	0	133	0	0	605	1,301
47,350	47,400	0	0	0	122	0	0	594	1,291
47,400	47,450	0	0	0	112	0	0	584	1,280
47,450	47,500	0	0	0	101	0	0	573	1,270
47,500	47,550	0	0	0	91	0	0	563	1,259
47,550	47,600	0	0	0	80	0	0	552	1,249
47,600	47,650	0	0	0	69	0	0	542	1,238
47,650	47,700	0	0	0	59	0	0	531	1,228
47,700	47,750	0	0	0	48	0	0	521	1,217
47,750	47,800	0	0	0	38	0	0	510	1,207
47,800	47,850	0	0	0	27	0	0	500	1,196
47,850	47,900	0	0	0	17	0	0	489	1,186
47,900	47,950	0	0	0	6	0	0	479	1,175
47,950	48,000	0	0	0	*	0	0	468	1,165
48,000	48,050	0	0	0	0	0	0	458	1,154
48,050	48,100	0	0	0	0	0	0	447	1,144
48,100	48,150	0	0	0	0	0	0	437	1,133
48,150	48,200	0	0	0	0	0	0	426	1,122
48,200	48,250	0	0	0	0	0	0	415	1,112
48,250	48,300	0	0	0	0	0	0	405	1,101
48,300	48,350	0	0	0	0	0	0	394	1,091
48,350	48,400	0	0	0	0	0	0	384	1,080
48,400	48,450	0	0	0	0	0	0	373	1,070
48,450	48,500	0	0	0	0	0	0	363	1,059
48,500	48,550	0	0	0	0	0	0	352	1,049
48,550	48,600	0	0	0	0	0	0	342	1,038
48,600	48,650	0	0	0	0	0	0	331	1,028
48,650	48,700	0	0	0	0	0	0	321	1,017
48,700	48,750	0	0	0	0	0	0	310	1,007
48,750	48,800	0	0	0	0	0	0	300	996
48,800	48,850	0	0	0	0	0	0	289	986
48,850	48,900	0	0	0	0	0	0	279	975
48,900	48,950	0	0	0	0	0	0	268	965
48,950	49,000	0	0	0	0	0	0	258	954
49,000	49,050	0	0	0	0	0	0	247	943
49,050	49,100	0	0	0	0	0	0	236	933
49,100	49,150	0	0	0	0	0	0	226	922
49,150	49,200	0	0	0	0	0	0	215	912
49,200	49,250	0	0	0	0	0	0	205	901
49,250	49,300	0	0	0	0	0	0	194	891
49,300	49,350	0	0	0	0	0	0	184	880
49,350	49,400	0	0	0	0	0	0	173	870
49,400	49,450	0	0	0	0	0	0	163	859
49,450	49,500	0	0	0	0	0	0	152	849
49,500	49,550	0	0	0	0	0	0	142	838
49,550	49,600	0	0	0	0	0	0	131	828
49,600	49,650	0	0	0	0	0	0	121	817
49,650	49,700	0	0	0	0	0	0	110	807
49,700	49,750	0	0	0	0	0	0	100	796
49,750	49,800	0	0	0	0	0	0	89	786
49,800	49,850	0	0	0	0	0	0	78	775
49,850	49,900	0	0	0	0	0	0	68	764
49,900	49,950	0	0	0	0	0	0	57	754
49,950	50,000	0	0	0	0	0	0	47	743
50,000	50,050	0	0	0	0	0	0	36	733
50,050	50,100	0	0	0	0	0	0	26	722
50,100	50,150	0	0	0	0	0	0	15	712
50,150	50,200	0	0	0	0	0	0	**	701
50,200	50,250	0	0	0	0	0	0	0	691
50,250	50,300	0	0	0	0	0	0	0	680
50,300	50,350	0	0	0	0	0	0	0	670
50,350	50,400	0	0	0	0	0	0	0	659
50,400	50,450	0	0	0	0	0	0	0	649
50,450	50,500	0	0	0	0	0	0	0	638
50,500	50,550	0	0	0	0	0	0	0	628
50,550	50,600	0	0	0	0	0	0	0	617
50,600	50,650	0	0	0	0	0	0	0	607
50,650	50,700	0	0	0	0	0	0	0	596
50,700	50,750	0	0	0	0	0	0	0	585
50,750	50,800	0	0	0	0	0	0	0	575
50,800	50,850	0	0	0	0	0	0	0	564
50,850	50,900	0	0	0	0	0	0	0	554
50,900	50,950	0	0	0	0	0	0	0	543
50,950	51,000	0	0	0	0	0	0	0	533
51,000	51,050	0	0	0	0	0	0	0	522
51,050	51,100	0	0	0	0	0	0	0	512
51,100	51,150	0	0	0	0	0	0	0	501
51,150	51,200	0	0	0	0	0	0	0	491
51,200	51,250	0	0	0	0	0	0	0	480
51,250	51,300	0	0	0	0	0	0	0	470
51,300	51,350	0	0	0	0	0	0	0	459
51,350	51,400	0	0	0	0	0	0	0	449
51,400	51,450	0	0	0	0	0	0	0	438
51,450	51,500	0	0	0	0	0	0	0	428
51,500	51,550	0	0	0	0	0	0	0	417
51,550	51,600	0	0	0	0	0	0	0	406
51,600	51,650	0	0	0	0	0	0	0	396
51,650	51,700	0	0	0	0	0	0	0	385
51,700	51,750	0	0	0	0	0	0	0	375
51,750	51,800	0	0	0	0	0	0	0	364
51,800	51,850	0	0	0	0	0	0	0	354
51,850	51,900	0	0	0	0	0	0	0	343
51,900	51,950	0	0	0	0	0	0	0	333
51,950	52,000	0	0	0	0	0	0	0	322

* If the amount you are looking up from the worksheet is at least $47,950 but less than $47,955, and you have three qualifying children, your credit is $1.
If the amount you are looking up from the worksheet is $47,955 or more, and you have three qualifying children, you can't take the credit.

** If the amount you are looking up from the worksheet is at least $50,150 but less than $50,198, and you have two qualifying children, your credit is $5.
If the amount you are looking up from the worksheet is $50,198 or more, and you have two qualifying children, you can't take the credit.

(Continued)

If the amount you are looking up from the worksheet is—		Single, head of household, or **qualifying widow(er)** and the number of children you have is—				Married filing jointly and the number of children you have is—				If the amount you are looking up from the worksheet is—		Single, head of household, or **qualifying widow(er)** and the number of children you have is—				Married filing jointly and the number of children you have is—			
		0	1	2	3	0	1	2	3			0	1	2	3	0	1	2	3
At least	But less than	Your credit is—				Your credit is—				At least	But less than	Your credit is—				Your credit is—			
52,000	52,050	0	0	0	0	0	0	0	312	52,800	52,850	0	0	0	0	0	0	0	143
52,050	52,100	0	0	0	0	0	0	0	301	52,850	52,900	0	0	0	0	0	0	0	133
52,100	52,150	0	0	0	0	0	0	0	291	52,900	52,950	0	0	0	0	0	0	0	122
52,150	52,200	0	0	0	0	0	0	0	280	52,950	53,000	0	0	0	0	0	0	0	112
52,200	52,250	0	0	0	0	0	0	0	270	53,000	53,050	0	0	0	0	0	0	0	101
52,250	52,300	0	0	0	0	0	0	0	259	53,050	53,100	0	0	0	0	0	0	0	91
52,300	52,350	0	0	0	0	0	0	0	248	53,100	53,150	0	0	0	0	0	0	0	80
52,350	52,400	0	0	0	0	0	0	0	238	53,150	53,200	0	0	0	0	0	0	0	69
52,400	52,450	0	0	0	0	0	0	0	227	53,200	53,250	0	0	0	0	0	0	0	59
52,450	52,500	0	0	0	0	0	0	0	217	53,250	53,300	0	0	0	0	0	0	0	48
52,500	52,550	0	0	0	0	0	0	0	206	53,300	53,350	0	0	0	0	0	0	0	38
52,550	52,600	0	0	0	0	0	0	0	196	53,350	53,400	0	0	0	0	0	0	0	27
52,600	52,650	0	0	0	0	0	0	0	185	53,400	53,450	0	0	0	0	0	0	0	17
52,650	52,700	0	0	0	0	0	0	0	175	53,450	53,500	0	0	0	0	0	0	0	6
52,700	52,750	0	0	0	0	0	0	0	164	53,500	53,505	0	0	0	0	0	0	0	1
52,750	52,800	0	0	0	0	0	0	0	154										

     Need more information or forms? Visit IRS.gov.

Line 67

Additional Child Tax Credit

What Is the Additional Child Tax Credit?

This credit is for certain people who have at least one qualifying child for the child tax credit (as defined in Steps 1, 2, and 3 of the instructions for line 6c). The additional child tax credit may give you a refund even if you do not owe any tax or didn't have any tax withheld.

Two Steps To Take the Additional Child Tax Credit!

Step 1. Be sure you figured the amount, if any, of your child tax credit. See the instructions for line 52.

Step 2. Read the TIP at the end of your Child Tax Credit Worksheet. Use Schedule 8812 to see if you can take the additional child tax credit, but only if you meet the condition given in that TIP.

Line 68

American Opportunity Credit

If you meet the requirements to claim an education credit (see the instructions for line 50), enter on line 68 the amount, if any, from Form 8863, line 8. You may be able to increase an education credit and reduce your total tax or increase your tax refund if the student chooses to include all or part of a Pell grant or certain other scholarships or fellowships in income. See Pub. 970 and the Instructions for Form 8863 for more information.

Line 69

Net Premium Tax Credit

The premium tax credit helps pay for health insurance purchased through the Marketplace. You may be eligible to claim the premium tax credit if you, your spouse, or a dependent enrolled in health insurance through the Marketplace. Eligible individuals may have advance payments of the premium tax credit made on their behalf directly to the insurance company. You (or whoev-

er enrolled you) should have received Form 1095-A from the Marketplace with information about your coverage and any advance credit payments. Complete Form 8962 to determine the amount of your premium tax credit, if any. If the premium tax credit you can claim exceeds your advance credit payments, your net premium tax credit will be shown on Form 8962, line 26. Enter that amount, if any, on Form 1040, line 69. For more information, see the Instructions for Form 8962.

Line 70

Amount Paid With Request for Extension To File

If you got an automatic extension of time to file Form 1040 by filing Form 4868 or by making a payment, enter the amount of the payment or any amount you paid with Form 4868. If you paid by debit or credit card, do not include on line 70 the convenience fee you were charged. Also, include any amounts paid with Form 2350.

 You may be able to deduct any credit or debit card convenience fees on your 2017 Schedule A.

Line 71

Excess Social Security and Tier 1 RRTA Tax Withheld

If you, or your spouse if filing a joint return, had more than one employer for 2016 and total wages of more than $118,500, too much social security or tier 1 railroad retirement (RRTA) tax may have been withheld. You can take a credit on this line for the amount withheld in excess of $7,347. But if any one employer withheld more than $7,347, you can't claim the excess on your return. The employer should adjust the tax for you. If the employer doesn't adjust the overcollection, you can file a claim for refund using Form 843. Figure this amount separately for you and your spouse.

You can't claim a refund for excess tier 2 RRTA tax on Form 1040. Instead, use Form 843.

For more details, see Pub. 505.

Line 72

Credit for Federal Tax on Fuels

Enter any credit for federal excise taxes paid on fuels that are ultimately used for a nontaxable purpose (for example, an off-highway business use). Attach Form 4136.

Line 73

Check the box(es) on line 73 to report any credit from Form 2439 or 8885.

If you are claiming a credit for repayment of amounts you included in your income in an earlier year because it appeared you had a right to the income, include the credit on line 73. Check box d and enter "I.R.C. 1341" in the space next to that box. See Pub. 525 for details about this credit.

If you made a tax payment that doesn't belong on any other line, include the payment on line 73. Check box d and enter "Tax" in the space next to that box.

If you check more than one box, enter the total of the line 73 credits and payments.

Refund

Line 75

Amount Overpaid

If line 75 is under $1, we will send a refund only on written request.

 If the amount you overpaid is large, you may want to decrease the amount of income tax withheld from your pay by filing a new Form W-4. See Income Tax Withholding and Estimated Tax Payments for 2017 *under* General Information, *later.*

Refund Offset

If you owe past-due federal tax, state income tax, state unemployment compensation debts, child support, spousal support, or certain federal nontax debts, such as student loans, all or part of the overpayment on line 75 may be used (offset) to pay the past-due amount. Off-

Need more information or forms? Visit IRS.gov.

sets for federal taxes are made by the IRS. All other offsets are made by the Treasury Department's Bureau of the Fiscal Service. For federal tax offsets, you will receive a notice from the IRS. For all other offsets, you will receive a notice from the Fiscal Service. To find out if you may have an offset or if you have any questions about it, contact the agency to which you owe the debt.

Injured Spouse

If you file a joint return and your spouse has not paid past-due federal tax, state income tax, state unemployment compensation debts, child support, spousal support, or a federal nontax debt, such as a student loan, part or all of the overpayment on line 75 may be used (offset) to pay the past-due amount. But your part of the overpayment may be refunded to you if certain conditions apply and you complete Form 8379. For details, use *Tax Topic 203* or see Form 8379.

Lines 76a Through 76d

Amount Refunded to You

If you want to check the status of your refund, just use the IRS2Go app or go to *IRS.gov/refunds*. See *Refund Information,* later. Information about your return will generally be available within 24 hours after the IRS receives your e-filed return, or 4 weeks after you mail your paper return. If you filed Form 8379 with your return, wait 14 weeks (11 weeks if you filed electronically). Have your 2016 tax return handy so you can enter your social security number, your filing status, and the exact whole dollar amount of your refund.

Where's My Refund will provide an actual personalized refund date as soon as the IRS processes your tax return and approves your refund.

Effect of refund on benefits. Any refund you receive can't be counted as income when determining if you or anyone else is eligible for benefits or assistance, or how much you or anyone else can receive, under any federal program or under any state or local program financed in whole or in part with federal funds. These programs include Temporary Assistance for Needy Families (TANF), Medicaid, Supplemental Security Income (SSI), and Supplemental Nutrition Assistance Program (food stamps). In addition, when determining eligibility, the refund can't be counted as a resource for at least 12 months after you receive it. Check with your local benefit coordinator to find out if your refund will affect your benefits.

DIRECT DEPOSIT
Simple. Safe. Secure.

Fast Refunds! Join the eight in 10 taxpayers who choose direct deposit—a fast, simple, safe, secure way to have your refund deposited automatically to your checking or savings account, including an individual retirement arrangement (IRA). See the information about IRAs later.

If you want us to directly deposit the amount shown on line 76a to your checking or savings account, including an IRA, at a bank or other financial institution (such as a mutual fund, brokerage firm, or credit union) in the United States:

• Complete lines 76b through 76d (if you want your refund deposited to only one account), or

• Check the box on line 76a and attach Form 8888 if you want to split the direct deposit of your refund into more than one account or use all or part of your refund to buy paper series I savings bonds.

If you do not want your refund directly deposited to your account, do not check the box on line 76a. Draw a line through the boxes on lines 76b and 76d. We will send you a check instead.

Account must be in your name. Do not request a deposit of your refund to an account that isn't in your name, such as your tax return preparer's account. Although you may owe your tax return preparer a fee for preparing your return, do not have any part of your refund deposited into the preparer's account to pay the fee.

The number of refunds that can be directly deposited to a single account or prepaid debit card is limited to three a year. After this limit is reached, paper checks will be sent instead. Learn more at *IRS.gov/depositlimit*.

Why Use Direct Deposit?

• You get your refund faster by direct deposit than you do by check.

• Payment is more secure. There is no check that can get lost or stolen.

• It is more convenient. You do not have to make a trip to the bank to deposit your check.

• It saves tax dollars. It costs the government less to refund by direct deposit.

• It's proven itself. Nearly 98% of social security and veterans' benefits are sent electronically using direct deposit.

 If you file a joint return and check the box on line 76a and attach Form 8888 or fill in lines 76b through 76d, your spouse may get at least part of the refund.

IRA. You can have your refund (or part of it) directly deposited to a traditional IRA, Roth IRA (including a *my*RA), or SEP-IRA, but not a SIMPLE IRA. You must establish the IRA at a bank or other financial institution before you request direct deposit. Make sure your direct deposit will be accepted. You must also notify the trustee or custodian of your account of the year to which the deposit is to be applied (unless the trustee or custodian won't accept a deposit for 2016). If you do not, the trustee or custodian can assume the deposit is for the year during which you are filing the return. For example, if you file your 2016 return during 2017 and do not notify the trustee or custodian in advance, the trustee or custodian can assume the deposit to your IRA is for 2017. If you designate your deposit to be for 2016, you must verify that the deposit was actually made to the account by the due date of the return (not counting extensions). If the deposit isn't made by that date, the deposit isn't an IRA contribution for 2016. In that case, you must file an amended 2016 return and reduce any IRA deduction and any retirement savings contributions credit you claimed.

You and your spouse, if filing jointly, each may be able to contribute up to $5,500 ($6,500 if age 50 or older at the end of 2016) to a traditional IRA or Roth IRA (including a myRA), for 2016. You may owe a penalty if your contributions exceed these limits, and the limits may be lower depending on your compensation and income. For more information on IRA contributions, see Pub. 590-A. If the limits on IRA contributions change for

2017, Pub. 590-A will have the new 2017 limits.

For more information on IRAs, see Pub. 590-A and Pub. 590-B.

*my*RA® . If you already have a *my*RA® account, you can request a deposit of your refund (or part of it) to your *my*RA account. A *my*RA is a starter retirement account offered by the Department of the Treasury. For more information on *my*RA and to open a *my*RA account on-line, visit *www.myRA.gov.*

TreasuryDirect®. You can request a deposit of your refund (or part of it) to a TreasuryDirect® online account to buy U.S. Treasury marketable securities and savings bonds. For more information, go to *go.usa.gov/3KvcP.*

Form 8888. You can have your refund directly deposited into more than one account or use it to buy up to $5,000 in paper series I savings bonds. You do not need a TreasuryDirect® account to do this. For more information, see the Form 8888 instructions.

Line 76a

You can't file Form 8888 to split your refund into more than one account or buy paper series I savings bonds if Form 8379 is filed with your return.

Line 76b

The routing number must be nine digits. The first two digits must be 01 through 12 or 21 through 32. On the sample check shown here, the routing number is 250250025. Charles and Mary Ellen Keys would use that routing number unless their financial institution instructed them to use a different routing number for direct deposits.

Ask your financial institution for the correct routing number to enter on line 76b if:

• The routing number on a deposit slip is different from the routing number on your checks,

• Your deposit is to a savings account that doesn't allow you to write checks,

• Your checks state they are payable through a financial institution different from the one at which you have your checking account, or

• Your deposit is to a *my*RA.

Sample Check—Lines 76b Through 76d

 The routing and account numbers may be in different places on your check.

Line 76c

Check the appropriate box for the type of account. Do not check more than one box. If the deposit is to an account such as an IRA, health savings account, brokerage account, or other similar account, ask your financial institution whether you should check the "Checking" or "Savings" box. You must check the correct box to ensure your deposit is accepted. If your deposit is to a *my*RA or a TreasuryDirect® online account, check the "Savings" box.

Line 76d

The account number can be up to 17 characters (both numbers and letters). Include hyphens but omit spaces and special symbols. Enter the number from left to right and leave any unused boxes blank. On the sample check shown here, the account number is 20202086. Do not include the check number.

If the direct deposit to your account(s) is different from the amount you expected, you will receive an explanation in the mail about 2 weeks after your refund is deposited.

Reasons Your Direct Deposit Request Will Be Rejected

If any of the following apply, your direct deposit request will be rejected and a check will be sent instead.

• You are asking to have a joint refund deposited to an individual account, and your financial institution(s) won't allow this. The IRS isn't responsible if a financial institution rejects a direct deposit.

• The name on your account doesn't match the name on the refund, and your financial institution(s) won't allow a refund to be deposited unless the name on the refund matches the name on the account.

• Three direct deposits of tax refunds have already been made to the same account or prepaid debit card.

• You haven't given a valid account number.

• You file your 2016 return after November 30, 2017.

• Any numbers or letters on lines 76b through 76d are crossed out or whited out.

 The IRS isn't responsible for a lost refund if you enter the wrong account information. Check with your financial institution to get the correct routing and account numbers and to make sure your direct deposit will be accepted.

Line 77

Applied to Your 2017 Estimated Tax

Enter on line 77 the amount, if any, of the overpayment on line 75 you want applied to your 2017 estimated tax. We will apply this amount to your account unless you include a statement requesting us to apply it to your spouse's account. Include your spouse's social security number in the statement.

Need more information or forms? Visit IRS.gov.

This election to apply part or all of the amount overpaid to your 2017 estimated tax can't be changed later.

Amount You Owe

 To avoid interest and penalties, pay your taxes in full by April 18, 2017. You do not have to pay if line 78 is under $1.

Include any estimated payments from line 79 in the amount you enter on line 78. Do not include any estimated payments for 2017 in this payment. Instead, make the estimated payment separately.

Bad check or payment. The penalty for writing a bad check to the IRS is $25 or 2% of the check, whichever is more. However, if the amount of the check is less than $25, the penalty equals the amount of the check. This also applies to other forms of payments if the IRS doesn't receive the funds. Use *Tax Topic 206*.

Line 78

Amount You Owe

IRS offers several payment options. You can pay online, by phone, mobile device, cash (maximum $1,000 per day and per transaction), check or money order. Go to *IRS.gov/payments* for payment options.

Pay Online

IRS offers an electronic payment option that is right for you. Paying online is convenient and secure and helps make sure we get your payments on time. To pay your taxes online or for more information, go to *IRS.gov/payments*. You can pay using any of the following methods.

• **IRS Direct Pay** for online transfers directly from your checking or savings account at no cost to you, go to *IRS.gov/payments*.

• **Pay by Card.** To pay by debit or credit card, go to *IRS.gov/payments*. A convenience fee is charged by these service providers.

• **Electronic Fund Withdrawal** (EFW) is an integrated *e-file*/e-pay option offered when filing your federal taxes electronically using tax preparation software, through a tax professional, or the IRS at *IRS.gov/payments*.

• **Online Payment Agreement.** If you cannot pay in full by the due date of your tax return you can apply for an online monthly installment agreement at *IRS.gov/payments*. Once you complete the online process, you will receive immediate notification of whether your agreement has been approved. A user fee charge is charged.

• **IRS2Go** is the mobile application of the IRS; you can access Direct Pay or Pay By Card by downloading the application.

Pay by Phone

Paying by phone is another safe and secure method of paying electronically. Use one of the following methods **(1)** call one of the debit or credit card service providers or **(2)** use the Electronic Federal Tax Payment System (EFTPS).

Debit or credit card. Call one of our service providers. Each charges a fee that varies by provider, card type, and payment amount.

> Link2Gov Corporation
> 1-888-PAY-1040™
> (1-888-729-1040)
> *www.PAY1040.com*
>
> WorldPay US, Inc.
> 1-844-729-8298
> (1-844-PAY-TAX-8™)
> *www.payUSAtax.com*
>
> Official Payments
> 1-888-UPAY-TAX™
> (1-888-872-9829)
> *www.officialpayments.com*

EFTPS. To use EFTPS, you must be enrolled either online or have an enrollment form mailed to you. To make a payment using EFTPS, call 1-800-555-4477 (English) or 1-800-244-4829 (Español). People who are deaf, hard of hearing, or have a speech disability and who have access to TTY/TDD equipment can call 1-800-733-4829. For more information about EFTPS, go to *IRS.gov/payments* or *www.eftps.gov*.

Pay by Mobile Device

To pay through your mobile device, download the IRS2Go app.

Pay by Cash

Cash is a new in-person payment option for individuals provided through retail partners with a maximum of $1,000 per day per transaction. To make a cash payment you must first be registered online at *www.officialpayments.com/fed* our Official Payment provider.

Pay by Check or Money Order

Before submitting a payment through the mail, please consider alternative methods. One of our safe, quick, and easy electronic payment options might be right for you. If you choose to mail a tax payment, make your check or money order payable to "United States Treasury" for the full amount due. Do not send cash. Do not attach the payment to your return. Write "2016 Form 1040" and your name, address, daytime phone number, and social security number (SSN) on your payment and attach Form 1040-V. For the most up-to-date information on Form 1040-V, go to *IRS.gov/form1040v*. If you are filing a joint return, enter the SSN shown first on your tax return.

To help us process your payment, enter the amount on the right side of the check like this: $ XXX.XX. Do not use dashes or lines (for example, do not enter "$ XXX–" or "$ XXX$^{xx}/_{100}$").

Mail your 2016 tax return, payment, and Form 1040-V to the address shown on the form that applies to you.

No checks of $100 million or more accepted. The IRS can't accept a single check (including a cashier's check) for amounts of $100,000,000 ($100 million) or more. If you are sending $100 million or more by check, you'll need to spread the payment over 2 or more checks with each check made out for an amount less than $100 million. This limit does not apply to other methods of payment (such as electronic payments). Please consider a method of payment other than check if the amount of the payment is over $100 million.

You may need to (a) increase the amount of income tax withheld from your pay by filing a new Form W-4, (b) increase the tax withheld from other income by filing Form W-4P or W-4V, or (c) make estimated tax payments for 2017. See Income Tax Withholding and Estimated Tax Payments for 2017 *under* General Information, *later.*

What If You Can't Pay?

If you can't pay the full amount shown on line 78 when you file, you can ask for:

- An installment agreement, or
- An extension of time to pay.

Installment agreement. Under an installment agreement, you can pay all or part of the tax you owe in monthly installments. However, even if an installment agreement is granted, you will be charged interest and may be charged a late payment penalty on the tax not paid by April 18, 2017. You must also pay a fee. To limit the interest and penalty charges, pay as much of the tax as possible when you file. But before requesting an installment agreement, you should consider other less costly alternatives, such as a bank loan or credit card payment.

To ask for an installment agreement, you can apply online or use Form 9465. To apply online, go to IRS.gov and click on *Apply for an Online Payment Plan*.

Extension of time to pay. If paying the tax when it is due would cause you an undue hardship, you can ask for an extension of time to pay by filing Form 1127 by April 18, 2017. An extension generally won't be granted for more than 6 months. You will be charged interest on the tax not paid by April 15, 2017. You must pay the tax before the extension runs out. Penalties and interest will be imposed until taxes are paid in full. For the most up-to-date information on Form 1127, go to *IRS.gov/form1127*.

Line 79

Estimated Tax Penalty

You may owe this penalty if:

- Line 78 is at least $1,000 and it is more than 10% of the tax shown on your return, or

- You didn't pay enough estimated tax by any of the due dates. This is true even if you are due a refund.

For most people, the "tax shown on your return" is the amount on your 2016 Form 1040, line 63, minus the total of any amounts shown on lines 61, 66a, 67, 68, 69, and 72 and Forms 8828, 4137, 5329 (Parts III through IX only), 8885, and 8919. Also subtract from line 63 any:

- Tax on an excess parachute payment,
- Excise tax on insider stock compensation of an expatriated corporation,
- Uncollected social security and Medicare or RRTA tax on tips or group-term life insurance, and
- Look-back interest due under section 167(g) or 460(b).

When figuring the amount on line 63, include household employment taxes only if line 64 is more than zero or you would owe the penalty even if you didn't include those taxes.

Exception. You won't owe the penalty if your 2015 tax return was for a tax year of 12 full months and either of the following applies.

1. You had no tax shown on your 2015 return and you were a U.S. citizen or resident for all of 2015.

2. The total of lines 64, 65, and 71 on your 2016 return is at least 100% of the tax shown on your 2015 return (110% of that amount if you aren't a farmer or fisherman, and your adjusted gross income (AGI) shown on your 2015 return was more than $150,000 (more than $75,000 if married filing separately for 2016)). Your estimated tax payments for 2016 must have been made on time and for the required amount.

For most people, the "tax shown on your 2015 return" is the amount on your 2015 Form 1040, line 63, minus the total of any amounts shown on lines 61, 66a, 67, 68, 69, and 72 and Forms 8828, 4137, 5329 (Parts III through IX only), 8885, and 8919. Also subtract from line 63 any:

- Tax on an excess parachute payment,
- Excise tax on insider stock compensation of an expatriated corporation,
- Uncollected social security and Medicare or RRTA tax on tips or group-term life insurance, and

- Look-back interest due under section 167(g) or 460(b).

When figuring the amount on line 63, include household employment taxes only if line 64 is more than zero or you would have owed the estimated tax penalty for 2015 even if you didn't include those taxes.

Figuring the Penalty

If the *Exception* just described doesn't apply and you choose to figure the penalty yourself, use Form 2210 (or 2210-F for farmers and fishermen).

Enter any penalty on line 79. Add the penalty to any tax due and enter the total on line 78.

However, if you have an overpayment on line 75, subtract the penalty from the amount you would otherwise enter on line 76a or line 77. Lines 76a, 77, and 79 must equal line 75.

If the penalty is more than the overpayment on line 75, enter -0- on lines 76a and 77. Then subtract line 75 from line 79 and enter the result on line 78.

Do not file Form 2210 with your return unless Form 2210 indicates that you must do so. Instead, keep it for your records.

 Because Form 2210 is complicated, you can leave line 79 blank and the IRS will figure the penalty and send you a bill. We won't charge you interest on the penalty if you pay by the date specified on the bill. If your income varied during the year, the annualized income installment method may reduce the amount of your penalty. But you must file Form 2210 because the IRS can't figure your penalty under this method. See the Instructions for Form 2210 for other situations in which you may be able to lower your penalty by filing Form 2210.

Third Party Designee

If you want to allow your preparer, a friend, a family member, or any other person you choose to discuss your 2016 tax return with the IRS, check the "Yes" box in the "Third Party Designee" area of your return. Also, enter the designee's name, phone number, and any five digits the designee chooses as his or her personal identification number (PIN).

Need more information or forms? Visit IRS.gov.

If you check the "Yes" box, you, and your spouse if filing a joint return, are authorizing the IRS to call the designee to answer any questions that may arise during the processing of your return. You are also authorizing the designee to:

• Give the IRS any information that is missing from your return,

• Call the IRS for information about the processing of your return or the status of your refund or payment(s),

• Receive copies of notices or transcripts related to your return, upon request, and

• Respond to certain IRS notices about math errors, offsets, and return preparation.

You aren't authorizing the designee to receive any refund check, bind you to anything (including any additional tax liability), or otherwise represent you before the IRS. If you want to expand the designee's authorization, see Pub. 947.

The authorization will automatically end no later than the due date (not counting extensions) for filing your 2017 tax return. This is April 17, 2018, for most people.

Sign Your Return

Form 1040 isn't considered a valid return unless you sign it. If you are filing a joint return, your spouse must also sign. If your spouse can't sign the return, see Pub. 501. Be sure to date your return and enter your occupation(s). If you have someone prepare your return, you are still responsible for the correctness of the return. If your return is signed by a representative for you, you must have a power of attorney attached that specifically authorizes the representative to sign your return. To do this, you can use Form 2848. If you are filing a joint return as a surviving spouse, see *Death of a Taxpayer,* later.

Court-Appointed Conservator, Guardian, or Other Fiduciary

If you are a court-appointed conservator, guardian, or other fiduciary for a mentally or physically incompetent individual who has to file Form 1040, sign your name for the individual and file Form 56.

Child's Return

If your child can't sign his or her return, either parent can sign the child's name in the space provided. Then, enter "By (your signature), parent for minor child."

Daytime Phone Number

Providing your daytime phone number may help speed the processing of your return. We may have questions about items on your return, such as the earned income credit or the credit for child and dependent care expenses. If you answer our questions over the phone, we may be able to continue processing your return without mailing you a letter. If you are filing a joint return, you can enter either your or your spouse's daytime phone number.

Electronic Return Signatures!

To file your return electronically, you must sign the return electronically using a personal identification number (PIN). If you are filing online using software, you must use a Self-Select PIN. If you are filing electronically using a tax practitioner, you can use a Self-Select PIN or a Practitioner PIN.

Self-Select PIN. The Self-Select PIN method allows you to create your own PIN. If you are married filing jointly, you and your spouse will each need to create a PIN and enter these PINs as your electronic signatures.

A PIN is any combination of five digits you choose except five zeros. If you use a PIN, there is nothing to sign and nothing to mail—not even your Forms W-2.

To verify your identity, you will be prompted to enter your adjusted gross income (AGI) from your originally filed 2015 federal income tax return, if applicable. Do not use your AGI from an amended return (Form 1040X) or a math error correction made by IRS. AGI is the amount shown on your 2015 Form 1040, line 38; Form 1040A, line 22; or Form 1040EZ, line 4. If you do not have your 2015 income tax return, call the IRS at 1-800-908-9946 to get a free transcript of your return or visit *IRS.gov/ transcript*. (If you filed electronically last year, you may use your prior year PIN to verify your identity instead of your prior year AGI. The prior year PIN

is the five digit PIN you used to electronically sign your 2015 return.) You will also be prompted to enter your date of birth (DOB).

 You can't use the Self-Select PIN method if you are a first-time filer under age 16 at the end of 2016.

Practitioner PIN. The Practitioner PIN method allows you to authorize your tax practitioner to enter or generate your PIN. The practitioner can provide you with details.

Form 8453. You must send in a paper Form 8453 if you have to attach certain forms or other documents that can't be electronically filed. See Form 8453.

Identity Protection PIN

For 2016, if you received an Identity Protection Personal Identification Number (IP PIN) from the IRS, enter it in the IP PIN spaces provided below your daytime phone number. You must correctly enter all six numbers of your IP PIN. If you didn't receive an IP PIN, leave these spaces blank.

 New IP PINs are issued every year. Enter the latest IP PIN you received. IP PINs for 2016 tax returns generally were sent in December 2016.

If you are filing a joint return and both taxpayers receive an IP PIN, only the taxpayer whose social security number (SSN) appears first on the tax return should enter his or her IP PIN. However, if you are filing electronically, both taxpayers must enter their IP PINs.

If you need more information, go to *IRS.gov/CP01A*. If you received an IP PIN but misplaced it, call 1-800-908-4490.

Paid Preparer Must Sign Your Return

Generally, anyone you pay to prepare your return must sign it and include their Preparer Tax Identification Number (PTIN) in the space provided. The preparer must give you a copy of the return for your records. Someone who prepares your return but doesn't charge you should not sign your return.

Assemble Your Return

Assemble any schedules and forms behind Form 1040 in order of the "Attachment Sequence No." shown in the upper right corner of the schedule or form. If you have supporting statements, arrange them in the same order as the schedules or forms they support and attach them last. Do not attach correspondence or other items unless required to do so. Attach Forms W-2 and 2439 to the front of Form 1040. If you received a Form W-2c (a corrected Form W-2), attach your original Forms W-2 and any Forms W-2c. Attach Forms W-2G and 1099-R to the front of Form 1040 if tax was withheld.

2016 Tax Table

See the instructions for line 44 to see if you must use the Tax Table below to figure your tax.

Example. Mr. and Mrs. Brown are filing a joint return. Their taxable income on Form 1040, line 43, is $25,300. First, they find the $25,300-25,350 taxable income line. Next, they find the column for married filing jointly and read down the column. The amount shown where the taxable income line and filing status column meet is $2,871. This is the tax amount they should enter on Form 1040, line 44.

Sample Table

At Least	But Less Than	Single	Married filing jointly*	Married filing separately	Head of a household
			Your tax is—		
25,200	25,250	3,320	2,856	3,320	3,121
25,250	25,300	3,328	2,864	3,328	3,129
25,300	25,350	3,335	(2,871)	3,335	3,136
25,350	25,400	3,343	2,879	3,343	3,144

If line 43 (taxable income) is—		And you are—			
At least	But less than	Single	Married filing jointly *	Married filing separately	Head of a household
			Your tax is—		
0	5	0	0	0	0
5	15	1	1	1	1
15	25	2	2	2	2
25	50	4	4	4	4
50	75	6	6	6	6
75	100	9	9	9	9
100	125	11	11	11	11
125	150	14	14	14	14
150	175	16	16	16	16
175	200	19	19	19	19
200	225	21	21	21	21
225	250	24	24	24	24
250	275	26	26	26	26
275	300	29	29	29	29
300	325	31	31	31	31
325	350	34	34	34	34
350	375	36	36	36	36
375	400	39	39	39	39
400	425	41	41	41	41
425	450	44	44	44	44
450	475	46	46	46	46
475	500	49	49	49	49
500	525	51	51	51	51
525	550	54	54	54	54
550	575	56	56	56	56
575	600	59	59	59	59
600	625	61	61	61	61
625	650	64	64	64	64
650	675	66	66	66	66
675	700	69	69	69	69
700	725	71	71	71	71
725	750	74	74	74	74
750	775	76	76	76	76
775	800	79	79	79	79
800	825	81	81	81	81
825	850	84	84	84	84
850	875	86	86	86	86
875	900	89	89	89	89
900	925	91	91	91	91
925	950	94	94	94	94
950	975	96	96	96	96
975	1,000	99	99	99	99

1,000

If line 43 (taxable income) is—		And you are—			
At least	But less than	Single	Married filing jointly *	Married filing separately	Head of a household
			Your tax is—		
1,000	1,025	101	101	101	101
1,025	1,050	104	104	104	104
1,050	1,075	106	106	106	106
1,075	1,100	109	109	109	109
1,100	1,125	111	111	111	111
1,125	1,150	114	114	114	114
1,150	1,175	116	116	116	116
1,175	1,200	119	119	119	119
1,200	1,225	121	121	121	121
1,225	1,250	124	124	124	124
1,250	1,275	126	126	126	126
1,275	1,300	129	129	129	129
1,300	1,325	131	131	131	131
1,325	1,350	134	134	134	134
1,350	1,375	136	136	136	136
1,375	1,400	139	139	139	139
1,400	1,425	141	141	141	141
1,425	1,450	144	144	144	144
1,450	1,475	146	146	146	146
1,475	1,500	149	149	149	149
1,500	1,525	151	151	151	151
1,525	1,550	154	154	154	154
1,550	1,575	156	156	156	156
1,575	1,600	159	159	159	159
1,600	1,625	161	161	161	161
1,625	1,650	164	164	164	164
1,650	1,675	166	166	166	166
1,675	1,700	169	169	169	169
1,700	1,725	171	171	171	171
1,725	1,750	174	174	174	174
1,750	1,775	176	176	176	176
1,775	1,800	179	179	179	179
1,800	1,825	181	181	181	181
1,825	1,850	184	184	184	184
1,850	1,875	186	186	186	186
1,875	1,900	189	189	189	189
1,900	1,925	191	191	191	191
1,925	1,950	194	194	194	194
1,950	1,975	196	196	196	196
1,975	2,000	199	199	199	199

2,000

If line 43 (taxable income) is—		And you are—			
At least	But less than	Single	Married filing jointly *	Married filing separately	Head of a household
			Your tax is—		
2,000	2,025	201	201	201	201
2,025	2,050	204	204	204	204
2,050	2,075	206	206	206	206
2,075	2,100	209	209	209	209
2,100	2,125	211	211	211	211
2,125	2,150	214	214	214	214
2,150	2,175	216	216	216	216
2,175	2,200	219	219	219	219
2,200	2,225	221	221	221	221
2,225	2,250	224	224	224	224
2,250	2,275	226	226	226	226
2,275	2,300	229	229	229	229
2,300	2,325	231	231	231	231
2,325	2,350	234	234	234	234
2,350	2,375	236	236	236	236
2,375	2,400	239	239	239	239
2,400	2,425	241	241	241	241
2,425	2,450	244	244	244	244
2,450	2,475	246	246	246	246
2,475	2,500	249	249	249	249
2,500	2,525	251	251	251	251
2,525	2,550	254	254	254	254
2,550	2,575	256	256	256	256
2,575	2,600	259	259	259	259
2,600	2,625	261	261	261	261
2,625	2,650	264	264	264	264
2,650	2,675	266	266	266	266
2,675	2,700	269	269	269	269
2,700	2,725	271	271	271	271
2,725	2,750	274	274	274	274
2,750	2,775	276	276	276	276
2,775	2,800	279	279	279	279
2,800	2,825	281	281	281	281
2,825	2,850	284	284	284	284
2,850	2,875	286	286	286	286
2,875	2,900	289	289	289	289
2,900	2,925	291	291	291	291
2,925	2,950	294	294	294	294
2,950	2,975	296	296	296	296
2,975	3,000	299	299	299	299

(Continued)

* This column must also be used by a qualifying widow(er).

3,000

At least	But less than	Single	Married filing jointly *	Married filing separately	Head of a household
		Your tax is—			
3,000	3,050	303	303	303	303
3,050	3,100	308	308	308	308
3,100	3,150	313	313	313	313
3,150	3,200	318	318	318	318
3,200	3,250	323	323	323	323
3,250	3,300	328	328	328	328
3,300	3,350	333	333	333	333
3,350	3,400	338	338	338	338
3,400	3,450	343	343	343	343
3,450	3,500	348	348	348	348
3,500	3,550	353	353	353	353
3,550	3,600	358	358	358	358
3,600	3,650	363	363	363	363
3,650	3,700	368	368	368	368
3,700	3,750	373	373	373	373
3,750	3,800	378	378	378	378
3,800	3,850	383	383	383	383
3,850	3,900	388	388	388	388
3,900	3,950	393	393	393	393
3,950	4,000	398	398	398	398

4,000

At least	But less than	Single	Married filing jointly *	Married filing separately	Head of a household
4,000	4,050	403	403	403	403
4,050	4,100	408	408	408	408
4,100	4,150	413	413	413	413
4,150	4,200	418	418	418	418
4,200	4,250	423	423	423	423
4,250	4,300	428	428	428	428
4,300	4,350	433	433	433	433
4,350	4,400	438	438	438	438
4,400	4,450	443	443	443	443
4,450	4,500	448	448	448	448
4,500	4,550	453	453	453	453
4,550	4,600	458	458	458	458
4,600	4,650	463	463	463	463
4,650	4,700	468	468	468	468
4,700	4,750	473	473	473	473
4,750	4,800	478	478	478	478
4,800	4,850	483	483	483	483
4,850	4,900	488	488	488	488
4,900	4,950	493	493	493	493
4,950	5,000	498	498	498	498

5,000

At least	But less than	Single	Married filing jointly *	Married filing separately	Head of a household
5,000	5,050	503	503	503	503
5,050	5,100	508	508	508	508
5,100	5,150	513	513	513	513
5,150	5,200	518	518	518	518
5,200	5,250	523	523	523	523
5,250	5,300	528	528	528	528
5,300	5,350	533	533	533	533
5,350	5,400	538	538	538	538
5,400	5,450	543	543	543	543
5,450	5,500	548	548	548	548
5,500	5,550	553	553	553	553
5,550	5,600	558	558	558	558
5,600	5,650	563	563	563	563
5,650	5,700	568	568	568	568
5,700	5,750	573	573	573	573
5,750	5,800	578	578	578	578
5,800	5,850	583	583	583	583
5,850	5,900	588	588	588	588
5,900	5,950	593	593	593	593
5,950	6,000	598	598	598	598

6,000

At least	But less than	Single	Married filing jointly *	Married filing separately	Head of a household
6,000	6,050	603	603	603	603
6,050	6,100	608	608	608	608
6,100	6,150	613	613	613	613
6,150	6,200	618	618	618	618
6,200	6,250	623	623	623	623
6,250	6,300	628	628	628	628
6,300	6,350	633	633	633	633
6,350	6,400	638	638	638	638
6,400	6,450	643	643	643	643
6,450	6,500	648	648	648	648
6,500	6,550	653	653	653	653
6,550	6,600	658	658	658	658
6,600	6,650	663	663	663	663
6,650	6,700	668	668	668	668
6,700	6,750	673	673	673	673
6,750	6,800	678	678	678	678
6,800	6,850	683	683	683	683
6,850	6,900	688	688	688	688
6,900	6,950	693	693	693	693
6,950	7,000	698	698	698	698

7,000

At least	But less than	Single	Married filing jointly *	Married filing separately	Head of a household
7,000	7,050	703	703	703	703
7,050	7,100	708	708	708	708
7,100	7,150	713	713	713	713
7,150	7,200	718	718	718	718
7,200	7,250	723	723	723	723
7,250	7,300	728	728	728	728
7,300	7,350	733	733	733	733
7,350	7,400	738	738	738	738
7,400	7,450	743	743	743	743
7,450	7,500	748	748	748	748
7,500	7,550	753	753	753	753
7,550	7,600	758	758	758	758
7,600	7,650	763	763	763	763
7,650	7,700	768	768	768	768
7,700	7,750	773	773	773	773
7,750	7,800	778	778	778	778
7,800	7,850	783	783	783	783
7,850	7,900	788	788	788	788
7,900	7,950	793	793	793	793
7,950	8,000	798	798	798	798

8,000

At least	But less than	Single	Married filing jointly *	Married filing separately	Head of a household
8,000	8,050	803	803	803	803
8,050	8,100	808	808	808	808
8,100	8,150	813	813	813	813
8,150	8,200	818	818	818	818
8,200	8,250	823	823	823	823
8,250	8,300	828	828	828	828
8,300	8,350	833	833	833	833
8,350	8,400	838	838	838	838
8,400	8,450	843	843	843	843
8,450	8,500	848	848	848	848
8,500	8,550	853	853	853	853
8,550	8,600	858	858	858	858
8,600	8,650	863	863	863	863
8,650	8,700	868	868	868	868
8,700	8,750	873	873	873	873
8,750	8,800	878	878	878	878
8,800	8,850	883	883	883	883
8,850	8,900	888	888	888	888
8,900	8,950	893	893	893	893
8,950	9,000	898	898	898	898

9,000

At least	But less than	Single	Married filing jointly *	Married filing separately	Head of a household
9,000	9,050	903	903	903	903
9,050	9,100	908	908	908	908
9,100	9,150	913	913	913	913
9,150	9,200	918	918	918	918
9,200	9,250	923	923	923	923
9,250	9,300	928	928	928	928
9,300	9,350	935	933	935	933
9,350	9,400	943	938	943	938
9,400	9,450	950	943	950	943
9,450	9,500	958	948	958	948
9,500	9,550	965	953	965	953
9,550	9,600	973	958	973	958
9,600	9,650	980	963	980	963
9,650	9,700	988	968	988	968
9,700	9,750	995	973	995	973
9,750	9,800	1,003	978	1,003	978
9,800	9,850	1,010	983	1,010	983
9,850	9,900	1,018	988	1,018	988
9,900	9,950	1,025	993	1,025	993
9,950	10,000	1,033	998	1,033	998

10,000

At least	But less than	Single	Married filing jointly *	Married filing separately	Head of a household
10,000	10,050	1,040	1,003	1,040	1,003
10,050	10,100	1,048	1,008	1,048	1,008
10,100	10,150	1,055	1,013	1,055	1,013
10,150	10,200	1,063	1,018	1,063	1,018
10,200	10,250	1,070	1,023	1,070	1,023
10,250	10,300	1,078	1,028	1,078	1,028
10,300	10,350	1,085	1,033	1,085	1,033
10,350	10,400	1,093	1,038	1,093	1,038
10,400	10,450	1,100	1,043	1,100	1,043
10,450	10,500	1,108	1,048	1,108	1,048
10,500	10,550	1,115	1,053	1,115	1,053
10,550	10,600	1,123	1,058	1,123	1,058
10,600	10,650	1,130	1,063	1,130	1,063
10,650	10,700	1,138	1,068	1,138	1,068
10,700	10,750	1,145	1,073	1,145	1,073
10,750	10,800	1,153	1,078	1,153	1,078
10,800	10,850	1,160	1,083	1,160	1,083
10,850	10,900	1,168	1,088	1,168	1,088
10,900	10,950	1,175	1,093	1,175	1,093
10,950	11,000	1,183	1,098	1,183	1,098

11,000

At least	But less than	Single	Married filing jointly *	Married filing separately	Head of a household
11,000	11,050	1,190	1,103	1,190	1,103
11,050	11,100	1,198	1,108	1,198	1,108
11,100	11,150	1,205	1,113	1,205	1,113
11,150	11,200	1,213	1,118	1,213	1,118
11,200	11,250	1,220	1,123	1,220	1,123
11,250	11,300	1,228	1,128	1,228	1,128
11,300	11,350	1,235	1,133	1,235	1,133
11,350	11,400	1,243	1,138	1,243	1,138
11,400	11,450	1,250	1,143	1,250	1,143
11,450	11,500	1,258	1,148	1,258	1,148
11,500	11,550	1,265	1,153	1,265	1,153
11,550	11,600	1,273	1,158	1,273	1,158
11,600	11,650	1,280	1,163	1,280	1,163
11,650	11,700	1,288	1,168	1,288	1,168
11,700	11,750	1,295	1,173	1,295	1,173
11,750	11,800	1,303	1,178	1,303	1,178
11,800	11,850	1,310	1,183	1,310	1,183
11,850	11,900	1,318	1,188	1,318	1,188
11,900	11,950	1,325	1,193	1,325	1,193
11,950	12,000	1,333	1,198	1,333	1,198

(Continued)

* This column must also be used by a qualifying widow(er).

Need more information or forms? Visit IRS.gov.

12,000

At least	But less than	Single	Married filing jointly *	Married filing separately	Head of a household
12,000	12,050	1,340	1,203	1,340	1,203
12,050	12,100	1,348	1,208	1,348	1,208
12,100	12,150	1,355	1,213	1,355	1,213
12,150	12,200	1,363	1,218	1,363	1,218
12,200	12,250	1,370	1,223	1,370	1,223
12,250	12,300	1,378	1,228	1,378	1,228
12,300	12,350	1,385	1,233	1,385	1,233
12,350	12,400	1,393	1,238	1,393	1,238
12,400	12,450	1,400	1,243	1,400	1,243
12,450	12,500	1,408	1,248	1,408	1,248
12,500	12,550	1,415	1,253	1,415	1,253
12,550	12,600	1,423	1,258	1,423	1,258
12,600	12,650	1,430	1,263	1,430	1,263
12,650	12,700	1,438	1,268	1,438	1,268
12,700	12,750	1,445	1,273	1,445	1,273
12,750	12,800	1,453	1,278	1,453	1,278
12,800	12,850	1,460	1,283	1,460	1,283
12,850	12,900	1,468	1,288	1,468	1,288
12,900	12,950	1,475	1,293	1,475	1,293
12,950	13,000	1,483	1,298	1,483	1,298

13,000

At least	But less than	Single	Married filing jointly *	Married filing separately	Head of a household
13,000	13,050	1,490	1,303	1,490	1,303
13,050	13,100	1,498	1,308	1,498	1,308
13,100	13,150	1,505	1,313	1,505	1,313
13,150	13,200	1,513	1,318	1,513	1,318
13,200	13,250	1,520	1,323	1,520	1,323
13,250	13,300	1,528	1,328	1,528	1,329
13,300	13,350	1,535	1,333	1,535	1,336
13,350	13,400	1,543	1,338	1,543	1,344
13,400	13,450	1,550	1,343	1,550	1,351
13,450	13,500	1,558	1,348	1,558	1,359
13,500	13,550	1,565	1,353	1,565	1,366
13,550	13,600	1,573	1,358	1,573	1,374
13,600	13,650	1,580	1,363	1,580	1,381
13,650	13,700	1,588	1,368	1,588	1,389
13,700	13,750	1,595	1,373	1,595	1,396
13,750	13,800	1,603	1,378	1,603	1,404
13,800	13,850	1,610	1,383	1,610	1,411
13,850	13,900	1,618	1,388	1,618	1,419
13,900	13,950	1,625	1,393	1,625	1,426
13,950	14,000	1,633	1,398	1,633	1,434

14,000

At least	But less than	Single	Married filing jointly *	Married filing separately	Head of a household
14,000	14,050	1,640	1,403	1,640	1,441
14,050	14,100	1,648	1,408	1,648	1,449
14,100	14,150	1,655	1,413	1,655	1,456
14,150	14,200	1,663	1,418	1,663	1,464
14,200	14,250	1,670	1,423	1,670	1,471
14,250	14,300	1,678	1,428	1,678	1,479
14,300	14,350	1,685	1,433	1,685	1,486
14,350	14,400	1,693	1,438	1,693	1,494
14,400	14,450	1,700	1,443	1,700	1,501
14,450	14,500	1,708	1,448	1,708	1,509
14,500	14,550	1,715	1,453	1,715	1,516
14,550	14,600	1,723	1,458	1,723	1,524
14,600	14,650	1,730	1,463	1,730	1,531
14,650	14,700	1,738	1,468	1,738	1,539
14,700	14,750	1,745	1,473	1,745	1,546
14,750	14,800	1,753	1,478	1,753	1,554
14,800	14,850	1,760	1,483	1,760	1,561
14,850	14,900	1,768	1,488	1,768	1,569
14,900	14,950	1,775	1,493	1,775	1,576
14,950	15,000	1,783	1,498	1,783	1,584

15,000

At least	But less than	Single	Married filing jointly *	Married filing separately	Head of a household
15,000	15,050	1,790	1,503	1,790	1,591
15,050	15,100	1,798	1,508	1,798	1,599
15,100	15,150	1,805	1,513	1,805	1,606
15,150	15,200	1,813	1,518	1,813	1,614
15,200	15,250	1,820	1,523	1,820	1,621
15,250	15,300	1,828	1,528	1,828	1,629
15,300	15,350	1,835	1,533	1,835	1,636
15,350	15,400	1,843	1,538	1,843	1,644
15,400	15,450	1,850	1,543	1,850	1,651
15,450	15,500	1,858	1,548	1,858	1,659
15,500	15,550	1,865	1,553	1,865	1,666
15,550	15,600	1,873	1,558	1,873	1,674
15,600	15,650	1,880	1,563	1,880	1,681
15,650	15,700	1,888	1,568	1,888	1,689
15,700	15,750	1,895	1,573	1,895	1,696
15,750	15,800	1,903	1,578	1,903	1,704
15,800	15,850	1,910	1,583	1,910	1,711
15,850	15,900	1,918	1,588	1,918	1,719
15,900	15,950	1,925	1,593	1,925	1,726
15,950	16,000	1,933	1,598	1,933	1,734

16,000

At least	But less than	Single	Married filing jointly *	Married filing separately	Head of a household
16,000	16,050	1,940	1,603	1,940	1,741
16,050	16,100	1,948	1,608	1,948	1,749
16,100	16,150	1,955	1,613	1,955	1,756
16,150	16,200	1,963	1,618	1,963	1,764
16,200	16,250	1,970	1,623	1,970	1,771
16,250	16,300	1,978	1,628	1,978	1,779
16,300	16,350	1,985	1,633	1,985	1,786
16,350	16,400	1,993	1,638	1,993	1,794
16,400	16,450	2,000	1,643	2,000	1,801
16,450	16,500	2,008	1,648	2,008	1,809
16,500	16,550	2,015	1,653	2,015	1,816
16,550	16,600	2,023	1,658	2,023	1,824
16,600	16,650	2,030	1,663	2,030	1,831
16,650	16,700	2,038	1,668	2,038	1,839
16,700	16,750	2,045	1,673	2,045	1,846
16,750	16,800	2,053	1,678	2,053	1,854
16,800	16,850	2,060	1,683	2,060	1,861
16,850	16,900	2,068	1,688	2,068	1,869
16,900	16,950	2,075	1,693	2,075	1,876
16,950	17,000	2,083	1,698	2,083	1,884

17,000

At least	But less than	Single	Married filing jointly *	Married filing separately	Head of a household
17,000	17,050	2,090	1,703	2,090	1,891
17,050	17,100	2,098	1,708	2,098	1,899
17,100	17,150	2,105	1,713	2,105	1,906
17,150	17,200	2,113	1,718	2,113	1,914
17,200	17,250	2,120	1,723	2,120	1,921
17,250	17,300	2,128	1,728	2,128	1,929
17,300	17,350	2,135	1,733	2,135	1,936
17,350	17,400	2,143	1,738	2,143	1,944
17,400	17,450	2,150	1,743	2,150	1,951
17,450	17,500	2,158	1,748	2,158	1,959
17,500	17,550	2,165	1,753	2,165	1,966
17,550	17,600	2,173	1,758	2,173	1,974
17,600	17,650	2,180	1,763	2,180	1,981
17,650	17,700	2,188	1,768	2,188	1,989
17,700	17,750	2,195	1,773	2,195	1,996
17,750	17,800	2,203	1,778	2,203	2,004
17,800	17,850	2,210	1,783	2,210	2,011
17,850	17,900	2,218	1,788	2,218	2,019
17,900	17,950	2,225	1,793	2,225	2,026
17,950	18,000	2,233	1,798	2,233	2,034

18,000

At least	But less than	Single	Married filing jointly *	Married filing separately	Head of a household
18,000	18,050	2,240	1,803	2,240	2,041
18,050	18,100	2,248	1,808	2,248	2,049
18,100	18,150	2,255	1,813	2,255	2,056
18,150	18,200	2,263	1,818	2,263	2,064
18,200	18,250	2,270	1,823	2,270	2,071
18,250	18,300	2,278	1,828	2,278	2,079
18,300	18,350	2,285	1,833	2,285	2,086
18,350	18,400	2,293	1,838	2,293	2,094
18,400	18,450	2,300	1,843	2,300	2,101
18,450	18,500	2,308	1,848	2,308	2,109
18,500	18,550	2,315	1,853	2,315	2,116
18,550	18,600	2,323	1,859	2,323	2,124
18,600	18,650	2,330	1,866	2,330	2,131
18,650	18,700	2,338	1,874	2,338	2,139
18,700	18,750	2,345	1,881	2,345	2,146
18,750	18,800	2,353	1,889	2,353	2,154
18,800	18,850	2,360	1,896	2,360	2,161
18,850	18,900	2,368	1,904	2,368	2,169
18,900	18,950	2,375	1,911	2,375	2,176
18,950	19,000	2,383	1,919	2,383	2,184

19,000

At least	But less than	Single	Married filing jointly *	Married filing separately	Head of a household
19,000	19,050	2,390	1,926	2,390	2,191
19,050	19,100	2,398	1,934	2,398	2,199
19,100	19,150	2,405	1,941	2,405	2,206
19,150	19,200	2,413	1,949	2,413	2,214
19,200	19,250	2,420	1,956	2,420	2,221
19,250	19,300	2,428	1,964	2,428	2,229
19,300	19,350	2,435	1,971	2,435	2,236
19,350	19,400	2,443	1,979	2,443	2,244
19,400	19,450	2,450	1,986	2,450	2,251
19,450	19,500	2,458	1,994	2,458	2,259
19,500	19,550	2,465	2,001	2,465	2,266
19,550	19,600	2,473	2,009	2,473	2,274
19,600	19,650	2,480	2,016	2,480	2,281
19,650	19,700	2,488	2,024	2,488	2,289
19,700	19,750	2,495	2,031	2,495	2,296
19,750	19,800	2,503	2,039	2,503	2,304
19,800	19,850	2,510	2,046	2,510	2,311
19,850	19,900	2,518	2,054	2,518	2,319
19,900	19,950	2,525	2,061	2,525	2,326
19,950	20,000	2,533	2,069	2,533	2,334

20,000

At least	But less than	Single	Married filing jointly *	Married filing separately	Head of a household
20,000	20,050	2,540	2,076	2,540	2,341
20,050	20,100	2,548	2,084	2,548	2,349
20,100	20,150	2,555	2,091	2,555	2,356
20,150	20,200	2,563	2,099	2,563	2,364
20,200	20,250	2,570	2,106	2,570	2,371
20,250	20,300	2,578	2,114	2,578	2,379
20,300	20,350	2,585	2,121	2,585	2,386
20,350	20,400	2,593	2,129	2,593	2,394
20,400	20,450	2,600	2,136	2,600	2,401
20,450	20,500	2,608	2,144	2,608	2,409
20,500	20,550	2,615	2,151	2,615	2,416
20,550	20,600	2,623	2,159	2,623	2,424
20,600	20,650	2,630	2,166	2,630	2,431
20,650	20,700	2,638	2,174	2,638	2,439
20,700	20,750	2,645	2,181	2,645	2,446
20,750	20,800	2,653	2,189	2,653	2,454
20,800	20,850	2,660	2,196	2,660	2,461
20,850	20,900	2,668	2,204	2,668	2,469
20,900	20,950	2,675	2,211	2,675	2,476
20,950	21,000	2,683	2,219	2,683	2,484

(Continued)

* This column must also be used by a qualifying widow(er).

If line 43 (taxable income) is—		And you are—				If line 43 (taxable income) is—		And you are—				If line 43 (taxable income) is—		And you are—			
At least	But less than	Single	Married filing jointly *	Married filing separately	Head of a household	At least	But less than	Single	Married filing jointly *	Married filing separately	Head of a household	At least	But less than	Single	Married filing jointly *	Married filing separately	Head of a household
		Your tax is—						Your tax is—						Your tax is—			
21,000						**24,000**						**27,000**					
21,000	21,050	2,690	2,226	2,690	2,491	24,000	24,050	3,140	2,676	3,140	2,941	27,000	27,050	3,590	3,126	3,590	3,391
21,050	21,100	2,698	2,234	2,698	2,499	24,050	24,100	3,148	2,684	3,148	2,949	27,050	27,100	3,598	3,134	3,598	3,399
21,100	21,150	2,705	2,241	2,705	2,506	24,100	24,150	3,155	2,691	3,155	2,956	27,100	27,150	3,605	3,141	3,605	3,406
21,150	21,200	2,713	2,249	2,713	2,514	24,150	24,200	3,163	2,699	3,163	2,964	27,150	27,200	3,613	3,149	3,613	3,414
21,200	21,250	2,720	2,256	2,720	2,521	24,200	24,250	3,170	2,706	3,170	2,971	27,200	27,250	3,620	3,156	3,620	3,421
21,250	21,300	2,728	2,264	2,728	2,529	24,250	24,300	3,178	2,714	3,178	2,979	27,250	27,300	3,628	3,164	3,628	3,429
21,300	21,350	2,735	2,271	2,735	2,536	24,300	24,350	3,185	2,721	3,185	2,986	27,300	27,350	3,635	3,171	3,635	3,436
21,350	21,400	2,743	2,279	2,743	2,544	24,350	24,400	3,193	2,729	3,193	2,994	27,350	27,400	3,643	3,179	3,643	3,444
21,400	21,450	2,750	2,286	2,750	2,551	24,400	24,450	3,200	2,736	3,200	3,001	27,400	27,450	3,650	3,186	3,650	3,451
21,450	21,500	2,758	2,294	2,758	2,559	24,450	24,500	3,208	2,744	3,208	3,009	27,450	27,500	3,658	3,194	3,658	3,459
21,500	21,550	2,765	2,301	2,765	2,566	24,500	24,550	3,215	2,751	3,215	3,016	27,500	27,550	3,665	3,201	3,665	3,466
21,550	21,600	2,773	2,309	2,773	2,574	24,550	24,600	3,223	2,759	3,223	3,024	27,550	27,600	3,673	3,209	3,673	3,474
21,600	21,650	2,780	2,316	2,780	2,581	24,600	24,650	3,230	2,766	3,230	3,031	27,600	27,650	3,680	3,216	3,680	3,481
21,650	21,700	2,788	2,324	2,788	2,589	24,650	24,700	3,238	2,774	3,238	3,039	27,650	27,700	3,688	3,224	3,688	3,489
21,700	21,750	2,795	2,331	2,795	2,596	24,700	24,750	3,245	2,781	3,245	3,046	27,700	27,750	3,695	3,231	3,695	3,496
21,750	21,800	2,803	2,339	2,803	2,604	24,750	24,800	3,253	2,789	3,253	3,054	27,750	27,800	3,703	3,239	3,703	3,504
21,800	21,850	2,810	2,346	2,810	2,611	24,800	24,850	3,260	2,796	3,260	3,061	27,800	27,850	3,710	3,246	3,710	3,511
21,850	21,900	2,818	2,354	2,818	2,619	24,850	24,900	3,268	2,804	3,268	3,069	27,850	27,900	3,718	3,254	3,718	3,519
21,900	21,950	2,825	2,361	2,825	2,626	24,900	24,950	3,275	2,811	3,275	3,076	27,900	27,950	3,725	3,261	3,725	3,526
21,950	22,000	2,833	2,369	2,833	2,634	24,950	25,000	3,283	2,819	3,283	3,084	27,950	28,000	3,733	3,269	3,733	3,534
22,000						**25,000**						**28,000**					
22,000	22,050	2,840	2,376	2,840	2,641	25,000	25,050	3,290	2,826	3,290	3,091	28,000	28,050	3,740	3,276	3,740	3,541
22,050	22,100	2,848	2,384	2,848	2,649	25,050	25,100	3,298	2,834	3,298	3,099	28,050	28,100	3,748	3,284	3,748	3,549
22,100	22,150	2,855	2,391	2,855	2,656	25,100	25,150	3,305	2,841	3,305	3,106	28,100	28,150	3,755	3,291	3,755	3,556
22,150	22,200	2,863	2,399	2,863	2,664	25,150	25,200	3,313	2,849	3,313	3,114	28,150	28,200	3,763	3,299	3,763	3,564
22,200	22,250	2,870	2,406	2,870	2,671	25,200	25,250	3,320	2,856	3,320	3,121	28,200	28,250	3,770	3,306	3,770	3,571
22,250	22,300	2,878	2,414	2,878	2,679	25,250	25,300	3,328	2,864	3,328	3,129	28,250	28,300	3,778	3,314	3,778	3,579
22,300	22,350	2,885	2,421	2,885	2,686	25,300	25,350	3,335	2,871	3,335	3,136	28,300	28,350	3,785	3,321	3,785	3,586
22,350	22,400	2,893	2,429	2,893	2,694	25,350	25,400	3,343	2,879	3,343	3,144	28,350	28,400	3,793	3,329	3,793	3,594
22,400	22,450	2,900	2,436	2,900	2,701	25,400	25,450	3,350	2,886	3,350	3,151	28,400	28,450	3,800	3,336	3,800	3,601
22,450	22,500	2,908	2,444	2,908	2,709	25,450	25,500	3,358	2,894	3,358	3,159	28,450	28,500	3,808	3,344	3,808	3,609
22,500	22,550	2,915	2,451	2,915	2,716	25,500	25,550	3,365	2,901	3,365	3,166	28,500	28,550	3,815	3,351	3,815	3,616
22,550	22,600	2,923	2,459	2,923	2,724	25,550	25,600	3,373	2,909	3,373	3,174	28,550	28,600	3,823	3,359	3,823	3,624
22,600	22,650	2,930	2,466	2,930	2,731	25,600	25,650	3,380	2,916	3,380	3,181	28,600	28,650	3,830	3,366	3,830	3,631
22,650	22,700	2,938	2,474	2,938	2,739	25,650	25,700	3,388	2,924	3,388	3,189	28,650	28,700	3,838	3,374	3,838	3,639
22,700	22,750	2,945	2,481	2,945	2,746	25,700	25,750	3,395	2,931	3,395	3,196	28,700	28,750	3,845	3,381	3,845	3,646
22,750	22,800	2,953	2,489	2,953	2,754	25,750	25,800	3,403	2,939	3,403	3,204	28,750	28,800	3,853	3,389	3,853	3,654
22,800	22,850	2,960	2,496	2,960	2,761	25,800	25,850	3,410	2,946	3,410	3,211	28,800	28,850	3,860	3,396	3,860	3,661
22,850	22,900	2,968	2,504	2,968	2,769	25,850	25,900	3,418	2,954	3,418	3,219	28,850	28,900	3,868	3,404	3,868	3,669
22,900	22,950	2,975	2,511	2,975	2,776	25,900	25,950	3,425	2,961	3,425	3,226	28,900	28,950	3,875	3,411	3,875	3,676
22,950	23,000	2,983	2,519	2,983	2,784	25,950	26,000	3,433	2,969	3,433	3,234	28,950	29,000	3,883	3,419	3,883	3,684
23,000						**26,000**						**29,000**					
23,000	23,050	2,990	2,526	2,990	2,791	26,000	26,050	3,440	2,976	3,440	3,241	29,000	29,050	3,890	3,426	3,890	3,691
23,050	23,100	2,998	2,534	2,998	2,799	26,050	26,100	3,448	2,984	3,448	3,249	29,050	29,100	3,898	3,434	3,898	3,699
23,100	23,150	3,005	2,541	3,005	2,806	26,100	26,150	3,455	2,991	3,455	3,256	29,100	29,150	3,905	3,441	3,905	3,706
23,150	23,200	3,013	2,549	3,013	2,814	26,150	26,200	3,463	2,999	3,463	3,264	29,150	29,200	3,913	3,449	3,913	3,714
23,200	23,250	3,020	2,556	3,020	2,821	26,200	26,250	3,470	3,006	3,470	3,271	29,200	29,250	3,920	3,456	3,920	3,721
23,250	23,300	3,028	2,564	3,028	2,829	26,250	26,300	3,478	3,014	3,478	3,279	29,250	29,300	3,928	3,464	3,928	3,729
23,300	23,350	3,035	2,571	3,035	2,836	26,300	26,350	3,485	3,021	3,485	3,286	29,300	29,350	3,935	3,471	3,935	3,736
23,350	23,400	3,043	2,579	3,043	2,844	26,350	26,400	3,493	3,029	3,493	3,294	29,350	29,400	3,943	3,479	3,943	3,744
23,400	23,450	3,050	2,586	3,050	2,851	26,400	26,450	3,500	3,036	3,500	3,301	29,400	29,450	3,950	3,486	3,950	3,751
23,450	23,500	3,058	2,594	3,058	2,859	26,450	26,500	3,508	3,044	3,508	3,309	29,450	29,500	3,958	3,494	3,958	3,759
23,500	23,550	3,065	2,601	3,065	2,866	26,500	26,550	3,515	3,051	3,515	3,316	29,500	29,550	3,965	3,501	3,965	3,766
23,550	23,600	3,073	2,609	3,073	2,874	26,550	26,600	3,523	3,059	3,523	3,324	29,550	29,600	3,973	3,509	3,973	3,774
23,600	23,650	3,080	2,616	3,080	2,881	26,600	26,650	3,530	3,066	3,530	3,331	29,600	29,650	3,980	3,516	3,980	3,781
23,650	23,700	3,088	2,624	3,088	2,889	26,650	26,700	3,538	3,074	3,538	3,339	29,650	29,700	3,988	3,524	3,988	3,789
23,700	23,750	3,095	2,631	3,095	2,896	26,700	26,750	3,545	3,081	3,545	3,346	29,700	29,750	3,995	3,531	3,995	3,796
23,750	23,800	3,103	2,639	3,103	2,904	26,750	26,800	3,553	3,089	3,553	3,354	29,750	29,800	4,003	3,539	4,003	3,804
23,800	23,850	3,110	2,646	3,110	2,911	26,800	26,850	3,560	3,096	3,560	3,361	29,800	29,850	4,010	3,546	4,010	3,811
23,850	23,900	3,118	2,654	3,118	2,919	26,850	26,900	3,568	3,104	3,568	3,369	29,850	29,900	4,018	3,554	4,018	3,819
23,900	23,950	3,125	2,661	3,125	2,926	26,900	26,950	3,575	3,111	3,575	3,376	29,900	29,950	4,025	3,561	4,025	3,826
23,950	24,000	3,133	2,669	3,133	2,934	26,950	27,000	3,583	3,119	3,583	3,384	29,950	30,000	4,033	3,569	4,033	3,834

(Continued)

* This column must also be used by a qualifying widow(er).

Need more information or forms? Visit IRS.gov.

If line 43 (taxable income) is—		And you are—				If line 43 (taxable income) is—		And you are—				If line 43 (taxable income) is—		And you are—			
At least	But less than	Single	Married filing jointly *	Married filing separately	Head of a household	At least	But less than	Single	Married filing jointly *	Married filing separately	Head of a household	At least	But less than	Single	Married filing jointly *	Married filing separately	Head of a household
		Your tax is—						Your tax is—						Your tax is—			

30,000 | 33,000 | 36,000

At least	But less than	Single	MFJ*	MFS	HoH	At least	But less than	Single	MFJ*	MFS	HoH	At least	But less than	Single	MFJ*	MFS	HoH
30,000	30,050	4,040	3,576	4,040	3,841	33,000	33,050	4,490	4,026	4,490	4,291	36,000	36,050	4,940	4,476	4,940	4,741
30,050	30,100	4,048	3,584	4,048	3,849	33,050	33,100	4,498	4,034	4,498	4,299	36,050	36,100	4,948	4,484	4,948	4,749
30,100	30,150	4,055	3,591	4,055	3,856	33,100	33,150	4,505	4,041	4,505	4,306	36,100	36,150	4,955	4,491	4,955	4,756
30,150	30,200	4,063	3,599	4,063	3,864	33,150	33,200	4,513	4,049	4,513	4,314	36,150	36,200	4,963	4,499	4,963	4,764
30,200	30,250	4,070	3,606	4,070	3,871	33,200	33,250	4,520	4,056	4,520	4,321	36,200	36,250	4,970	4,506	4,970	4,771
30,250	30,300	4,078	3,614	4,078	3,879	33,250	33,300	4,528	4,064	4,528	4,329	36,250	36,300	4,978	4,514	4,978	4,779
30,300	30,350	4,085	3,621	4,085	3,886	33,300	33,350	4,535	4,071	4,535	4,336	36,300	36,350	4,985	4,521	4,985	4,786
30,350	30,400	4,093	3,629	4,093	3,894	33,350	33,400	4,543	4,079	4,543	4,344	36,350	36,400	4,993	4,529	4,993	4,794
30,400	30,450	4,100	3,636	4,100	3,901	33,400	33,450	4,550	4,086	4,550	4,351	36,400	36,450	5,000	4,536	5,000	4,801
30,450	30,500	4,108	3,644	4,108	3,909	33,450	33,500	4,558	4,094	4,558	4,359	36,450	36,500	5,008	4,544	5,008	4,809
30,500	30,550	4,115	3,651	4,115	3,916	33,500	33,550	4,565	4,101	4,565	4,366	36,500	36,550	5,015	4,551	5,015	4,816
30,550	30,600	4,123	3,659	4,123	3,924	33,550	33,600	4,573	4,109	4,573	4,374	36,550	36,600	5,023	4,559	5,023	4,824
30,600	30,650	4,130	3,666	4,130	3,931	33,600	33,650	4,580	4,116	4,580	4,381	36,600	36,650	5,030	4,566	5,030	4,831
30,650	30,700	4,138	3,674	4,138	3,939	33,650	33,700	4,588	4,124	4,588	4,389	36,650	36,700	5,038	4,574	5,038	4,839
30,700	30,750	4,145	3,681	4,145	3,946	33,700	33,750	4,595	4,131	4,595	4,396	36,700	36,750	5,045	4,581	5,045	4,846
30,750	30,800	4,153	3,689	4,153	3,954	33,750	33,800	4,603	4,139	4,603	4,404	36,750	36,800	5,053	4,589	5,053	4,854
30,800	30,850	4,160	3,696	4,160	3,961	33,800	33,850	4,610	4,146	4,610	4,411	36,800	36,850	5,060	4,596	5,060	4,861
30,850	30,900	4,168	3,704	4,168	3,969	33,850	33,900	4,618	4,154	4,618	4,419	36,850	36,900	5,068	4,604	5,068	4,869
30,900	30,950	4,175	3,711	4,175	3,976	33,900	33,950	4,625	4,161	4,625	4,426	36,900	36,950	5,075	4,611	5,075	4,876
30,950	31,000	4,183	3,719	4,183	3,984	33,950	34,000	4,633	4,169	4,633	4,434	36,950	37,000	5,083	4,619	5,083	4,884

31,000 | 34,000 | 37,000

At least	But less than	Single	MFJ*	MFS	HoH	At least	But less than	Single	MFJ*	MFS	HoH	At least	But less than	Single	MFJ*	MFS	HoH
31,000	31,050	4,190	3,726	4,190	3,991	34,000	34,050	4,640	4,176	4,640	4,441	37,000	37,050	5,090	4,626	5,090	4,891
31,050	31,100	4,198	3,734	4,198	3,999	34,050	34,100	4,648	4,184	4,648	4,449	37,050	37,100	5,098	4,634	5,098	4,899
31,100	31,150	4,205	3,741	4,205	4,006	34,100	34,150	4,655	4,191	4,655	4,456	37,100	37,150	5,105	4,641	5,105	4,906
31,150	31,200	4,213	3,749	4,213	4,014	34,150	34,200	4,663	4,199	4,663	4,464	37,150	37,200	5,113	4,649	5,113	4,914
31,200	31,250	4,220	3,756	4,220	4,021	34,200	34,250	4,670	4,206	4,670	4,471	37,200	37,250	5,120	4,656	5,120	4,921
31,250	31,300	4,228	3,764	4,228	4,029	34,250	34,300	4,678	4,214	4,678	4,479	37,250	37,300	5,128	4,664	5,128	4,929
31,300	31,350	4,235	3,771	4,235	4,036	34,300	34,350	4,685	4,221	4,685	4,486	37,300	37,350	5,135	4,671	5,135	4,936
31,350	31,400	4,243	3,779	4,243	4,044	34,350	34,400	4,693	4,229	4,693	4,494	37,350	37,400	5,143	4,679	5,143	4,944
31,400	31,450	4,250	3,786	4,250	4,051	34,400	34,450	4,700	4,236	4,700	4,501	37,400	37,450	5,150	4,686	5,150	4,951
31,450	31,500	4,258	3,794	4,258	4,059	34,450	34,500	4,708	4,244	4,708	4,509	37,450	37,500	5,158	4,694	5,158	4,959
31,500	31,550	4,265	3,801	4,265	4,066	34,500	34,550	4,715	4,251	4,715	4,516	37,500	37,550	5,165	4,701	5,165	4,966
31,550	31,600	4,273	3,809	4,273	4,074	34,550	34,600	4,723	4,259	4,723	4,524	37,550	37,600	5,173	4,709	5,173	4,974
31,600	31,650	4,280	3,816	4,280	4,081	34,600	34,650	4,730	4,266	4,730	4,531	37,600	37,650	5,180	4,716	5,180	4,981
31,650	31,700	4,288	3,824	4,288	4,089	34,650	34,700	4,738	4,274	4,738	4,539	37,650	37,700	5,190	4,724	5,190	4,989
31,700	31,750	4,295	3,831	4,295	4,096	34,700	34,750	4,745	4,281	4,745	4,546	37,700	37,750	5,203	4,731	5,203	4,996
31,750	31,800	4,303	3,839	4,303	4,104	34,750	34,800	4,753	4,289	4,753	4,554	37,750	37,800	5,215	4,739	5,215	5,004
31,800	31,850	4,310	3,846	4,310	4,111	34,800	34,850	4,760	4,296	4,760	4,561	37,800	37,850	5,228	4,746	5,228	5,011
31,850	31,900	4,318	3,854	4,318	4,119	34,850	34,900	4,768	4,304	4,768	4,569	37,850	37,900	5,240	4,754	5,240	5,019
31,900	31,950	4,325	3,861	4,325	4,126	34,900	34,950	4,775	4,311	4,775	4,576	37,900	37,950	5,253	4,761	5,253	5,026
31,950	32,000	4,333	3,869	4,333	4,134	34,950	35,000	4,783	4,319	4,783	4,584	37,950	38,000	5,265	4,769	5,265	5,034

32,000 | 35,000 | 38,000

At least	But less than	Single	MFJ*	MFS	HoH	At least	But less than	Single	MFJ*	MFS	HoH	At least	But less than	Single	MFJ*	MFS	HoH
32,000	32,050	4,340	3,876	4,340	4,141	35,000	35,050	4,790	4,326	4,790	4,591	38,000	38,050	5,278	4,776	5,278	5,041
32,050	32,100	4,348	3,884	4,348	4,149	35,050	35,100	4,798	4,334	4,798	4,599	38,050	38,100	5,290	4,784	5,290	5,049
32,100	32,150	4,355	3,891	4,355	4,156	35,100	35,150	4,805	4,341	4,805	4,606	38,100	38,150	5,303	4,791	5,303	5,056
32,150	32,200	4,363	3,899	4,363	4,164	35,150	35,200	4,813	4,349	4,813	4,614	38,150	38,200	5,315	4,799	5,315	5,064
32,200	32,250	4,370	3,906	4,370	4,171	35,200	35,250	4,820	4,356	4,820	4,621	38,200	38,250	5,328	4,806	5,328	5,071
32,250	32,300	4,378	3,914	4,378	4,179	35,250	35,300	4,828	4,364	4,828	4,629	38,250	38,300	5,340	4,814	5,340	5,079
32,300	32,350	4,385	3,921	4,385	4,186	35,300	35,350	4,835	4,371	4,835	4,636	38,300	38,350	5,353	4,821	5,353	5,086
32,350	32,400	4,393	3,929	4,393	4,194	35,350	35,400	4,843	4,379	4,843	4,644	38,350	38,400	5,365	4,829	5,365	5,094
32,400	32,450	4,400	3,936	4,400	4,201	35,400	35,450	4,850	4,386	4,850	4,651	38,400	38,450	5,378	4,836	5,378	5,101
32,450	32,500	4,408	3,944	4,408	4,209	35,450	35,500	4,858	4,394	4,858	4,659	38,450	38,500	5,390	4,844	5,390	5,109
32,500	32,550	4,415	3,951	4,415	4,216	35,500	35,550	4,865	4,401	4,865	4,666	38,500	38,550	5,403	4,851	5,403	5,116
32,550	32,600	4,423	3,959	4,423	4,224	35,550	35,600	4,873	4,409	4,873	4,674	38,550	38,600	5,415	4,859	5,415	5,124
32,600	32,650	4,430	3,966	4,430	4,231	35,600	35,650	4,880	4,416	4,880	4,681	38,600	38,650	5,428	4,866	5,428	5,131
32,650	32,700	4,438	3,974	4,438	4,239	35,650	35,700	4,888	4,424	4,888	4,689	38,650	38,700	5,440	4,874	5,440	5,139
32,700	32,750	4,445	3,981	4,445	4,246	35,700	35,750	4,895	4,431	4,895	4,696	38,700	38,750	5,453	4,881	5,453	5,146
32,750	32,800	4,453	3,989	4,453	4,254	35,750	35,800	4,903	4,439	4,903	4,704	38,750	38,800	5,465	4,889	5,465	5,154
32,800	32,850	4,460	3,996	4,460	4,261	35,800	35,850	4,910	4,446	4,910	4,711	38,800	38,850	5,478	4,896	5,478	5,161
32,850	32,900	4,468	4,004	4,468	4,269	35,850	35,900	4,918	4,454	4,918	4,719	38,850	38,900	5,490	4,904	5,490	5,169
32,900	32,950	4,475	4,011	4,475	4,276	35,900	35,950	4,925	4,461	4,925	4,726	38,900	38,950	5,503	4,911	5,503	5,176
32,950	33,000	4,483	4,019	4,483	4,284	35,950	36,000	4,933	4,469	4,933	4,734	38,950	39,000	5,515	4,919	5,515	5,184

* This column must also be used by a qualifying widow(er).

(Continued)

39,000

If line 43 (taxable income) is—		And you are—			
At least	But less than	Single	Married filing jointly *	Married filing separately	Head of a household
		Your tax is—			
39,000	39,050	5,528	4,926	5,528	5,191
39,050	39,100	5,540	4,934	5,540	5,199
39,100	39,150	5,553	4,941	5,553	5,206
39,150	39,200	5,565	4,949	5,565	5,214
39,200	39,250	5,578	4,956	5,578	5,221
39,250	39,300	5,590	4,964	5,590	5,229
39,300	39,350	5,603	4,971	5,603	5,236
39,350	39,400	5,615	4,979	5,615	5,244
39,400	39,450	5,628	4,986	5,628	5,251
39,450	39,500	5,640	4,994	5,640	5,259
39,500	39,550	5,653	5,001	5,653	5,266
39,550	39,600	5,665	5,009	5,665	5,274
39,600	39,650	5,678	5,016	5,678	5,281
39,650	39,700	5,690	5,024	5,690	5,289
39,700	39,750	5,703	5,031	5,703	5,296
39,750	39,800	5,715	5,039	5,715	5,304
39,800	39,850	5,728	5,046	5,728	5,311
39,850	39,900	5,740	5,054	5,740	5,319
39,900	39,950	5,753	5,061	5,753	5,326
39,950	40,000	5,765	5,069	5,765	5,334

40,000

At least	But less than	Single	Married filing jointly *	Married filing separately	Head of a household
40,000	40,050	5,778	5,076	5,778	5,341
40,050	40,100	5,790	5,084	5,790	5,349
40,100	40,150	5,803	5,091	5,803	5,356
40,150	40,200	5,815	5,099	5,815	5,364
40,200	40,250	5,828	5,106	5,828	5,371
40,250	40,300	5,840	5,114	5,840	5,379
40,300	40,350	5,853	5,121	5,853	5,386
40,350	40,400	5,865	5,129	5,865	5,394
40,400	40,450	5,878	5,136	5,878	5,401
40,450	40,500	5,890	5,144	5,890	5,409
40,500	40,550	5,903	5,151	5,903	5,416
40,550	40,600	5,915	5,159	5,915	5,424
40,600	40,650	5,928	5,166	5,928	5,431
40,650	40,700	5,940	5,174	5,940	5,439
40,700	40,750	5,953	5,181	5,953	5,446
40,750	40,800	5,965	5,189	5,965	5,454
40,800	40,850	5,978	5,196	5,978	5,461
40,850	40,900	5,990	5,204	5,990	5,469
40,900	40,950	6,003	5,211	6,003	5,476
40,950	41,000	6,015	5,219	6,015	5,484

41,000

At least	But less than	Single	Married filing jointly *	Married filing separately	Head of a household
41,000	41,050	6,028	5,226	6,028	5,491
41,050	41,100	6,040	5,234	6,040	5,499
41,100	41,150	6,053	5,241	6,053	5,506
41,150	41,200	6,065	5,249	6,065	5,514
41,200	41,250	6,078	5,256	6,078	5,521
41,250	41,300	6,090	5,264	6,090	5,529
41,300	41,350	6,103	5,271	6,103	5,536
41,350	41,400	6,115	5,279	6,115	5,544
41,400	41,450	6,128	5,286	6,128	5,551
41,450	41,500	6,140	5,294	6,140	5,559
41,500	41,550	6,153	5,301	6,153	5,566
41,550	41,600	6,165	5,309	6,165	5,574
41,600	41,650	6,178	5,316	6,178	5,581
41,650	41,700	6,190	5,324	6,190	5,589
41,700	41,750	6,203	5,331	6,203	5,596
41,750	41,800	6,215	5,339	6,215	5,604
41,800	41,850	6,228	5,346	6,228	5,611
41,850	41,900	6,240	5,354	6,240	5,619
41,900	41,950	6,253	5,361	6,253	5,626
41,950	42,000	6,265	5,369	6,265	5,634

42,000

If line 43 (taxable income) is—		And you are—			
At least	But less than	Single	Married filing jointly *	Married filing separately	Head of a household
		Your tax is—			
42,000	42,050	6,278	5,376	6,278	5,641
42,050	42,100	6,290	5,384	6,290	5,649
42,100	42,150	6,303	5,391	6,303	5,656
42,150	42,200	6,315	5,399	6,315	5,664
42,200	42,250	6,328	5,406	6,328	5,671
42,250	42,300	6,340	5,414	6,340	5,679
42,300	42,350	6,353	5,421	6,353	5,686
42,350	42,400	6,365	5,429	6,365	5,694
42,400	42,450	6,378	5,436	6,378	5,701
42,450	42,500	6,390	5,444	6,390	5,709
42,500	42,550	6,403	5,451	6,403	5,716
42,550	42,600	6,415	5,459	6,415	5,724
42,600	42,650	6,428	5,466	6,428	5,731
42,650	42,700	6,440	5,474	6,440	5,739
42,700	42,750	6,453	5,481	6,453	5,746
42,750	42,800	6,465	5,489	6,465	5,754
42,800	42,850	6,478	5,496	6,478	5,761
42,850	42,900	6,490	5,504	6,490	5,769
42,900	42,950	6,503	5,511	6,503	5,776
42,950	43,000	6,515	5,519	6,515	5,784

43,000

At least	But less than	Single	Married filing jointly *	Married filing separately	Head of a household
43,000	43,050	6,528	5,526	6,528	5,791
43,050	43,100	6,540	5,534	6,540	5,799
43,100	43,150	6,553	5,541	6,553	5,806
43,150	43,200	6,565	5,549	6,565	5,814
43,200	43,250	6,578	5,556	6,578	5,821
43,250	43,300	6,590	5,564	6,590	5,829
43,300	43,350	6,603	5,571	6,603	5,836
43,350	43,400	6,615	5,579	6,615	5,844
43,400	43,450	6,628	5,586	6,628	5,851
43,450	43,500	6,640	5,594	6,640	5,859
43,500	43,550	6,653	5,601	6,653	5,866
43,550	43,600	6,665	5,609	6,665	5,874
43,600	43,650	6,678	5,616	6,678	5,881
43,650	43,700	6,690	5,624	6,690	5,889
43,700	43,750	6,703	5,631	6,703	5,896
43,750	43,800	6,715	5,639	6,715	5,904
43,800	43,850	6,728	5,646	6,728	5,911
43,850	43,900	6,740	5,654	6,740	5,919
43,900	43,950	6,753	5,661	6,753	5,926
43,950	44,000	6,765	5,669	6,765	5,934

44,000

At least	But less than	Single	Married filing jointly *	Married filing separately	Head of a household
44,000	44,050	6,778	5,676	6,778	5,941
44,050	44,100	6,790	5,684	6,790	5,949
44,100	44,150	6,803	5,691	6,803	5,956
44,150	44,200	6,815	5,699	6,815	5,964
44,200	44,250	6,828	5,706	6,828	5,971
44,250	44,300	6,840	5,714	6,840	5,979
44,300	44,350	6,853	5,721	6,853	5,986
44,350	44,400	6,865	5,729	6,865	5,994
44,400	44,450	6,878	5,736	6,878	6,001
44,450	44,500	6,890	5,744	6,890	6,009
44,500	44,550	6,903	5,751	6,903	6,016
44,550	44,600	6,915	5,759	6,915	6,024
44,600	44,650	6,928	5,766	6,928	6,031
44,650	44,700	6,940	5,774	6,940	6,039
44,700	44,750	6,953	5,781	6,953	6,046
44,750	44,800	6,965	5,789	6,965	6,054
44,800	44,850	6,978	5,796	6,978	6,061
44,850	44,900	6,990	5,804	6,990	6,069
44,900	44,950	7,003	5,811	7,003	6,076
44,950	45,000	7,015	5,819	7,015	6,084

45,000

If line 43 (taxable income) is—		And you are—			
At least	But less than	Single	Married filing jointly *	Married filing separately	Head of a household
		Your tax is—			
45,000	45,050	7,028	5,826	7,028	6,091
45,050	45,100	7,040	5,834	7,040	6,099
45,100	45,150	7,053	5,841	7,053	6,106
45,150	45,200	7,065	5,849	7,065	6,114
45,200	45,250	7,078	5,856	7,078	6,121
45,250	45,300	7,090	5,864	7,090	6,129
45,300	45,350	7,103	5,871	7,103	6,136
45,350	45,400	7,115	5,879	7,115	6,144
45,400	45,450	7,128	5,886	7,128	6,151
45,450	45,500	7,140	5,894	7,140	6,159
45,500	45,550	7,153	5,901	7,153	6,166
45,550	45,600	7,165	5,909	7,165	6,174
45,600	45,650	7,178	5,916	7,178	6,181
45,650	45,700	7,190	5,924	7,190	6,189
45,700	45,750	7,203	5,931	7,203	6,196
45,750	45,800	7,215	5,939	7,215	6,204
45,800	45,850	7,228	5,946	7,228	6,211
45,850	45,900	7,240	5,954	7,240	6,219
45,900	45,950	7,253	5,961	7,253	6,226
45,950	46,000	7,265	5,969	7,265	6,234

46,000

At least	But less than	Single	Married filing jointly *	Married filing separately	Head of a household
46,000	46,050	7,278	5,976	7,278	6,241
46,050	46,100	7,290	5,984	7,290	6,249
46,100	46,150	7,303	5,991	7,303	6,256
46,150	46,200	7,315	5,999	7,315	6,264
46,200	46,250	7,328	6,006	7,328	6,271
46,250	46,300	7,340	6,014	7,340	6,279
46,300	46,350	7,353	6,021	7,353	6,286
46,350	46,400	7,365	6,029	7,365	6,294
46,400	46,450	7,378	6,036	7,378	6,301
46,450	46,500	7,390	6,044	7,390	6,309
46,500	46,550	7,403	6,051	7,403	6,316
46,550	46,600	7,415	6,059	7,415	6,324
46,600	46,650	7,428	6,066	7,428	6,331
46,650	46,700	7,440	6,074	7,440	6,339
46,700	46,750	7,453	6,081	7,453	6,346
46,750	46,800	7,465	6,089	7,465	6,354
46,800	46,850	7,478	6,096	7,478	6,361
46,850	46,900	7,490	6,104	7,490	6,369
46,900	46,950	7,503	6,111	7,503	6,376
46,950	47,000	7,515	6,119	7,515	6,384

47,000

At least	But less than	Single	Married filing jointly *	Married filing separately	Head of a household
47,000	47,050	7,528	6,126	7,528	6,391
47,050	47,100	7,540	6,134	7,540	6,399
47,100	47,150	7,553	6,141	7,553	6,406
47,150	47,200	7,565	6,149	7,565	6,414
47,200	47,250	7,578	6,156	7,578	6,421
47,250	47,300	7,590	6,164	7,590	6,429
47,300	47,350	7,603	6,171	7,603	6,436
47,350	47,400	7,615	6,179	7,615	6,444
47,400	47,450	7,628	6,186	7,628	6,451
47,450	47,500	7,640	6,194	7,640	6,459
47,500	47,550	7,653	6,201	7,653	6,466
47,550	47,600	7,665	6,209	7,665	6,474
47,600	47,650	7,678	6,216	7,678	6,481
47,650	47,700	7,690	6,224	7,690	6,489
47,700	47,750	7,703	6,231	7,703	6,496
47,750	47,800	7,715	6,239	7,715	6,504
47,800	47,850	7,728	6,246	7,728	6,511
47,850	47,900	7,740	6,254	7,740	6,519
47,900	47,950	7,753	6,261	7,753	6,526
47,950	48,000	7,765	6,269	7,765	6,534

* This column must also be used by a qualifying widow(er).

(Continued)

Need more information or forms? Visit IRS.gov.

If line 43 (taxable income) is—		And you are—			
At least	But less than	Single	Married filing jointly *	Married filing separately	Head of a household
		Your tax is—			

48,000

At least	But less than	Single	MFJ *	MFS	HoH
48,000	48,050	7,778	6,276	7,778	6,541
48,050	48,100	7,790	6,284	7,790	6,549
48,100	48,150	7,803	6,291	7,803	6,556
48,150	48,200	7,815	6,299	7,815	6,564
48,200	48,250	7,828	6,306	7,828	6,571
48,250	48,300	7,840	6,314	7,840	6,579
48,300	48,350	7,853	6,321	7,853	6,586
48,350	48,400	7,865	6,329	7,865	6,594
48,400	48,450	7,878	6,336	7,878	6,601
48,450	48,500	7,890	6,344	7,890	6,609
48,500	48,550	7,903	6,351	7,903	6,616
48,550	48,600	7,915	6,359	7,915	6,624
48,600	48,650	7,928	6,366	7,928	6,631
48,650	48,700	7,940	6,374	7,940	6,639
48,700	48,750	7,953	6,381	7,953	6,646
48,750	48,800	7,965	6,389	7,965	6,654
48,800	48,850	7,978	6,396	7,978	6,661
48,850	48,900	7,990	6,404	7,990	6,669
48,900	48,950	8,003	6,411	8,003	6,676
48,950	49,000	8,015	6,419	8,015	6,684

49,000

At least	But less than	Single	MFJ *	MFS	HoH
49,000	49,050	8,028	6,426	8,028	6,691
49,050	49,100	8,040	6,434	8,040	6,699
49,100	49,150	8,053	6,441	8,053	6,706
49,150	49,200	8,065	6,449	8,065	6,714
49,200	49,250	8,078	6,456	8,078	6,721
49,250	49,300	8,090	6,464	8,090	6,729
49,300	49,350	8,103	6,471	8,103	6,736
49,350	49,400	8,115	6,479	8,115	6,744
49,400	49,450	8,128	6,486	8,128	6,751
49,450	49,500	8,140	6,494	8,140	6,759
49,500	49,550	8,153	6,501	8,153	6,766
49,550	49,600	8,165	6,509	8,165	6,774
49,600	49,650	8,178	6,516	8,178	6,781
49,650	49,700	8,190	6,524	8,190	6,789
49,700	49,750	8,203	6,531	8,203	6,796
49,750	49,800	8,215	6,539	8,215	6,804
49,800	49,850	8,228	6,546	8,228	6,811
49,850	49,900	8,240	6,554	8,240	6,819
49,900	49,950	8,253	6,561	8,253	6,826
49,950	50,000	8,265	6,569	8,265	6,834

50,000

At least	But less than	Single	MFJ *	MFS	HoH
50,000	50,050	8,278	6,576	8,278	6,841
50,050	50,100	8,290	6,584	8,290	6,849
50,100	50,150	8,303	6,591	8,303	6,856
50,150	50,200	8,315	6,599	8,315	6,864
50,200	50,250	8,328	6,606	8,328	6,871
50,250	50,300	8,340	6,614	8,340	6,879
50,300	50,350	8,353	6,621	8,353	6,886
50,350	50,400	8,365	6,629	8,365	6,894
50,400	50,450	8,378	6,636	8,378	6,904
50,450	50,500	8,390	6,644	8,390	6,916
50,500	50,550	8,403	6,651	8,403	6,929
50,550	50,600	8,415	6,659	8,415	6,941
50,600	50,650	8,428	6,666	8,428	6,954
50,650	50,700	8,440	6,674	8,440	6,966
50,700	50,750	8,453	6,681	8,453	6,979
50,750	50,800	8,465	6,689	8,465	6,991
50,800	50,850	8,478	6,696	8,478	7,004
50,850	50,900	8,490	6,704	8,490	7,016
50,900	50,950	8,503	6,711	8,503	7,029
50,950	51,000	8,515	6,719	8,515	7,041

51,000

At least	But less than	Single	MFJ *	MFS	HoH
51,000	51,050	8,528	6,726	8,528	7,054
51,050	51,100	8,540	6,734	8,540	7,066
51,100	51,150	8,553	6,741	8,553	7,079
51,150	51,200	8,565	6,749	8,565	7,091
51,200	51,250	8,578	6,756	8,578	7,104
51,250	51,300	8,590	6,764	8,590	7,116
51,300	51,350	8,603	6,771	8,603	7,129
51,350	51,400	8,615	6,779	8,615	7,141
51,400	51,450	8,628	6,786	8,628	7,154
51,450	51,500	8,640	6,794	8,640	7,166
51,500	51,550	8,653	6,801	8,653	7,179
51,550	51,600	8,665	6,809	8,665	7,191
51,600	51,650	8,678	6,816	8,678	7,204
51,650	51,700	8,690	6,824	8,690	7,216
51,700	51,750	8,703	6,831	8,703	7,229
51,750	51,800	8,715	6,839	8,715	7,241
51,800	51,850	8,728	6,846	8,728	7,254
51,850	51,900	8,740	6,854	8,740	7,266
51,900	51,950	8,753	6,861	8,753	7,279
51,950	52,000	8,765	6,869	8,765	7,291

52,000

At least	But less than	Single	MFJ *	MFS	HoH
52,000	52,050	8,778	6,876	8,778	7,304
52,050	52,100	8,790	6,884	8,790	7,316
52,100	52,150	8,803	6,891	8,803	7,329
52,150	52,200	8,815	6,899	8,815	7,341
52,200	52,250	8,828	6,906	8,828	7,354
52,250	52,300	8,840	6,914	8,840	7,366
52,300	52,350	8,853	6,921	8,853	7,379
52,350	52,400	8,865	6,929	8,865	7,391
52,400	52,450	8,878	6,936	8,878	7,404
52,450	52,500	8,890	6,944	8,890	7,416
52,500	52,550	8,903	6,951	8,903	7,429
52,550	52,600	8,915	6,959	8,915	7,441
52,600	52,650	8,928	6,966	8,928	7,454
52,650	52,700	8,940	6,974	8,940	7,466
52,700	52,750	8,953	6,981	8,953	7,479
52,750	52,800	8,965	6,989	8,965	7,491
52,800	52,850	8,978	6,996	8,978	7,504
52,850	52,900	8,990	7,004	8,990	7,516
52,900	52,950	9,003	7,011	9,003	7,529
52,950	53,000	9,015	7,019	9,015	7,541

53,000

At least	But less than	Single	MFJ *	MFS	HoH
53,000	53,050	9,028	7,026	9,028	7,554
53,050	53,100	9,040	7,034	9,040	7,566
53,100	53,150	9,053	7,041	9,053	7,579
53,150	53,200	9,065	7,049	9,065	7,591
53,200	53,250	9,078	7,056	9,078	7,604
53,250	53,300	9,090	7,064	9,090	7,616
53,300	53,350	9,103	7,071	9,103	7,629
53,350	53,400	9,115	7,079	9,115	7,641
53,400	53,450	9,128	7,086	9,128	7,654
53,450	53,500	9,140	7,094	9,140	7,666
53,500	53,550	9,153	7,101	9,153	7,679
53,550	53,600	9,165	7,109	9,165	7,691
53,600	53,650	9,178	7,116	9,178	7,704
53,650	53,700	9,190	7,124	9,190	7,716
53,700	53,750	9,203	7,131	9,203	7,729
53,750	53,800	9,215	7,139	9,215	7,741
53,800	53,850	9,228	7,146	9,228	7,754
53,850	53,900	9,240	7,154	9,240	7,766
53,900	53,950	9,253	7,161	9,253	7,779
53,950	54,000	9,265	7,169	9,265	7,791

54,000

At least	But less than	Single	MFJ *	MFS	HoH
54,000	54,050	9,278	7,176	9,278	7,804
54,050	54,100	9,290	7,184	9,290	7,816
54,100	54,150	9,303	7,191	9,303	7,829
54,150	54,200	9,315	7,199	9,315	7,841
54,200	54,250	9,328	7,206	9,328	7,854
54,250	54,300	9,340	7,214	9,340	7,866
54,300	54,350	9,353	7,221	9,353	7,879
54,350	54,400	9,365	7,229	9,365	7,891
54,400	54,450	9,378	7,236	9,378	7,904
54,450	54,500	9,390	7,244	9,390	7,916
54,500	54,550	9,403	7,251	9,403	7,929
54,550	54,600	9,415	7,259	9,415	7,941
54,600	54,650	9,428	7,266	9,428	7,954
54,650	54,700	9,440	7,274	9,440	7,966
54,700	54,750	9,453	7,281	9,453	7,979
54,750	54,800	9,465	7,289	9,465	7,991
54,800	54,850	9,478	7,296	9,478	8,004
54,850	54,900	9,490	7,304	9,490	8,016
54,900	54,950	9,503	7,311	9,503	8,029
54,950	55,000	9,515	7,319	9,515	8,041

55,000

At least	But less than	Single	MFJ *	MFS	HoH
55,000	55,050	9,528	7,326	9,528	8,054
55,050	55,100	9,540	7,334	9,540	8,066
55,100	55,150	9,553	7,341	9,553	8,079
55,150	55,200	9,565	7,349	9,565	8,091
55,200	55,250	9,578	7,356	9,578	8,104
55,250	55,300	9,590	7,364	9,590	8,116
55,300	55,350	9,603	7,371	9,603	8,129
55,350	55,400	9,615	7,379	9,615	8,141
55,400	55,450	9,628	7,386	9,628	8,154
55,450	55,500	9,640	7,394	9,640	8,166
55,500	55,550	9,653	7,401	9,653	8,179
55,550	55,600	9,665	7,409	9,665	8,191
55,600	55,650	9,678	7,416	9,678	8,204
55,650	55,700	9,690	7,424	9,690	8,216
55,700	55,750	9,703	7,431	9,703	8,229
55,750	55,800	9,715	7,439	9,715	8,241
55,800	55,850	9,728	7,446	9,728	8,254
55,850	55,900	9,740	7,454	9,740	8,266
55,900	55,950	9,753	7,461	9,753	8,279
55,950	56,000	9,765	7,469	9,765	8,291

56,000

At least	But less than	Single	MFJ *	MFS	HoH
56,000	56,050	9,778	7,476	9,778	8,304
56,050	56,100	9,790	7,484	9,790	8,316
56,100	56,150	9,803	7,491	9,803	8,329
56,150	56,200	9,815	7,499	9,815	8,341
56,200	56,250	9,828	7,506	9,828	8,354
56,250	56,300	9,840	7,514	9,840	8,366
56,300	56,350	9,853	7,521	9,853	8,379
56,350	56,400	9,865	7,529	9,865	8,391
56,400	56,450	9,878	7,536	9,878	8,404
56,450	56,500	9,890	7,544	9,890	8,416
56,500	56,550	9,903	7,551	9,903	8,429
56,550	56,600	9,915	7,559	9,915	8,441
56,600	56,650	9,928	7,566	9,928	8,454
56,650	56,700	9,940	7,574	9,940	8,466
56,700	56,750	9,953	7,581	9,953	8,479
56,750	56,800	9,965	7,589	9,965	8,491
56,800	56,850	9,978	7,596	9,978	8,504
56,850	56,900	9,990	7,604	9,990	8,516
56,900	56,950	10,003	7,611	10,003	8,529
56,950	57,000	10,015	7,619	10,015	8,541

(Continued)

* This column must also be used by a qualifying widow(er).

Need more information or forms? Visit IRS.gov.

57,000

At least	But less than	Single	Married filing jointly *	Married filing separately	Head of a household
		Your tax is—			
57,000	57,050	10,028	7,626	10,028	8,554
57,050	57,100	10,040	7,634	10,040	8,566
57,100	57,150	10,053	7,641	10,053	8,579
57,150	57,200	10,065	7,649	10,065	8,591
57,200	57,250	10,078	7,656	10,078	8,604
57,250	57,300	10,090	7,664	10,090	8,616
57,300	57,350	10,103	7,671	10,103	8,629
57,350	57,400	10,115	7,679	10,115	8,641
57,400	57,450	10,128	7,686	10,128	8,654
57,450	57,500	10,140	7,694	10,140	8,666
57,500	57,550	10,153	7,701	10,153	8,679
57,550	57,600	10,165	7,709	10,165	8,691
57,600	57,650	10,178	7,716	10,178	8,704
57,650	57,700	10,190	7,724	10,190	8,716
57,700	57,750	10,203	7,731	10,203	8,729
57,750	57,800	10,215	7,739	10,215	8,741
57,800	57,850	10,228	7,746	10,228	8,754
57,850	57,900	10,240	7,754	10,240	8,766
57,900	57,950	10,253	7,761	10,253	8,779
57,950	58,000	10,265	7,769	10,265	8,791

58,000

At least	But less than	Single	Married filing jointly *	Married filing separately	Head of a household
58,000	58,050	10,278	7,776	10,278	8,804
58,050	58,100	10,290	7,784	10,290	8,816
58,100	58,150	10,303	7,791	10,303	8,829
58,150	58,200	10,315	7,799	10,315	8,841
58,200	58,250	10,328	7,806	10,328	8,854
58,250	58,300	10,340	7,814	10,340	8,866
58,300	58,350	10,353	7,821	10,353	8,879
58,350	58,400	10,365	7,829	10,365	8,891
58,400	58,450	10,378	7,836	10,378	8,904
58,450	58,500	10,390	7,844	10,390	8,916
58,500	58,550	10,403	7,851	10,403	8,929
58,550	58,600	10,415	7,859	10,415	8,941
58,600	58,650	10,428	7,866	10,428	8,954
58,650	58,700	10,440	7,874	10,440	8,966
58,700	58,750	10,453	7,881	10,453	8,979
58,750	58,800	10,465	7,889	10,465	8,991
58,800	58,850	10,478	7,896	10,478	9,004
58,850	58,900	10,490	7,904	10,490	9,016
58,900	58,950	10,503	7,911	10,503	9,029
58,950	59,000	10,515	7,919	10,515	9,041

59,000

At least	But less than	Single	Married filing jointly *	Married filing separately	Head of a household
59,000	59,050	10,528	7,926	10,528	9,054
59,050	59,100	10,540	7,934	10,540	9,066
59,100	59,150	10,553	7,941	10,553	9,079
59,150	59,200	10,565	7,949	10,565	9,091
59,200	59,250	10,578	7,956	10,578	9,104
59,250	59,300	10,590	7,964	10,590	9,116
59,300	59,350	10,603	7,971	10,603	9,129
59,350	59,400	10,615	7,979	10,615	9,141
59,400	59,450	10,628	7,986	10,628	9,154
59,450	59,500	10,640	7,994	10,640	9,166
59,500	59,550	10,653	8,001	10,653	9,179
59,550	59,600	10,665	8,009	10,665	9,191
59,600	59,650	10,678	8,016	10,678	9,204
59,650	59,700	10,690	8,024	10,690	9,216
59,700	59,750	10,703	8,031	10,703	9,229
59,750	59,800	10,715	8,039	10,715	9,241
59,800	59,850	10,728	8,046	10,728	9,254
59,850	59,900	10,740	8,054	10,740	9,266
59,900	59,950	10,753	8,061	10,753	9,279
59,950	60,000	10,765	8,069	10,765	9,291

60,000

At least	But less than	Single	Married filing jointly *	Married filing separately	Head of a household
60,000	60,050	10,778	8,076	10,778	9,304
60,050	60,100	10,790	8,084	10,790	9,316
60,100	60,150	10,803	8,091	10,803	9,329
60,150	60,200	10,815	8,099	10,815	9,341
60,200	60,250	10,828	8,106	10,828	9,354
60,250	60,300	10,840	8,114	10,840	9,366
60,300	60,350	10,853	8,121	10,853	9,379
60,350	60,400	10,865	8,129	10,865	9,391
60,400	60,450	10,878	8,136	10,878	9,404
60,450	60,500	10,890	8,144	10,890	9,416
60,500	60,550	10,903	8,151	10,903	9,429
60,550	60,600	10,915	8,159	10,915	9,441
60,600	60,650	10,928	8,166	10,928	9,454
60,650	60,700	10,940	8,174	10,940	9,466
60,700	60,750	10,953	8,181	10,953	9,479
60,750	60,800	10,965	8,189	10,965	9,491
60,800	60,850	10,978	8,196	10,978	9,504
60,850	60,900	10,990	8,204	10,990	9,516
60,900	60,950	11,003	8,211	11,003	9,529
60,950	61,000	11,015	8,219	11,015	9,541

61,000

At least	But less than	Single	Married filing jointly *	Married filing separately	Head of a household
61,000	61,050	11,028	8,226	11,028	9,554
61,050	61,100	11,040	8,234	11,040	9,566
61,100	61,150	11,053	8,241	11,053	9,579
61,150	61,200	11,065	8,249	11,065	9,591
61,200	61,250	11,078	8,256	11,078	9,604
61,250	61,300	11,090	8,264	11,090	9,616
61,300	61,350	11,103	8,271	11,103	9,629
61,350	61,400	11,115	8,279	11,115	9,641
61,400	61,450	11,128	8,286	11,128	9,654
61,450	61,500	11,140	8,294	11,140	9,666
61,500	61,550	11,153	8,301	11,153	9,679
61,550	61,600	11,165	8,309	11,165	9,691
61,600	61,650	11,178	8,316	11,178	9,704
61,650	61,700	11,190	8,324	11,190	9,716
61,700	61,750	11,203	8,331	11,203	9,729
61,750	61,800	11,215	8,339	11,215	9,741
61,800	61,850	11,228	8,346	11,228	9,754
61,850	61,900	11,240	8,354	11,240	9,766
61,900	61,950	11,253	8,361	11,253	9,779
61,950	62,000	11,265	8,369	11,265	9,791

62,000

At least	But less than	Single	Married filing jointly *	Married filing separately	Head of a household
62,000	62,050	11,278	8,376	11,278	9,804
62,050	62,100	11,290	8,384	11,290	9,816
62,100	62,150	11,303	8,391	11,303	9,829
62,150	62,200	11,315	8,399	11,315	9,841
62,200	62,250	11,328	8,406	11,328	9,854
62,250	62,300	11,340	8,414	11,340	9,866
62,300	62,350	11,353	8,421	11,353	9,879
62,350	62,400	11,365	8,429	11,365	9,891
62,400	62,450	11,378	8,436	11,378	9,904
62,450	62,500	11,390	8,444	11,390	9,916
62,500	62,550	11,403	8,451	11,403	9,929
62,550	62,600	11,415	8,459	11,415	9,941
62,600	62,650	11,428	8,466	11,428	9,954
62,650	62,700	11,440	8,474	11,440	9,966
62,700	62,750	11,453	8,481	11,453	9,979
62,750	62,800	11,465	8,489	11,465	9,991
62,800	62,850	11,478	8,496	11,478	10,004
62,850	62,900	11,490	8,504	11,490	10,016
62,900	62,950	11,503	8,511	11,503	10,029
62,950	63,000	11,515	8,519	11,515	10,041

63,000

At least	But less than	Single	Married filing jointly *	Married filing separately	Head of a household
63,000	63,050	11,528	8,526	11,528	10,054
63,050	63,100	11,540	8,534	11,540	10,066
63,100	63,150	11,553	8,541	11,553	10,079
63,150	63,200	11,565	8,549	11,565	10,091
63,200	63,250	11,578	8,556	11,578	10,104
63,250	63,300	11,590	8,564	11,590	10,116
63,300	63,350	11,603	8,571	11,603	10,129
63,350	63,400	11,615	8,579	11,615	10,141
63,400	63,450	11,628	8,586	11,628	10,154
63,450	63,500	11,640	8,594	11,640	10,166
63,500	63,550	11,653	8,601	11,653	10,179
63,550	63,600	11,665	8,609	11,665	10,191
63,600	63,650	11,678	8,616	11,678	10,204
63,650	63,700	11,690	8,624	11,690	10,216
63,700	63,750	11,703	8,631	11,703	10,229
63,750	63,800	11,715	8,639	11,715	10,241
63,800	63,850	11,728	8,646	11,728	10,254
63,850	63,900	11,740	8,654	11,740	10,266
63,900	63,950	11,753	8,661	11,753	10,279
63,950	64,000	11,765	8,669	11,765	10,291

64,000

At least	But less than	Single	Married filing jointly *	Married filing separately	Head of a household
64,000	64,050	11,778	8,676	11,778	10,304
64,050	64,100	11,790	8,684	11,790	10,316
64,100	64,150	11,803	8,691	11,803	10,329
64,150	64,200	11,815	8,699	11,815	10,341
64,200	64,250	11,828	8,706	11,828	10,354
64,250	64,300	11,840	8,714	11,840	10,366
64,300	64,350	11,853	8,721	11,853	10,379
64,350	64,400	11,865	8,729	11,865	10,391
64,400	64,450	11,878	8,736	11,878	10,404
64,450	64,500	11,890	8,744	11,890	10,416
64,500	64,550	11,903	8,751	11,903	10,429
64,550	64,600	11,915	8,759	11,915	10,441
64,600	64,650	11,928	8,766	11,928	10,454
64,650	64,700	11,940	8,774	11,940	10,466
64,700	64,750	11,953	8,781	11,953	10,479
64,750	64,800	11,965	8,789	11,965	10,491
64,800	64,850	11,978	8,796	11,978	10,504
64,850	64,900	11,990	8,804	11,990	10,516
64,900	64,950	12,003	8,811	12,003	10,529
64,950	65,000	12,015	8,819	12,015	10,541

65,000

At least	But less than	Single	Married filing jointly *	Married filing separately	Head of a household
65,000	65,050	12,028	8,826	12,028	10,554
65,050	65,100	12,040	8,834	12,040	10,566
65,100	65,150	12,053	8,841	12,053	10,579
65,150	65,200	12,065	8,849	12,065	10,591
65,200	65,250	12,078	8,856	12,078	10,604
65,250	65,300	12,090	8,864	12,090	10,616
65,300	65,350	12,103	8,871	12,103	10,629
65,350	65,400	12,115	8,879	12,115	10,641
65,400	65,450	12,128	8,886	12,128	10,654
65,450	65,500	12,140	8,894	12,140	10,666
65,500	65,550	12,153	8,901	12,153	10,679
65,550	65,600	12,165	8,909	12,165	10,691
65,600	65,650	12,178	8,916	12,178	10,704
65,650	65,700	12,190	8,924	12,190	10,716
65,700	65,750	12,203	8,931	12,203	10,729
65,750	65,800	12,215	8,939	12,215	10,741
65,800	65,850	12,228	8,946	12,228	10,754
65,850	65,900	12,240	8,954	12,240	10,766
65,900	65,950	12,253	8,961	12,253	10,779
65,950	66,000	12,265	8,969	12,265	10,791

* This column must also be used by a qualifying widow(er).

(Continued)

Need more information or forms? Visit IRS.gov.

If line 43 (taxable income) is—		And you are—			
At least	But less than	Single	Married filing jointly *	Married filing separately	Head of a household
		Your tax is—			

66,000

At least	But less than	Single	Married filing jointly *	Married filing separately	Head of a household
66,000	66,050	12,278	8,976	12,278	10,804
66,050	66,100	12,290	8,984	12,290	10,816
66,100	66,150	12,303	8,991	12,303	10,829
66,150	66,200	12,315	8,999	12,315	10,841
66,200	66,250	12,328	9,006	12,328	10,854
66,250	66,300	12,340	9,014	12,340	10,866
66,300	66,350	12,353	9,021	12,353	10,879
66,350	66,400	12,365	9,029	12,365	10,891
66,400	66,450	12,378	9,036	12,378	10,904
66,450	66,500	12,390	9,044	12,390	10,916
66,500	66,550	12,403	9,051	12,403	10,929
66,550	66,600	12,415	9,059	12,415	10,941
66,600	66,650	12,428	9,066	12,428	10,954
66,650	66,700	12,440	9,074	12,440	10,966
66,700	66,750	12,453	9,081	12,453	10,979
66,750	66,800	12,465	9,089	12,465	10,991
66,800	66,850	12,478	9,096	12,478	11,004
66,850	66,900	12,490	9,104	12,490	11,016
66,900	66,950	12,503	9,111	12,503	11,029
66,950	67,000	12,515	9,119	12,515	11,041

67,000

At least	But less than	Single	Married filing jointly *	Married filing separately	Head of a household
67,000	67,050	12,528	9,126	12,528	11,054
67,050	67,100	12,540	9,134	12,540	11,066
67,100	67,150	12,553	9,141	12,553	11,079
67,150	67,200	12,565	9,149	12,565	11,091
67,200	67,250	12,578	9,156	12,578	11,104
67,250	67,300	12,590	9,164	12,590	11,116
67,300	67,350	12,603	9,171	12,603	11,129
67,350	67,400	12,615	9,179	12,615	11,141
67,400	67,450	12,628	9,186	12,628	11,154
67,450	67,500	12,640	9,194	12,640	11,166
67,500	67,550	12,653	9,201	12,653	11,179
67,550	67,600	12,665	9,209	12,665	11,191
67,600	67,650	12,678	9,216	12,678	11,204
67,650	67,700	12,690	9,224	12,690	11,216
67,700	67,750	12,703	9,231	12,703	11,229
67,750	67,800	12,715	9,239	12,715	11,241
67,800	67,850	12,728	9,246	12,728	11,254
67,850	67,900	12,740	9,254	12,740	11,266
67,900	67,950	12,753	9,261	12,753	11,279
67,950	68,000	12,765	9,269	12,765	11,291

68,000

At least	But less than	Single	Married filing jointly *	Married filing separately	Head of a household
68,000	68,050	12,778	9,276	12,778	11,304
68,050	68,100	12,790	9,284	12,790	11,316
68,100	68,150	12,803	9,291	12,803	11,329
68,150	68,200	12,815	9,299	12,815	11,341
68,200	68,250	12,828	9,306	12,828	11,354
68,250	68,300	12,840	9,314	12,840	11,366
68,300	68,350	12,853	9,321	12,853	11,379
68,350	68,400	12,865	9,329	12,865	11,391
68,400	68,450	12,878	9,336	12,878	11,404
68,450	68,500	12,890	9,344	12,890	11,416
68,500	68,550	12,903	9,351	12,903	11,429
68,550	68,600	12,915	9,359	12,915	11,441
68,600	68,650	12,928	9,366	12,928	11,454
68,650	68,700	12,940	9,374	12,940	11,466
68,700	68,750	12,953	9,381	12,953	11,479
68,750	68,800	12,965	9,389	12,965	11,491
68,800	68,850	12,978	9,396	12,978	11,504
68,850	68,900	12,990	9,404	12,990	11,516
68,900	68,950	13,003	9,411	13,003	11,529
68,950	69,000	13,015	9,419	13,015	11,541

69,000

At least	But less than	Single	Married filing jointly *	Married filing separately	Head of a household
69,000	69,050	13,028	9,426	13,028	11,554
69,050	69,100	13,040	9,434	13,040	11,566
69,100	69,150	13,053	9,441	13,053	11,579
69,150	69,200	13,065	9,449	13,065	11,591
69,200	69,250	13,078	9,456	13,078	11,604
69,250	69,300	13,090	9,464	13,090	11,616
69,300	69,350	13,103	9,471	13,103	11,629
69,350	69,400	13,115	9,479	13,115	11,641
69,400	69,450	13,128	9,486	13,128	11,654
69,450	69,500	13,140	9,494	13,140	11,666
69,500	69,550	13,153	9,501	13,153	11,679
69,550	69,600	13,165	9,509	13,165	11,691
69,600	69,650	13,178	9,516	13,178	11,704
69,650	69,700	13,190	9,524	13,190	11,716
69,700	69,750	13,203	9,531	13,203	11,729
69,750	69,800	13,215	9,539	13,215	11,741
69,800	69,850	13,228	9,546	13,228	11,754
69,850	69,900	13,240	9,554	13,240	11,766
69,900	69,950	13,253	9,561	13,253	11,779
69,950	70,000	13,265	9,569	13,265	11,791

70,000

At least	But less than	Single	Married filing jointly *	Married filing separately	Head of a household
70,000	70,050	13,278	9,576	13,278	11,804
70,050	70,100	13,290	9,584	13,290	11,816
70,100	70,150	13,303	9,591	13,303	11,829
70,150	70,200	13,315	9,599	13,315	11,841
70,200	70,250	13,328	9,606	13,328	11,854
70,250	70,300	13,340	9,614	13,340	11,866
70,300	70,350	13,353	9,621	13,353	11,879
70,350	70,400	13,365	9,629	13,365	11,891
70,400	70,450	13,378	9,636	13,378	11,904
70,450	70,500	13,390	9,644	13,390	11,916
70,500	70,550	13,403	9,651	13,403	11,929
70,550	70,600	13,415	9,659	13,415	11,941
70,600	70,650	13,428	9,666	13,428	11,954
70,650	70,700	13,440	9,674	13,440	11,966
70,700	70,750	13,453	9,681	13,453	11,979
70,750	70,800	13,465	9,689	13,465	11,991
70,800	70,850	13,478	9,696	13,478	12,004
70,850	70,900	13,490	9,704	13,490	12,016
70,900	70,950	13,503	9,711	13,503	12,029
70,950	71,000	13,515	9,719	13,515	12,041

71,000

At least	But less than	Single	Married filing jointly *	Married filing separately	Head of a household
71,000	71,050	13,528	9,726	13,528	12,054
71,050	71,100	13,540	9,734	13,540	12,066
71,100	71,150	13,553	9,741	13,553	12,079
71,150	71,200	13,565	9,749	13,565	12,091
71,200	71,250	13,578	9,756	13,578	12,104
71,250	71,300	13,590	9,764	13,590	12,116
71,300	71,350	13,603	9,771	13,603	12,129
71,350	71,400	13,615	9,779	13,615	12,141
71,400	71,450	13,628	9,786	13,628	12,154
71,450	71,500	13,640	9,794	13,640	12,166
71,500	71,550	13,653	9,801	13,653	12,179
71,550	71,600	13,665	9,809	13,665	12,191
71,600	71,650	13,678	9,816	13,678	12,204
71,650	71,700	13,690	9,824	13,690	12,216
71,700	71,750	13,703	9,831	13,703	12,229
71,750	71,800	13,715	9,839	13,715	12,241
71,800	71,850	13,728	9,846	13,728	12,254
71,850	71,900	13,740	9,854	13,740	12,266
71,900	71,950	13,753	9,861	13,753	12,279
71,950	72,000	13,765	9,869	13,765	12,291

72,000

At least	But less than	Single	Married filing jointly *	Married filing separately	Head of a household
72,000	72,050	13,778	9,876	13,778	12,304
72,050	72,100	13,790	9,884	13,790	12,316
72,100	72,150	13,803	9,891	13,803	12,329
72,150	72,200	13,815	9,899	13,815	12,341
72,200	72,250	13,828	9,906	13,828	12,354
72,250	72,300	13,840	9,914	13,840	12,366
72,300	72,350	13,853	9,921	13,853	12,379
72,350	72,400	13,865	9,929	13,865	12,391
72,400	72,450	13,878	9,936	13,878	12,404
72,450	72,500	13,890	9,944	13,890	12,416
72,500	72,550	13,903	9,951	13,903	12,429
72,550	72,600	13,915	9,959	13,915	12,441
72,600	72,650	13,928	9,966	13,928	12,454
72,650	72,700	13,940	9,974	13,940	12,466
72,700	72,750	13,953	9,981	13,953	12,479
72,750	72,800	13,965	9,989	13,965	12,491
72,800	72,850	13,978	9,996	13,978	12,504
72,850	72,900	13,990	10,004	13,990	12,516
72,900	72,950	14,003	10,011	14,003	12,529
72,950	73,000	14,015	10,019	14,015	12,541

73,000

At least	But less than	Single	Married filing jointly *	Married filing separately	Head of a household
73,000	73,050	14,028	10,026	14,028	12,554
73,050	73,100	14,040	10,034	14,040	12,566
73,100	73,150	14,053	10,041	14,053	12,579
73,150	73,200	14,065	10,049	14,065	12,591
73,200	73,250	14,078	10,056	14,078	12,604
73,250	73,300	14,090	10,064	14,090	12,616
73,300	73,350	14,103	10,071	14,103	12,629
73,350	73,400	14,115	10,079	14,115	12,641
73,400	73,450	14,128	10,086	14,128	12,654
73,450	73,500	14,140	10,094	14,140	12,666
73,500	73,550	14,153	10,101	14,153	12,679
73,550	73,600	14,165	10,109	14,165	12,691
73,600	73,650	14,178	10,116	14,178	12,704
73,650	73,700	14,190	10,124	14,190	12,716
73,700	73,750	14,203	10,131	14,203	12,729
73,750	73,800	14,215	10,139	14,215	12,741
73,800	73,850	14,228	10,146	14,228	12,754
73,850	73,900	14,240	10,154	14,240	12,766
73,900	73,950	14,253	10,161	14,253	12,779
73,950	74,000	14,265	10,169	14,265	12,791

74,000

At least	But less than	Single	Married filing jointly *	Married filing separately	Head of a household
74,000	74,050	14,278	10,176	14,278	12,804
74,050	74,100	14,290	10,184	14,290	12,816
74,100	74,150	14,303	10,191	14,303	12,829
74,150	74,200	14,315	10,199	14,315	12,841
74,200	74,250	14,328	10,206	14,328	12,854
74,250	74,300	14,340	10,214	14,340	12,866
74,300	74,350	14,353	10,221	14,353	12,879
74,350	74,400	14,365	10,229	14,365	12,891
74,400	74,450	14,378	10,236	14,378	12,904
74,450	74,500	14,390	10,244	14,390	12,916
74,500	74,550	14,403	10,251	14,403	12,929
74,550	74,600	14,415	10,259	14,415	12,941
74,600	74,650	14,428	10,266	14,428	12,954
74,650	74,700	14,440	10,274	14,440	12,966
74,700	74,750	14,453	10,281	14,453	12,979
74,750	74,800	14,465	10,289	14,465	12,991
74,800	74,850	14,478	10,296	14,478	13,004
74,850	74,900	14,490	10,304	14,490	13,016
74,900	74,950	14,503	10,311	14,503	13,029
74,950	75,000	14,515	10,319	14,515	13,041

* This column must also be used by a qualifying widow(er).

(Continued)

75,000

At least	But less than	Single	Married filing jointly *	Married filing separately	Head of a household
75,000	75,050	14,528	10,326	14,528	13,054
75,050	75,100	14,540	10,334	14,540	13,066
75,100	75,150	14,553	10,341	14,553	13,079
75,150	75,200	14,565	10,349	14,565	13,091
75,200	75,250	14,578	10,356	14,578	13,104
75,250	75,300	14,590	10,364	14,590	13,116
75,300	75,350	14,603	10,374	14,603	13,129
75,350	75,400	14,615	10,386	14,615	13,141
75,400	75,450	14,628	10,399	14,628	13,154
75,450	75,500	14,640	10,411	14,640	13,166
75,500	75,550	14,653	10,424	14,653	13,179
75,550	75,600	14,665	10,436	14,665	13,191
75,600	75,650	14,678	10,449	14,678	13,204
75,650	75,700	14,690	10,461	14,690	13,216
75,700	75,750	14,703	10,474	14,703	13,229
75,750	75,800	14,715	10,486	14,715	13,241
75,800	75,850	14,728	10,499	14,728	13,254
75,850	75,900	14,740	10,511	14,740	13,266
75,900	75,950	14,753	10,524	14,753	13,279
75,950	76,000	14,765	10,536	14,766	13,291

76,000

At least	But less than	Single	Married filing jointly *	Married filing separately	Head of a household
76,000	76,050	14,778	10,549	14,780	13,304
76,050	76,100	14,790	10,561	14,794	13,316
76,100	76,150	14,803	10,574	14,808	13,329
76,150	76,200	14,815	10,586	14,822	13,341
76,200	76,250	14,828	10,599	14,836	13,354
76,250	76,300	14,840	10,611	14,850	13,366
76,300	76,350	14,853	10,624	14,864	13,379
76,350	76,400	14,865	10,636	14,878	13,391
76,400	76,450	14,878	10,649	14,892	13,404
76,450	76,500	14,890	10,661	14,906	13,416
76,500	76,550	14,903	10,674	14,920	13,429
76,550	76,600	14,915	10,686	14,934	13,441
76,600	76,650	14,928	10,699	14,948	13,454
76,650	76,700	14,940	10,711	14,962	13,466
76,700	76,750	14,953	10,724	14,976	13,479
76,750	76,800	14,965	10,736	14,990	13,491
76,800	76,850	14,978	10,749	15,004	13,504
76,850	76,900	14,990	10,761	15,018	13,516
76,900	76,950	15,003	10,774	15,032	13,529
76,950	77,000	15,015	10,786	15,046	13,541

77,000

At least	But less than	Single	Married filing jointly *	Married filing separately	Head of a household
77,000	77,050	15,028	10,799	15,060	13,554
77,050	77,100	15,040	10,811	15,074	13,566
77,100	77,150	15,053	10,824	15,088	13,579
77,150	77,200	15,065	10,836	15,102	13,591
77,200	77,250	15,078	10,849	15,116	13,604
77,250	77,300	15,090	10,861	15,130	13,616
77,300	77,350	15,103	10,874	15,144	13,629
77,350	77,400	15,115	10,886	15,158	13,641
77,400	77,450	15,128	10,899	15,172	13,654
77,450	77,500	15,140	10,911	15,186	13,666
77,500	77,550	15,153	10,924	15,200	13,679
77,550	77,600	15,165	10,936	15,214	13,691
77,600	77,650	15,178	10,949	15,228	13,704
77,650	77,700	15,190	10,961	15,242	13,716
77,700	77,750	15,203	10,974	15,256	13,729
77,750	77,800	15,215	10,986	15,270	13,741
77,800	77,850	15,228	10,999	15,284	13,754
77,850	77,900	15,240	11,011	15,298	13,766
77,900	77,950	15,253	11,024	15,312	13,779
77,950	78,000	15,265	11,036	15,326	13,791

78,000

At least	But less than	Single	Married filing jointly *	Married filing separately	Head of a household
78,000	78,050	15,278	11,049	15,340	13,804
78,050	78,100	15,290	11,061	15,354	13,816
78,100	78,150	15,303	11,074	15,368	13,829
78,150	78,200	15,315	11,086	15,382	13,841
78,200	78,250	15,328	11,099	15,396	13,854
78,250	78,300	15,340	11,111	15,410	13,866
78,300	78,350	15,353	11,124	15,424	13,879
78,350	78,400	15,365	11,136	15,438	13,891
78,400	78,450	15,378	11,149	15,452	13,904
78,450	78,500	15,390	11,161	15,466	13,916
78,500	78,550	15,403	11,174	15,480	13,929
78,550	78,600	15,415	11,186	15,494	13,941
78,600	78,650	15,428	11,199	15,508	13,954
78,650	78,700	15,440	11,211	15,522	13,966
78,700	78,750	15,453	11,224	15,536	13,979
78,750	78,800	15,465	11,236	15,550	13,991
78,800	78,850	15,478	11,249	15,564	14,004
78,850	78,900	15,490	11,261	15,578	14,016
78,900	78,950	15,503	11,274	15,592	14,029
78,950	79,000	15,515	11,286	15,606	14,041

79,000

At least	But less than	Single	Married filing jointly *	Married filing separately	Head of a household
79,000	79,050	15,528	11,299	15,620	14,054
79,050	79,100	15,540	11,311	15,634	14,066
79,100	79,150	15,553	11,324	15,648	14,079
79,150	79,200	15,565	11,336	15,662	14,091
79,200	79,250	15,578	11,349	15,676	14,104
79,250	79,300	15,590	11,361	15,690	14,116
79,300	79,350	15,603	11,374	15,704	14,129
79,350	79,400	15,615	11,386	15,718	14,141
79,400	79,450	15,628	11,399	15,732	14,154
79,450	79,500	15,640	11,411	15,746	14,166
79,500	79,550	15,653	11,424	15,760	14,179
79,550	79,600	15,665	11,436	15,774	14,191
79,600	79,650	15,678	11,449	15,788	14,204
79,650	79,700	15,690	11,461	15,802	14,216
79,700	79,750	15,703	11,474	15,816	14,229
79,750	79,800	15,715	11,486	15,830	14,241
79,800	79,850	15,728	11,499	15,844	14,254
79,850	79,900	15,740	11,511	15,858	14,266
79,900	79,950	15,753	11,524	15,872	14,279
79,950	80,000	15,765	11,536	15,886	14,291

80,000

At least	But less than	Single	Married filing jointly *	Married filing separately	Head of a household
80,000	80,050	15,778	11,549	15,900	14,304
80,050	80,100	15,790	11,561	15,914	14,316
80,100	80,150	15,803	11,574	15,928	14,329
80,150	80,200	15,815	11,586	15,942	14,341
80,200	80,250	15,828	11,599	15,956	14,354
80,250	80,300	15,840	11,611	15,970	14,366
80,300	80,350	15,853	11,624	15,984	14,379
80,350	80,400	15,865	11,636	15,998	14,391
80,400	80,450	15,878	11,649	16,012	14,404
80,450	80,500	15,890	11,661	16,026	14,416
80,500	80,550	15,903	11,674	16,040	14,429
80,550	80,600	15,915	11,686	16,054	14,441
80,600	80,650	15,928	11,699	16,068	14,454
80,650	80,700	15,940	11,711	16,082	14,466
80,700	80,750	15,953	11,724	16,096	14,479
80,750	80,800	15,965	11,736	16,110	14,491
80,800	80,850	15,978	11,749	16,124	14,504
80,850	80,900	15,990	11,761	16,138	14,516
80,900	80,950	16,003	11,774	16,152	14,529
80,950	81,000	16,015	11,786	16,166	14,541

81,000

At least	But less than	Single	Married filing jointly *	Married filing separately	Head of a household
81,000	81,050	16,028	11,799	16,180	14,554
81,050	81,100	16,040	11,811	16,194	14,566
81,100	81,150	16,053	11,824	16,208	14,579
81,150	81,200	16,065	11,836	16,222	14,591
81,200	81,250	16,078	11,849	16,236	14,604
81,250	81,300	16,090	11,861	16,250	14,616
81,300	81,350	16,103	11,874	16,264	14,629
81,350	81,400	16,115	11,886	16,278	14,641
81,400	81,450	16,128	11,899	16,292	14,654
81,450	81,500	16,140	11,911	16,306	14,666
81,500	81,550	16,153	11,924	16,320	14,679
81,550	81,600	16,165	11,936	16,334	14,691
81,600	81,650	16,178	11,949	16,348	14,704
81,650	81,700	16,190	11,961	16,362	14,716
81,700	81,750	16,203	11,974	16,376	14,729
81,750	81,800	16,215	11,986	16,390	14,741
81,800	81,850	16,228	11,999	16,404	14,754
81,850	81,900	16,240	12,011	16,418	14,766
81,900	81,950	16,253	12,024	16,432	14,779
81,950	82,000	16,265	12,036	16,446	14,791

82,000

At least	But less than	Single	Married filing jointly *	Married filing separately	Head of a household
82,000	82,050	16,278	12,049	16,460	14,804
82,050	82,100	16,290	12,061	16,474	14,816
82,100	82,150	16,303	12,074	16,488	14,829
82,150	82,200	16,315	12,086	16,502	14,841
82,200	82,250	16,328	12,099	16,516	14,854
82,250	82,300	16,340	12,111	16,530	14,866
82,300	82,350	16,353	12,124	16,544	14,879
82,350	82,400	16,365	12,136	16,558	14,891
82,400	82,450	16,378	12,149	16,572	14,904
82,450	82,500	16,390	12,161	16,586	14,916
82,500	82,550	16,403	12,174	16,600	14,929
82,550	82,600	16,415	12,186	16,614	14,941
82,600	82,650	16,428	12,199	16,628	14,954
82,650	82,700	16,440	12,211	16,642	14,966
82,700	82,750	16,453	12,224	16,656	14,979
82,750	82,800	16,465	12,236	16,670	14,991
82,800	82,850	16,478	12,249	16,684	15,004
82,850	82,900	16,490	12,261	16,698	15,016
82,900	82,950	16,503	12,274	16,712	15,029
82,950	83,000	16,515	12,286	16,726	15,041

83,000

At least	But less than	Single	Married filing jointly *	Married filing separately	Head of a household
83,000	83,050	16,528	12,299	16,740	15,054
83,050	83,100	16,540	12,311	16,754	15,066
83,100	83,150	16,553	12,324	16,768	15,079
83,150	83,200	16,565	12,336	16,782	15,091
83,200	83,250	16,578	12,349	16,796	15,104
83,250	83,300	16,590	12,361	16,810	15,116
83,300	83,350	16,603	12,374	16,824	15,129
83,350	83,400	16,615	12,386	16,838	15,141
83,400	83,450	16,628	12,399	16,852	15,154
83,450	83,500	16,640	12,411	16,866	15,166
83,500	83,550	16,653	12,424	16,880	15,179
83,550	83,600	16,665	12,436	16,894	15,191
83,600	83,650	16,678	12,449	16,908	15,204
83,650	83,700	16,690	12,461	16,922	15,216
83,700	83,750	16,703	12,474	16,936	15,229
83,750	83,800	16,715	12,486	16,950	15,241
83,800	83,850	16,728	12,499	16,964	15,254
83,850	83,900	16,740	12,511	16,978	15,266
83,900	83,950	16,753	12,524	16,992	15,279
83,950	84,000	16,765	12,536	17,006	15,291

(Continued)

* This column must also be used by a qualifying widow(er).

Need more information or forms? Visit IRS.gov.

84,000

At least	But less than	Single	Married filing jointly *	Married filing separately	Head of a household
84,000	84,050	16,778	12,549	17,020	15,304
84,050	84,100	16,790	12,561	17,034	15,316
84,100	84,150	16,803	12,574	17,048	15,329
84,150	84,200	16,815	12,586	17,062	15,341
84,200	84,250	16,828	12,599	17,076	15,354
84,250	84,300	16,840	12,611	17,090	15,366
84,300	84,350	16,853	12,624	17,104	15,379
84,350	84,400	16,865	12,636	17,118	15,391
84,400	84,450	16,878	12,649	17,132	15,404
84,450	84,500	16,890	12,661	17,146	15,416
84,500	84,550	16,903	12,674	17,160	15,429
84,550	84,600	16,915	12,686	17,174	15,441
84,600	84,650	16,928	12,699	17,188	15,454
84,650	84,700	16,940	12,711	17,202	15,466
84,700	84,750	16,953	12,724	17,216	15,479
84,750	84,800	16,965	12,736	17,230	15,491
84,800	84,850	16,978	12,749	17,244	15,504
84,850	84,900	16,990	12,761	17,258	15,516
84,900	84,950	17,003	12,774	17,272	15,529
84,950	85,000	17,015	12,786	17,286	15,541

85,000

At least	But less than	Single	Married filing jointly *	Married filing separately	Head of a household
85,000	85,050	17,028	12,799	17,300	15,554
85,050	85,100	17,040	12,811	17,314	15,566
85,100	85,150	17,053	12,824	17,328	15,579
85,150	85,200	17,065	12,836	17,342	15,591
85,200	85,250	17,078	12,849	17,356	15,604
85,250	85,300	17,090	12,861	17,370	15,616
85,300	85,350	17,103	12,874	17,384	15,629
85,350	85,400	17,115	12,886	17,398	15,641
85,400	85,450	17,128	12,899	17,412	15,654
85,450	85,500	17,140	12,911	17,426	15,666
85,500	85,550	17,153	12,924	17,440	15,679
85,550	85,600	17,165	12,936	17,454	15,691
85,600	85,650	17,178	12,949	17,468	15,704
85,650	85,700	17,190	12,961	17,482	15,716
85,700	85,750	17,203	12,974	17,496	15,729
85,750	85,800	17,215	12,986	17,510	15,741
85,800	85,850	17,228	12,999	17,524	15,754
85,850	85,900	17,240	13,011	17,538	15,766
85,900	85,950	17,253	13,024	17,552	15,779
85,950	86,000	17,265	13,036	17,566	15,791

86,000

At least	But less than	Single	Married filing jointly *	Married filing separately	Head of a household
86,000	86,050	17,278	13,049	17,580	15,804
86,050	86,100	17,290	13,061	17,594	15,816
86,100	86,150	17,303	13,074	17,608	15,829
86,150	86,200	17,315	13,086	17,622	15,841
86,200	86,250	17,328	13,099	17,636	15,854
86,250	86,300	17,340	13,111	17,650	15,866
86,300	86,350	17,353	13,124	17,664	15,879
86,350	86,400	17,365	13,136	17,678	15,891
86,400	86,450	17,378	13,149	17,692	15,904
86,450	86,500	17,390	13,161	17,706	15,916
86,500	86,550	17,403	13,174	17,720	15,929
86,550	86,600	17,415	13,186	17,734	15,941
86,600	86,650	17,428	13,199	17,748	15,954
86,650	86,700	17,440	13,211	17,762	15,966
86,700	86,750	17,453	13,224	17,776	15,979
86,750	86,800	17,465	13,236	17,790	15,991
86,800	86,850	17,478	13,249	17,804	16,004
86,850	86,900	17,490	13,261	17,818	16,016
86,900	86,950	17,503	13,274	17,832	16,029
86,950	87,000	17,515	13,286	17,846	16,041

87,000

At least	But less than	Single	Married filing jointly *	Married filing separately	Head of a household
87,000	87,050	17,528	13,299	17,860	16,054
87,050	87,100	17,540	13,311	17,874	16,066
87,100	87,150	17,553	13,324	17,888	16,079
87,150	87,200	17,565	13,336	17,902	16,091
87,200	87,250	17,578	13,349	17,916	16,104
87,250	87,300	17,590	13,361	17,930	16,116
87,300	87,350	17,603	13,374	17,944	16,129
87,350	87,400	17,615	13,386	17,958	16,141
87,400	87,450	17,628	13,399	17,972	16,154
87,450	87,500	17,640	13,411	17,986	16,166
87,500	87,550	17,653	13,424	18,000	16,179
87,550	87,600	17,665	13,436	18,014	16,191
87,600	87,650	17,678	13,449	18,028	16,204
87,650	87,700	17,690	13,461	18,042	16,216
87,700	87,750	17,703	13,474	18,056	16,229
87,750	87,800	17,715	13,486	18,070	16,241
87,800	87,850	17,728	13,499	18,084	16,254
87,850	87,900	17,740	13,511	18,098	16,266
87,900	87,950	17,753	13,524	18,112	16,279
87,950	88,000	17,765	13,536	18,126	16,291

88,000

At least	But less than	Single	Married filing jointly *	Married filing separately	Head of a household
88,000	88,050	17,778	13,549	18,140	16,304
88,050	88,100	17,790	13,561	18,154	16,316
88,100	88,150	17,803	13,574	18,168	16,329
88,150	88,200	17,815	13,586	18,182	16,341
88,200	88,250	17,828	13,599	18,196	16,354
88,250	88,300	17,840	13,611	18,210	16,366
88,300	88,350	17,853	13,624	18,224	16,379
88,350	88,400	17,865	13,636	18,238	16,391
88,400	88,450	17,878	13,649	18,252	16,404
88,450	88,500	17,890	13,661	18,266	16,416
88,500	88,550	17,903	13,674	18,280	16,429
88,550	88,600	17,915	13,686	18,294	16,441
88,600	88,650	17,928	13,699	18,308	16,454
88,650	88,700	17,940	13,711	18,322	16,466
88,700	88,750	17,953	13,724	18,336	16,479
88,750	88,800	17,965	13,736	18,350	16,491
88,800	88,850	17,978	13,749	18,364	16,504
88,850	88,900	17,990	13,761	18,378	16,516
88,900	88,950	18,003	13,774	18,392	16,529
88,950	89,000	18,015	13,786	18,406	16,541

89,000

At least	But less than	Single	Married filing jointly *	Married filing separately	Head of a household
89,000	89,050	18,028	13,799	18,420	16,554
89,050	89,100	18,040	13,811	18,434	16,566
89,100	89,150	18,053	13,824	18,448	16,579
89,150	89,200	18,065	13,836	18,462	16,591
89,200	89,250	18,078	13,849	18,476	16,604
89,250	89,300	18,090	13,861	18,490	16,616
89,300	89,350	18,103	13,874	18,504	16,629
89,350	89,400	18,115	13,886	18,518	16,641
89,400	89,450	18,128	13,899	18,532	16,654
89,450	89,500	18,140	13,911	18,546	16,666
89,500	89,550	18,153	13,924	18,560	16,679
89,550	89,600	18,165	13,936	18,574	16,691
89,600	89,650	18,178	13,949	18,588	16,704
89,650	89,700	18,190	13,961	18,602	16,716
89,700	89,750	18,203	13,974	18,616	16,729
89,750	89,800	18,215	13,986	18,630	16,741
89,800	89,850	18,228	13,999	18,644	16,754
89,850	89,900	18,240	14,011	18,658	16,766
89,900	89,950	18,253	14,024	18,672	16,779
89,950	90,000	18,265	14,036	18,686	16,791

90,000

At least	But less than	Single	Married filing jointly *	Married filing separately	Head of a household
90,000	90,050	18,278	14,049	18,700	16,804
90,050	90,100	18,290	14,061	18,714	16,816
90,100	90,150	18,303	14,074	18,728	16,829
90,150	90,200	18,315	14,086	18,742	16,841
90,200	90,250	18,328	14,099	18,756	16,854
90,250	90,300	18,340	14,111	18,770	16,866
90,300	90,350	18,353	14,124	18,784	16,879
90,350	90,400	18,365	14,136	18,798	16,891
90,400	90,450	18,378	14,149	18,812	16,904
90,450	90,500	18,390	14,161	18,826	16,916
90,500	90,550	18,403	14,174	18,840	16,929
90,550	90,600	18,415	14,186	18,854	16,941
90,600	90,650	18,428	14,199	18,868	16,954
90,650	90,700	18,440	14,211	18,882	16,966
90,700	90,750	18,453	14,224	18,896	16,979
90,750	90,800	18,465	14,236	18,910	16,991
90,800	90,850	18,478	14,249	18,924	17,004
90,850	90,900	18,490	14,261	18,938	17,016
90,900	90,950	18,503	14,274	18,952	17,029
90,950	91,000	18,515	14,286	18,966	17,041

91,000

At least	But less than	Single	Married filing jointly *	Married filing separately	Head of a household
91,000	91,050	18,528	14,299	18,980	17,054
91,050	91,100	18,540	14,311	18,994	17,066
91,100	91,150	18,553	14,324	19,008	17,079
91,150	91,200	18,566	14,336	19,022	17,091
91,200	91,250	18,580	14,349	19,036	17,104
91,250	91,300	18,594	14,361	19,050	17,116
91,300	91,350	18,608	14,374	19,064	17,129
91,350	91,400	18,622	14,386	19,078	17,141
91,400	91,450	18,636	14,399	19,092	17,154
91,450	91,500	18,650	14,411	19,106	17,166
91,500	91,550	18,664	14,424	19,120	17,179
91,550	91,600	18,678	14,436	19,134	17,191
91,600	91,650	18,692	14,449	19,148	17,204
91,650	91,700	18,706	14,461	19,162	17,216
91,700	91,750	18,720	14,474	19,176	17,229
91,750	91,800	18,734	14,486	19,190	17,241
91,800	91,850	18,748	14,499	19,204	17,254
91,850	91,900	18,762	14,511	19,218	17,266
91,900	91,950	18,776	14,524	19,232	17,279
91,950	92,000	18,790	14,536	19,246	17,291

92,000

At least	But less than	Single	Married filing jointly *	Married filing separately	Head of a household
92,000	92,050	18,804	14,549	19,260	17,304
92,050	92,100	18,818	14,561	19,274	17,316
92,100	92,150	18,832	14,574	19,288	17,329
92,150	92,200	18,846	14,586	19,302	17,341
92,200	92,250	18,860	14,599	19,316	17,354
92,250	92,300	18,874	14,611	19,330	17,366
92,300	92,350	18,888	14,624	19,344	17,379
92,350	92,400	18,902	14,636	19,358	17,391
92,400	92,450	18,916	14,649	19,372	17,404
92,450	92,500	18,930	14,661	19,386	17,416
92,500	92,550	18,944	14,674	19,400	17,429
92,550	92,600	18,958	14,686	19,414	17,441
92,600	92,650	18,972	14,699	19,428	17,454
92,650	92,700	18,986	14,711	19,442	17,466
92,700	92,750	19,000	14,724	19,456	17,479
92,750	92,800	19,014	14,736	19,470	17,491
92,800	92,850	19,028	14,749	19,484	17,504
92,850	92,900	19,042	14,761	19,498	17,516
92,900	92,950	19,056	14,774	19,512	17,529
92,950	93,000	19,070	14,786	19,526	17,541

(Continued)

* This column must also be used by a qualifying widow(er).

If line 43 (taxable income) is—		And you are—			
At least	But less than	Single	Married filing jointly *	Married filing separately	Head of a household
		Your tax is—			

93,000

At least	But less than	Single	Married filing jointly *	Married filing separately	Head of a household
93,000	93,050	19,084	14,799	19,540	17,554
93,050	93,100	19,098	14,811	19,554	17,566
93,100	93,150	19,112	14,824	19,568	17,579
93,150	93,200	19,126	14,836	19,582	17,591
93,200	93,250	19,140	14,849	19,596	17,604
93,250	93,300	19,154	14,861	19,610	17,616
93,300	93,350	19,168	14,874	19,624	17,629
93,350	93,400	19,182	14,886	19,638	17,641
93,400	93,450	19,196	14,899	19,652	17,654
93,450	93,500	19,210	14,911	19,666	17,666
93,500	93,550	19,224	14,924	19,680	17,679
93,550	93,600	19,238	14,936	19,694	17,691
93,600	93,650	19,252	14,949	19,708	17,704
93,650	93,700	19,266	14,961	19,722	17,716
93,700	93,750	19,280	14,974	19,736	17,729
93,750	93,800	19,294	14,986	19,750	17,741
93,800	93,850	19,308	14,999	19,764	17,754
93,850	93,900	19,322	15,011	19,778	17,766
93,900	93,950	19,336	15,024	19,792	17,779
93,950	94,000	19,350	15,036	19,806	17,791

94,000

At least	But less than	Single	Married filing jointly *	Married filing separately	Head of a household
94,000	94,050	19,364	15,049	19,820	17,804
94,050	94,100	19,378	15,061	19,834	17,816
94,100	94,150	19,392	15,074	19,848	17,829
94,150	94,200	19,406	15,086	19,862	17,841
94,200	94,250	19,420	15,099	19,876	17,854
94,250	94,300	19,434	15,111	19,890	17,866
94,300	94,350	19,448	15,124	19,904	17,879
94,350	94,400	19,462	15,136	19,918	17,891
94,400	94,450	19,476	15,149	19,932	17,904
94,450	94,500	19,490	15,161	19,946	17,916
94,500	94,550	19,504	15,174	19,960	17,929
94,550	94,600	19,518	15,186	19,974	17,941
94,600	94,650	19,532	15,199	19,988	17,954
94,650	94,700	19,546	15,211	20,002	17,966
94,700	94,750	19,560	15,224	20,016	17,979
94,750	94,800	19,574	15,236	20,030	17,991
94,800	94,850	19,588	15,249	20,044	18,004
94,850	94,900	19,602	15,261	20,058	18,016
94,900	94,950	19,616	15,274	20,072	18,029
94,950	95,000	19,630	15,286	20,086	18,041

95,000

At least	But less than	Single	Married filing jointly *	Married filing separately	Head of a household
95,000	95,050	19,644	15,299	20,100	18,054
95,050	95,100	19,658	15,311	20,114	18,066
95,100	95,150	19,672	15,324	20,128	18,079
95,150	95,200	19,686	15,336	20,142	18,091
95,200	95,250	19,700	15,349	20,156	18,104
95,250	95,300	19,714	15,361	20,170	18,116
95,300	95,350	19,728	15,374	20,184	18,129
95,350	95,400	19,742	15,386	20,198	18,141
95,400	95,450	19,756	15,399	20,212	18,154
95,450	95,500	19,770	15,411	20,226	18,166
95,500	95,550	19,784	15,424	20,240	18,179
95,550	95,600	19,798	15,436	20,254	18,191
95,600	95,650	19,812	15,449	20,268	18,204
95,650	95,700	19,826	15,461	20,282	18,216
95,700	95,750	19,840	15,474	20,296	18,229
95,750	95,800	19,854	15,486	20,310	18,241
95,800	95,850	19,868	15,499	20,324	18,254
95,850	95,900	19,882	15,511	20,338	18,266
95,900	95,950	19,896	15,524	20,352	18,279
95,950	96,000	19,910	15,536	20,366	18,291

96,000

At least	But less than	Single	Married filing jointly *	Married filing separately	Head of a household
96,000	96,050	19,924	15,549	20,380	18,304
96,050	96,100	19,938	15,561	20,394	18,316
96,100	96,150	19,952	15,574	20,408	18,329
96,150	96,200	19,966	15,586	20,422	18,341
96,200	96,250	19,980	15,599	20,436	18,354
96,250	96,300	19,994	15,611	20,450	18,366
96,300	96,350	20,008	15,624	20,464	18,379
96,350	96,400	20,022	15,636	20,478	18,391
96,400	96,450	20,036	15,649	20,492	18,404
96,450	96,500	20,050	15,661	20,506	18,416
96,500	96,550	20,064	15,674	20,520	18,429
96,550	96,600	20,078	15,686	20,534	18,441
96,600	96,650	20,092	15,699	20,548	18,454
96,650	96,700	20,106	15,711	20,562	18,466
96,700	96,750	20,120	15,724	20,576	18,479
96,750	96,800	20,134	15,736	20,590	18,491
96,800	96,850	20,148	15,749	20,604	18,504
96,850	96,900	20,162	15,761	20,618	18,516
96,900	96,950	20,176	15,774	20,632	18,529
96,950	97,000	20,190	15,786	20,646	18,541

97,000

At least	But less than	Single	Married filing jointly *	Married filing separately	Head of a household
97,000	97,050	20,204	15,799	20,660	18,554
97,050	97,100	20,218	15,811	20,674	18,566
97,100	97,150	20,232	15,824	20,688	18,579
97,150	97,200	20,246	15,836	20,702	18,591
97,200	97,250	20,260	15,849	20,716	18,604
97,250	97,300	20,274	15,861	20,730	18,616
97,300	97,350	20,288	15,874	20,744	18,629
97,350	97,400	20,302	15,886	20,758	18,641
97,400	97,450	20,316	15,899	20,772	18,654
97,450	97,500	20,330	15,911	20,786	18,666
97,500	97,550	20,344	15,924	20,800	18,679
97,550	97,600	20,358	15,936	20,814	18,691
97,600	97,650	20,372	15,949	20,828	18,704
97,650	97,700	20,386	15,961	20,842	18,716
97,700	97,750	20,400	15,974	20,856	18,729
97,750	97,800	20,414	15,986	20,870	18,741
97,800	97,850	20,428	15,999	20,884	18,754
97,850	97,900	20,442	16,011	20,898	18,766
97,900	97,950	20,456	16,024	20,912	18,779
97,950	98,000	20,470	16,036	20,926	18,791

98,000

At least	But less than	Single	Married filing jointly *	Married filing separately	Head of a household
98,000	98,050	20,484	16,049	20,940	18,804
98,050	98,100	20,498	16,061	20,954	18,816
98,100	98,150	20,512	16,074	20,968	18,829
98,150	98,200	20,526	16,086	20,982	18,841
98,200	98,250	20,540	16,099	20,996	18,854
98,250	98,300	20,554	16,111	21,010	18,866
98,300	98,350	20,568	16,124	21,024	18,879
98,350	98,400	20,582	16,136	21,038	18,891
98,400	98,450	20,596	16,149	21,052	18,904
98,450	98,500	20,610	16,161	21,066	18,916
98,500	98,550	20,624	16,174	21,080	18,929
98,550	98,600	20,638	16,186	21,094	18,941
98,600	98,650	20,652	16,199	21,108	18,954
98,650	98,700	20,666	16,211	21,122	18,966
98,700	98,750	20,680	16,224	21,136	18,979
98,750	98,800	20,694	16,236	21,150	18,991
98,800	98,850	20,708	16,249	21,164	19,004
98,850	98,900	20,722	16,261	21,178	19,016
98,900	98,950	20,736	16,274	21,192	19,029
98,950	99,000	20,750	16,286	21,206	19,041

99,000

At least	But less than	Single	Married filing jointly *	Married filing separately	Head of a household
99,000	99,050	20,764	16,299	21,220	19,054
99,050	99,100	20,778	16,311	21,234	19,066
99,100	99,150	20,792	16,324	21,248	19,079
99,150	99,200	20,806	16,336	21,262	19,091
99,200	99,250	20,820	16,349	21,276	19,104
99,250	99,300	20,834	16,361	21,290	19,116
99,300	99,350	20,848	16,374	21,304	19,129
99,350	99,400	20,862	16,386	21,318	19,141
99,400	99,450	20,876	16,399	21,332	19,154
99,450	99,500	20,890	16,411	21,346	19,166
99,500	99,550	20,904	16,424	21,360	19,179
99,550	99,600	20,918	16,436	21,374	19,191
99,600	99,650	20,932	16,449	21,388	19,204
99,650	99,700	20,946	16,461	21,402	19,216
99,700	99,750	20,960	16,474	21,416	19,229
99,750	99,800	20,974	16,486	21,430	19,241
99,800	99,850	20,988	16,499	21,444	19,254
99,850	99,900	21,002	16,511	21,458	19,266
99,900	99,950	21,016	16,524	21,472	19,279
99,950	100,000	21,030	16,536	21,486	19,291

$100,000 or over
use the Tax Computation Worksheet

* This column must also be used by a qualifying widow(er).

Need more information or forms? Visit IRS.gov.

2016 Tax Computation Worksheet—Line 44

 See the instructions for line 44 to see if you must use the worksheet below to figure your tax.

Note. If you are required to use this worksheet to figure the tax on an amount from another form or worksheet, such as the Qualified Dividends and Capital Gain Tax Worksheet, the Schedule D Tax Worksheet, Schedule J, Form 8615, or the Foreign Earned Income Tax Worksheet, enter the amount from that form or worksheet in column (a) of the row that applies to the amount you are looking up. Enter the result on the appropriate line of the form or worksheet that you are completing.

Section A—Use if your filing status is **Single.** Complete the row below that applies to you.

Taxable income. If line 43 is—	(a) Enter the amount from line 43	(b) Multiplication amount	(c) Multiply (a) by (b)	(d) Subtraction amount	Tax. Subtract (d) from (c). Enter the result here and on Form 1040, line 44
At least $100,000 but not over $190,150	$	× 28% (0.28)	$	$ 6,963.25	$
Over $190,150 but not over $413,350	$	× 33% (0.33)	$	$ 16,470.75	$
Over $413,350 but not over $415,050	$	× 35% (0.35)	$	$ 24,737.75	$
Over $415,050	$	× 39.6% (0.396)	$	$ 43,830.05	$

Section B—Use if your filing status is **Married filing jointly** or **Qualifying widow(er).** Complete the row below that applies to you.

Taxable income. If line 43 is—	(a) Enter the amount from line 43	(b) Multiplication amount	(c) Multiply (a) by (b)	(d) Subtraction amount	Tax. Subtract (d) from (c). Enter the result here and on Form 1040, line 44
At least $100,000 but not over $151,900	$	× 25% (0.25)	$	$ 8,457.50	$
Over $151,900 but not over $231,450	$	× 28% (0.28)	$	$ 13,014.50	$
Over $231,450 but not over $413,350	$	× 33% (0.33)	$	$ 24,587.00	$
Over $413,350 but not over $466,950	$	× 35% (0.35)	$	$ 32,854.00	$
Over $466,950	$	× 39.6% (0.396)	$	$ 54,333.70	$

Section C—Use if your filing status is **Married filing separately.** Complete the row below that applies to you.

Taxable income. If line 43 is—	(a) Enter the amount from line 43	(b) Multiplication amount	(c) Multiply (a) by (b)	(d) Subtraction amount	Tax. Subtract (d) from (c). Enter the result here and on Form 1040, line 44
At least $100,000 but not over $115,725	$	× 28% (0.28)	$	$ 6,507.25	$
Over $115,725 but not over $206,675	$	× 33% (0.33)	$	$ 12,293.50	$
Over $206,675 but not over $233,475	$	× 35% (0.35)	$	$ 16,427.00	$
Over $233,475	$	× 39.6% (0.396)	$	$ 27,166.85	$

Section D—Use if your filing status is **Head of household.** Complete the row below that applies to you.

Taxable income. If line 43 is—	(a) Enter the amount from line 43	(b) Multiplication amount	(c) Multiply (a) by (b)	(d) Subtraction amount	Tax. Subtract (d) from (c). Enter the result here and on Form 1040, line 44
At least $100,000 but not over $130,150	$	× 25% (0.25)	$	$ 5,702.50	$
Over $130,150 but not over $210,800	$	× 28% (0.28)	$	$ 9,607.00	$
Over $210,800 but not over $413,350	$	× 33% (0.33)	$	$ 20,147.00	$
Over $413,350 but not over $441,000	$	× 35% (0.35)	$	$ 28,414.00	$
Over $441,000	$	× 39.6% (0.396)	$	$ 48,700.00	$

General Information

The IRS Mission. Provide America's taxpayers top-quality service by helping them understand and meet their tax responsibilities and enforce the law with integrity and fairness to all.

How To Avoid Common Mistakes

Mistakes can delay your refund or result in notices being sent to you. One of the best ways to file an accurate return is to file electronically. Tax software does the math for you and will help you avoid mistakes. You may be eligible to use free tax software that will take the guesswork out of preparing your return. Free File makes available free brand-name software and free *e-file*. Visit *IRS.gov/freefile* for details. Join the eight in 10 taxpayers who get their refunds faster by using direct deposit and *e-file*.

- Make sure you entered the correct name and social security number (SSN) for each dependent you claim on line 6c. Check that each dependent's name and SSN agrees with his or her social security card. For each child under age 17 who is a qualifying child for the child tax credit, make sure you checked the box in line 6c, column (4).
- Check your math, especially for the child tax credit, earned income credit (EIC), taxable social security benefits, total income, itemized deductions or standard deduction, deduction for exemptions, taxable income, total tax, federal income tax withheld, and refund or amount you owe.
- Be sure you used the correct method to figure your tax. See the instructions for line 44.
- Be sure to enter your SSN in the space provided on page 1 of Form 1040. If you are married filing a joint or separate return, also enter your spouse's SSN. Be sure to enter your SSN in the space next to your name. Check that your name and SSN agree with your social security card.
- Make sure your name and address are correct. Enter your (and your spouse's) name in the same order as shown on your last return.
- If you live in an apartment, be sure to include your apartment number in your address.

- If you are taking the standard deduction, see the instructions for line 40 to be sure you entered the correct amount.
- If you received capital gain distributions but weren't required to file Schedule D, make sure you checked the box on line 13.
- If you are taking the EIC, be sure you used the correct column of the EIC Table for your filing status and the number of children you have.
- Remember to sign and date Form 1040 and enter your occupation(s).
- Attach your Form(s) W-2 and other required forms and schedules. Put all forms and schedules in the proper order. See *Assemble Your Return,* earlier.
- If you owe tax and are paying by check or money order, be sure to include all the required information on your payment. See the instructions for line 78 for details.
- Do not file more than one original return for the same year, even if you haven't gotten your refund or haven't heard from the IRS since you filed. Filing more than one original return for the same year, or sending in more than one copy of the same return (unless we ask you to do so), could delay your refund.

Innocent Spouse Relief

Generally, both you and your spouse are each responsible for paying the full amount of tax, interest, and penalties on your joint return. However, you may qualify for relief from liability for tax on a joint return if (a) there is an understatement of tax because your spouse omitted income or claimed false deductions or credits, (b) you are divorced, separated, or no longer living with your spouse, or (c) given all the facts and circumstances, it wouldn't be fair to hold you liable for the tax. You may also qualify for relief if you were a married resident of a community property state but didn't file a joint return and are now liable for an unpaid or understated tax. File Form 8857 to request relief. In some cases, Form 8857 may need to be

filed within 2 years of the date on which the IRS first attempted to collect the tax from you. Do not file Form 8857 with your Form 1040. For more information, see Pub. 971 and Form 8857 or you can call the Innocent Spouse office toll-free at 1-855-851-2009.

Income Tax Withholding and Estimated Tax Payments for 2017

If the amount you owe or the amount you overpaid is large, you may want to file a new Form W-4 with your employer to change the amount of income tax withheld from your 2017 pay. For details on how to complete Form W-4, see Pub. 505. If you have pension or annuity income, use Form W-4P. If you receive certain government payments (such as unemployment compensation or social security benefits), you can have tax withheld from those payments by giving the payer Form W-4V.

 You can use the IRS Withholding Calculator instead of Pub. 505 or the worksheets included with Form W-4 or W-4P, to determine whether you need to have your withholding increased or decreased.

In general, you do not have to make estimated tax payments if you expect that your 2017 Form 1040 will show a tax refund or a tax balance due of less than $1,000. If your total estimated tax for 2017 is $1,000 or more, see Form 1040-ES and Pub. 505 for a worksheet you can use to see if you have to make estimated tax payments. For more details, see Pub. 505.

Secure Your Tax Records From Identity Theft

Identity theft occurs when someone uses your personal information, such as your name, social security number (SSN), or other identifying information, without your permission, to commit fraud or other crimes. An identity thief may use your SSN to get a job or may file a tax return using your SSN to receive a refund.

To reduce your risk:
- Protect your SSN,
- Ensure your employer is protecting your SSN, and
- Be careful when choosing a tax preparer.

If your tax records are affected by identity theft and you receive a notice from the IRS, respond right away to the name and phone number printed on the IRS notice or letter. For more information, see Pub. 5027.

If your SSN has been lost or stolen or you suspect you are a victim of tax-related identity theft, visit *IRS.gov/ identitytheft* to learn what steps you should take.

Victims of identity theft who are experiencing economic harm or a systemic problem, or are seeking help in resolving tax problems that haven't been resolved through normal channels, may be eligible for Taxpayer Advocate Service (TAS) assistance. You can reach TAS by calling the National Taxpayer Advocate helpline at 1-877-777-4778. People who are deaf, hard of hearing, or have a speech disability and who have access to TTY/TDD equipment can call 1-800-829-4059. Deaf or hard-of-hearing individuals can also contact the IRS through relay services such as the Federal Relay Service available at *www.gsa.gov/fedrelay*.

Protect yourself from suspicious emails or phishing schemes. Phishing is the creation and use of email and websites designed to mimic legitimate business emails and websites. The most common form is sending an email to a user falsely claiming to be an established legitimate enterprise in an attempt to scam the user into surrendering private information that will be used for identity theft.

The IRS doesn't initiate contacts with taxpayers via emails. Also, the IRS doesn't request detailed personal information through email or ask taxpayers for the PIN numbers, passwords, or similar secret access information for their credit card, bank, or other financial accounts.

If you receive an unsolicited email claiming to be from the IRS, forward the message to *phishing@irs.gov*. You may also report misuse of the IRS name, logo, forms, or other IRS property to the Treasury Inspector General for Tax Administration toll-free at 1-800-366-4484. People who are deaf, hard of hearing, or have a speech disability and who have access to TTY/TDD equipment can call 1-800-877-8339. You can forward suspicious emails to the Federal Trade Commission at *spam@uce.gov* or contact them at *www.ftc.gov/idtheft* or 1-877-IDTHEFT (1-877-438-4338). People who are deaf, hard of hearing, or have a speech disability and who have access to TTY/TDD equipment can call 1-866-653-4261.

Visit IRS.gov and enter "identity theft" in the search box to learn more about identity theft and how to reduce your risk.

How Do You Make a Gift To Reduce Debt Held By the Public?

If you wish to do so, make a check payable to "Bureau of the Fiscal Service." You can send it to: Bureau of the Fiscal Service, Attn: Dept G, P.O. Box 2188, Parkersburg, WV 26106-2188. Or you can enclose the check with your income tax return when you file. In the memo section of the check, make a note that it is a gift to reduce the debt held by the public. Do not add your gift to any tax you may owe. See the instructions for line 78 for details on how to pay any tax you owe. For information on how to make this type of gift online, go to *www.treasurydirect.gov* and click on "How To Make a Contribution to Reduce the Debt."

 You may be able to deduct this gift on your 2017 tax return.

How Long Should Records Be Kept?

Keep a copy of your tax return, worksheets you used, and records of all items appearing on it (such as Forms W-2 and 1099) until the statute of limitations runs out for that return. Usually, this is 3 years from the date the return was due or filed or 2 years from the date the tax was

paid, whichever is later. You should keep some records longer. For example, keep property records (including those on your home) as long as they are needed to figure the basis of the original or replacement property. For more details, see chapter 1 of Pub. 17.

Amended Return

File Form 1040X to change a return you already filed. Generally, Form 1040X must be filed within 3 years after the date the original return was filed or within 2 years after the date the tax was paid, whichever is later. But you may have more time to file Form 1040X if you live in a federally declared disaster area or you are physically or mentally unable to manage your financial affairs. See Pub. 556 for details.

Use the *Where's My Amended Return* application on IRS.gov to track the status of your amended return. It can take up to 3 weeks from the date you mailed it to show up in our system.

Need a Copy of Your Tax Return Information?

Tax return transcripts are free and generally are used to validate income and tax filing status for mortgage applications, student and small business loan applications, and during tax preparation. To get a free transcript:
- Visit *IRS.gov/transcript*,
- Use Form 4506-T or 4506T-EZ, or
- Call us at 1-800-908-9946.

If you need a copy of your actual tax return, use Form 4506. There is a fee for each return requested. See Form 4506 for the current fee. If your main home, principal place of business, or tax records are located in a federally declared disaster area, this fee will be waived.

Death of a Taxpayer

If a taxpayer died before filing a return for 2016, the taxpayer's spouse or personal representative may have to file and sign a return for that taxpayer. A personal representative can be an executor, administrator, or anyone who is in charge of the deceased taxpayer's property. If the deceased taxpayer didn't have to file a return but had tax withheld, a return must be filed to get a refund. The person who files the return must enter "Deceased," the deceased taxpayer's name, and the date of death across the top of the return. If this information isn't provided, it may delay the processing of the return.

If your spouse died in 2016 and you didn't remarry in 2016, or if your spouse died in 2017 before filing a return for 2016, you can file a joint return. A joint return should show your spouse's 2016 income before death and your income for all of 2016. Enter "Filing as surviving spouse" in the area where you sign the return. If someone else is the personal representative, he or she must also sign.

The surviving spouse or personal representative should promptly notify all payers of income, including financial institutions, of the taxpayer's death. This will ensure the proper reporting of income earned by the taxpayer's estate or heirs. A deceased taxpayer's social security number shouldn't be used for tax years after the year of death, except for estate tax return purposes.

Claiming a Refund for a Deceased Taxpayer

If you are filing a joint return as a surviving spouse, you only need to file the tax return to claim the refund. If you are a court-appointed representative, file the return and include a copy of the certificate that shows your appointment. All other filers requesting the deceased taxpayer's refund must file the return and attach Form 1310.

For more details, use *Tax Topic 356* or see Pub. 559.

Past Due Returns

If you or someone you know needs to file past due tax returns, use *Tax Topic 153* or go to *IRS.gov/individuals* for help in filing those returns. Send the return to the address that applies to you in the latest Form 1040 instructions. For example, if you are filing a 2013 return in 2017, use the address at the end of these instructions. However, if you got an IRS notice, mail the return to the address in the notice.

How To Get Tax Help

If you have questions about a tax issue, need help preparing your tax return, or want to download free publications, forms, or instructions, go to IRS.gov and find resources that can help you right away.

Preparing and filing your tax return. Find free options to prepare and file your return on IRS.gov or in your local community if you qualify.

The Volunteer Income Tax Assistance (VITA) program offers free tax help to people who generally make $54,000 or less, persons with disabilities, the elderly, and limited-English-speaking taxpayers who need help preparing their own tax returns. The Tax Counseling for the Elderly (TCE) program offers free tax help for all taxpayers, particularly those who are 60 years of age and older. TCE volunteers specialize in answering questions about pensions and retirement-related issues unique to seniors.

You can go to IRS.gov and click on the Filing tab to see your options for preparing and filing your return which include the following.
- **Free File.** Go to *IRS.gov/freefile*. See if you qualify to use brand-name software to prepare and *e-file* your federal tax return for free.
- **VITA.** Go to *IRS.gov/vita*, download the free IRS2Go app, or call 1-800-906-9887 to find the nearest VITA location for free tax preparation.
- **TCE.** Go to *IRS.gov/tce*, download the free IRS2Go app, or call 1-888-227-7669 to find the nearest TCE location for free tax preparation.

Getting answers to your tax law questions. On IRS.gov get answers to your tax questions anytime, anywhere.
- Go to *IRS.gov/help* or *IRS.gov/letushelp* pages for a variety of tools that will help you get answers to some of the most common tax questions.
- Go to *IRS.gov/ita* for the Interactive Tax Assistant, a tool that will ask you questions on a number of tax law topics and provide answers. You can print the entire interview and the final response for your records.
- Go to *IRS.gov/pub17* to get Pub. 17, Your Federal Income Tax for Individuals, which features details on tax-saving opportunities, 2016 tax changes, and thousands of interactive links to help you find answers to your questions. View it online in HTML or as a PDF or, better yet, download it to your mobile device to enjoy eBook features.

- You may also be able to access tax law information in your electronic filing software.

Getting tax forms and publications. Go to *IRS.gov/forms* to view, download, or print all of the forms and publications you may need. You can also download and view popular tax publications and instructions (including the 1040 instructions) on mobile devices as an eBook at no charge. Or, you can go to *IRS.gov/orderforms* to place an order and have forms mailed to you within 10 business days.

Using direct deposit. The fastest way to receive a tax refund is to combine direct deposit and IRS *e-file*. Direct deposit securely and electronically transfers your refund directly into your financial account. Eight in 10 taxpayers use direct deposit to receive their refund. IRS issues more than 90% of refunds in less than 21 days.

Delayed refund for returns claiming certain credits. Due to changes in the law, the IRS can't issue refunds before February 15, 2017, for returns that claim the earned income credit (EIC) or the additional child tax credit (ACTC). This applies to the entire refund, not just the portion associated with these credits.

Getting a transcript or copy of a return. The quickest way to get a copy of your tax transcript is to go to *IRS.gov/transcripts*. Click on either "Get Transcript Online" or "Get Transcript by Mail" to order a copy of your transcript. If you prefer, you can:
- Order your transcript by calling 1-800-908-9946.
- Mail Form 4506-T or Form 4506T-EZ (both available on IRS.gov).

Using online tools to help prepare your return. Go to *IRS.gov/tools* for the following.
- The *Earned Income Tax Credit Assistant* (*IRS.gov/eic*) determines if you are eligible for the EIC.
- The *Online EIN Application* (*IRS.gov/ein*) helps you get an employer identification number.
- The *IRS Withholding Calculator* (*IRS.gov/w4app*) estimates the amount you should have withheld from your paycheck for federal income tax purposes.
- The *First Time Homebuyer Credit Account Look-up* (*IRS.gov/homebuyer*)

tool provides information on your repayments and account balance.

• The *Sales Tax Deduction Calculator* (*IRS.gov/salestax*) figures the amount you can claim if you itemize deductions on Schedule A (Form 1040), choose not to claim state and local income taxes, and you didn't save your receipts showing the sales tax you paid.

For help with the alternative minimum tax, go to *IRS.gov/amt*.

Resolving tax-related identity theft issues.

• The IRS doesn't initiate contact with taxpayers by email or telephone to request personal or financial information. This includes any type of electronic communication, such as text messages and social media channels.

• Go to *IRS.gov/idprotection* for information and videos.

• If your SSN has been lost or stolen or you suspect you are a victim of tax-related identity theft, visit *IRS.gov/id* to learn what steps you should take.

• See *Secure Your Tax Records From Identity Theft* under *General Information*, earlier.

Checking on the status of your refund.

• Go to *IRS.gov/refunds*.

• Due to changes in the law, the IRS can't issue refunds before February 15, 2017, for returns that claim the EIC or ACTC. This applies to the entire refund, not just the portion associated with these credits.

• Download the official IRS2Go app to your mobile device to check your refund status.

• Call the automated refund hotline at 1-800-829-1954. See *Refund Information*, later.

Making a tax payment. The IRS uses the latest encryption technology to ensure your electronic payments are safe and secure. You can make electronic payments online, by phone, and from a mobile device using the IRS2Go app. Paying electronically is quick, easy, and faster than mailing in a check or money order. Go to *IRS.gov/payments* to make a payment using any of the following options.

• *IRS Direct Pay*: Pay your individual tax bill or estimated tax payment directly from your checking or savings account at no cost to you.

• **Debit or credit card:** Choose an approved payment processor to pay online, by phone, and by mobile device.

• **Electronic Funds Withdrawal:** Offered only when filing your federal taxes using tax preparation software or through a tax professional.

• **Electronic Federal Tax Payment System:** Best option for businesses. Enrollment is required.

• **Check or money order:** Mail your payment to the address listed on the notice or instructions.

• **Cash:** If cash is your only option, you may be able to pay your taxes at a participating retail store.

What if I can't pay now? Go to *IRS.gov/payments* for more information about your options.

• Apply for an *online payment agreement* (*IRS.gov/opa*) to meet your tax obligation in monthly installments if you can't pay your taxes in full today. Once you complete the online process, you will receive immediate notification of whether your agreement has been approved.

• Use the *Offer in Compromise Pre-Qualifier* (*IRS.gov/oic*) to see if you can settle your tax debt for less than the full amount you owe.

Checking the status of an amended return. Go to IRS.gov and click on *Where's My Amended Return?* (*IRS.gov/wmar*) under the "Tools" bar to track the status of Form 1040X amended returns. Please note that it can take up to 3 weeks from the date you mailed your amended return for it to show up in our system and processing it can take up to 16 weeks.

Understanding an IRS notice or letter. Go to *IRS.gov/notices* to find additional information about responding to an IRS notice or letter.

Contacting your local IRS office. Keep in mind, many questions can be resolved on IRS.gov without visiting an IRS Tax Assistance Center (TAC). Go to *IRS.gov/letushelp* for the topics people ask about most. If you still need help, IRS TACs provide help when a tax issue can't be handled online or by phone. All TACs now provide service by appointment so you'll know in advance that you can get the service you need without waiting. Before you visit, go to *IRS.gov/taclocator* to find the nearest TAC, check hours, available

services, and appointment options. Or, on the IRS2Go app, under the Stay Connected tab, choose the Contact Us option and click on "Local Offices."

Watching IRS videos. The IRS Video portal *IRSvideos.gov* contains video and audio presentations for individuals, small businesses, and tax professionals.

Getting tax information in other languages. For taxpayers whose native language isn't English, we have the following resources available. Taxpayers can find information on IRS.gov in the following languages.

• *Spanish* (*IRS.gov/spanish*).
• *Chinese* (*IRS.gov/chinese*).
• *Vietnamese* (*IRS.gov/vietnamese*).
• *Korean* (*IRS.gov/korean*).
• *Russian* (*IRS.gov/russian*).

The IRS TACs provide over-the-phone interpreter service in over 170 languages, and the service is available free to taxpayers.

Interest and Penalties

You do not have to figure the amount of any interest or penalties you may owe. Because figuring these amounts can be complicated, we will do it for you if you want. We will send you a bill for any amount due.

If you include interest or penalties (other than the estimated tax penalty) with your payment, identify and enter the amount in the bottom margin of Form 1040, page 2. Do not include interest or penalties (other than the estimated tax penalty) in the amount you owe on line 78.

Interest

We will charge you interest on taxes not paid by their due date, even if an extension of time to file is granted. We will also charge you interest on penalties imposed for failure to file, negligence, fraud, substantial valuation misstatements, substantial understatements of tax, and reportable transaction understatements. Interest is charged on the penalty from the due date of the return (including extensions).

Penalties

Late filing. If you do not file your return by the due date (including extensions), the penalty is usually 5% of the amount due for each month or part of a month your return is late, unless you have a reasonable explanation. If you do, include it with your return. The penalty can be as much as 25% of the tax due. The penalty is 15% per month, up to a maximum of 75%, if the failure to file is fraudulent. If your return is more than 60 days late, the minimum penalty will be $205 or the amount of any tax you owe, whichever is smaller.

Late payment of tax. If you pay your taxes late, the penalty is usually ½ of 1% of the unpaid amount for each month or part of a month the tax isn't paid. The penalty can be as much as 25% of the unpaid amount. It applies to any unpaid tax on the return. This penalty is in addition to interest charges on late payments.

Frivolous return. In addition to any other penalties, the law imposes a penalty of $5,000 for filing a frivolous return. A frivolous return is one that doesn't contain information needed to figure the correct tax or shows a substantially incorrect tax because you take a frivolous position or desire to delay or interfere with the tax laws. This includes altering or striking out the preprinted language above the space where you sign. For a list of positions identified as frivolous, see Notice 2010-33, 2010-17 I.R.B. 609, available at *IRS.gov/irb/2010-17_IRB/ar13.html*.

Other. Other penalties can be imposed for negligence, substantial understatement of tax, reportable transaction understatements, filing an erroneous refund claim, and fraud. Criminal penalties may be imposed for willful failure to file, tax evasion, making a false statement, or identity theft. See Pub. 17 for details on some of these penalties.

Taxpayer Bill of Rights

All taxpayers have fundamental rights they should be aware of when dealing with the IRS. The Taxpayer Bill of Rights, which the IRS adopted in June of 2014, takes existing rights in the tax code and groups them into the following 10 broad categories, making them easier to understand. Explore your rights and our obligations to protect them.

The right to be informed. Taxpayers have the right to know what they need to do to comply with the tax laws. They are entitled to clear explanations of the laws and IRS procedures in all tax forms, instructions, publications, notices, and correspondence. They have the right to be informed of IRS decisions about their tax accounts and to receive clear explanations of the outcomes.

The right to quality service. Taxpayers have the right to receive prompt, courteous, and professional assistance in their dealings with the IRS, to be spoken to in a way they can easily understand, to receive clear and easily understandable communications from the IRS, and to speak to a supervisor about inadequate service.

The right to pay no more than the correct amount of tax. Taxpayers have the right to pay only the amount of tax legally due, including interest and penalties, and to have the IRS apply all tax payments properly.

The right to challenge the IRS's position and be heard. Taxpayers have the right to raise objections and provide additional documentation in response to formal IRS actions or proposed actions, to expect that the IRS will consider their timely objections and documentation promptly and fairly, and to receive a response if the IRS does not agree with their position.

The right to appeal an IRS decision in an independent forum. Taxpayers are entitled to a fair and impartial administrative appeal of most IRS decisions, including many penalties, and have the right to receive a written response regarding the Office of Appeals' decision. Taxpayers generally have the right to take their cases to court.

The right to finality. Taxpayers have the right to know the maximum amount of time they have to challenge the IRS's position as well as the maximum amount of time the IRS has to audit a particular tax year or collect a tax debt. Taxpayers have the right to know when the IRS has finished an audit.

The right to privacy. Taxpayers have the right to expect that any IRS inquiry, examination, or enforcement action will comply with the law and be no more intrusive than necessary, and will respect all due process rights, including search and seizure protections and will provide, where applicable, a collection due process hearing.

The right to confidentiality. Taxpayers have the right to expect that any information they provide to the IRS will not be disclosed unless authorized by the taxpayer or by law. Taxpayers have the right to expect appropriate action will be taken against employees, return preparers, and others who wrongfully use or disclose taxpayer return information.

The right to retain representation. Taxpayers have the right to retain an authorized representative of their choice to represent them in their dealings with the IRS. Taxpayers have the right to seek assistance from a *Low Income Taxpayer Clinic* if they can't afford representation.

The right to a fair and just tax system. Taxpayers have the right to expect the tax system to consider facts and circumstances that might affect their underlying liabilities, ability to pay, or ability to provide information timely. Taxpayers have the right to receive assistance from the *Taxpayer Advocate Service* if they are experiencing financial difficulty or if the IRS has not resolved their tax issues properly and timely through its normal channels.

Learn more at *IRS.gov/taxpayerrights*.

Refund Information

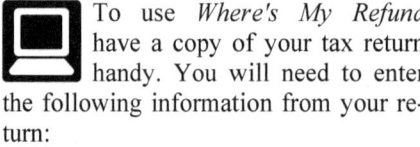 To check the status of your refund go to *Where's My Refund* at *IRS.gov/refunds*, or use the free IRS2Go app, 24 hours a day, 7 days a week. Information about your return will generally be available within 24 hours after the IRS receives your e-filed return, or 4 weeks after you mail a paper return. But if you filed Form 8379 with your return, allow 14 weeks (11 weeks if you filed electronically) before checking your refund status.

Due to changes in the law, the IRS can't issue refunds before February 15, 2017, for returns that claim the earned income credit or the additional child tax credit. This delay applies to the entire refund, not just the portion associated with these credits. Because of the time it generally takes banking or financial systems to process deposits, if you claimed either or both of these credits, it is unlikely that your refund will arrive in your bank account or on a debit card before the week of February 27 (assuming your return has no processing issues and you elect direct deposit). Because many financial institutions do not process payments on weekends or holidays, the three-day holiday weekend that includes Presidents Day may also affect when you receive your refund.

If you filed your return before February 15 and claimed the earned income credit or the additional child tax credit, you can start to check *Where's My Refund* on IRS.gov and the IRS2Go phone mobile app a few days after February 15 for the status of your refund.

 To use *Where's My Refund* have a copy of your tax return handy. You will need to enter the following information from your return:

- Your social security number (or individual taxpayer identification number),
- Your filing status, and
- The exact whole dollar amount of your refund.

Where's My Refund will provide an actual personalized refund date as soon as the IRS processes your tax return and approves your refund.

 Updates to refund status are made once a day - usually at night.

If you do not have Internet access, you can call 1-800-829-1954 24 hours a day, 7 days a week, for automated refund information. Our phone and walk-in assistors can research the status of your refund only if it's been 21 days or more since you filed electronically or more than 6 weeks since you mailed your paper return.

Do not send in a copy of your return unless asked to do so.

To get a refund, you generally must file your return within 3 years from the date the return was due (including extensions).

Where's My Refund doesn't track refunds that are claimed on an amended tax return.

Refund information also is available in Spanish at *IRS.gov/spanish* and 1-800-829-1954.

Tax Topics

You can read these Tax Topics at *IRS.gov/taxtopics*.

List of Tax Topics

All topics are available in Spanish (and most topics are available in Chinese, Korean, Vietnamese, and Russian).

Topic No.	Subject
	IRS Help Available
101	IRS services—Volunteer tax assistance, outreach programs, and identity theft
102	Tax assistance for individuals with disabilities
103	Tax help for small businesses and the self-employed
104	Taxpayer Advocate Service—Your voice at the IRS
105	Armed Forces tax information
107	Tax relief in disaster situations
	IRS Procedures
151	Your appeal rights
152	Refund information
153	What to do if you haven't filed your tax return
154	Form W-2 and Form 1099-R (What to do if incorrect or not received)
155	Forms and publications—How to order
156	Copy or transcript of your tax return—How to get one
157	Change your address—How to notify the IRS
158	Paying your taxes and ensuring proper credit of payments
159	Prior year(s) Form W-2 (How to get a copy)
161	Returning an erroneous refund—Paper check or direct deposit
	Collection
201	The collection process
202	Tax payment options
203	Refund offsets for unpaid child support, certain federal and state debts, and unemployment compensation debts
204	Offers in compromise
205	Innocent spouse relief (Including separation of liability and equitable relief)
206	Dishonored payments
	Alternative Filing Methods
253	Substitute tax forms
254	How to choose a tax return preparer
255	Signing your return electronically

Topic No.	Subject
	General Information
301	When, how, and where to file
303	Checklist of common errors when preparing your tax return
304	Extensions of time to file your tax return
305	Recordkeeping
306	Penalty for underpayment of estimated tax
307	Backup withholding
308	Amended returns
309	Roth IRA contributions
310	Coverdell education savings accounts
311	Power of attorney information
312	Disclosure authorizations
313	Qualified tuition programs (QTPs)
	Which Forms to File
352	Which form—1040, 1040A, or 1040EZ?
356	Decedents
	Types of Income
401	Wages and salaries
403	Interest received
404	Dividends
407	Business income
409	Capital gains and losses
410	Pensions and annuities
411	Pensions—The general rule and the simplified method
412	Lump-sum distributions
413	Rollovers from retirement plans
414	Rental income and expenses
415	Renting residential and vacation property
416	Farming and fishing income
417	Earnings for clergy
418	Unemployment compensation
419	Gambling income and losses
420	Bartering income
421	Scholarships, fellowship grants, and other grants
423	Social security and equivalent railroad retirement benefits
424	401(k) plans
425	Passive activities—Losses and credits
427	Stock options
429	Traders in securities (Information for Form 1040 filers)
430	Receipt of stock in a demutualization
431	Canceled debt—Is it taxable or not?
432	Form 1099-A (Acquisition or Abandonment of Secured Property)

Topic No.	Subject
	and Form 1099-C (Cancellation of Debt)
	Adjustments to Income
451	Individual retirement arrangements (IRAs)
452	Alimony
453	Bad debt deduction
455	Moving expenses
456	Student loan interest deduction
457	Tuition and fees deduction
458	Educator expense deduction
	Itemized Deductions
501	Should I itemize?
502	Medical and dental expenses
503	Deductible taxes
504	Home mortgage points
505	Interest expense
506	Charitable contributions
508	Miscellaneous expenses
509	Business use of home
510	Business use of car
511	Business travel expenses
512	Business entertainment expenses
513	Work-related education expenses
514	Employee business expenses
515	Casualty, disaster, and theft losses (including federally declared disaster areas)
	Tax Computation
551	Standard deduction
552	Tax and credits figured by the IRS
553	Tax on a child's investment and other unearned income (Kiddie tax)
554	Self-employment tax
556	Alternative minimum tax
557	Additional tax on early distributions from traditional and Roth IRAs
558	Additional tax on early distributions from retirement plans, other than IRAs
559	Net Investment Income Tax
560	Additional Medicare Tax
561	Individual shared responsibility provision
	Tax Credits
601	Earned income credit
602	Child and dependent care credit
607	Adoption credit and adoption assistance programs
608	Excess social security and RRTA tax withheld
610	Retirement savings contributions credit
611	Repayment of the first-time homebuyer credit

List of Tax Topics

(Continued)

Tax Topic numbers are effective January 2, 2017.

Disclosure, Privacy Act, and Paperwork Reduction Act Notice

The IRS Restructuring and Reform Act of 1998, the Privacy Act of 1974, and the Paperwork Reduction Act of 1980 require that when we ask you for information we must first tell you our legal right to ask for the information, why we are asking for it, and how it will be used. We must also tell you what could happen if we do not receive it and whether your response is voluntary, required to obtain a benefit, or mandatory under the law.

This notice applies to all papers you file with us, including this tax return. It also applies to any questions we need to ask you so we can complete, correct, or process your return; figure your tax; and collect tax, interest, or penalties.

Our legal right to ask for information is Internal Revenue Code sections 6001, 6011, and 6012(a), and their regulations. They say that you must file a return or statement with us for any tax you are liable for. Your response is mandatory under these sections. Code section 6109 requires you to provide your identifying number on the return. This is so we know who you are, and can process your return and other papers. You must fill in all parts of the tax form that apply to you. But you do not have to check the boxes for the Presidential Election Campaign Fund or for the third-party designee. You also do not have to provide your daytime phone number.

You are not required to provide the information requested on a form that is subject to the Paperwork Reduction Act unless the form displays a valid OMB control number. Books or records relating to a form or its instructions must be retained as long as their contents may become material in the administration of any Internal Revenue law.

We ask for tax return information to carry out the tax laws of the United States. We need it to figure and collect the right amount of tax.

If you do not file a return, do not provide the information we ask for, or provide fraudulent information, you may be charged penalties and be subject to criminal prosecution. We may also have to disallow the exemptions, exclusions, credits, deductions, or adjustments shown on the tax return. This could make the tax higher or delay any refund. Interest may also be charged.

Generally, tax returns and return information are confidential, as stated in Code section 6103. However, Code section 6103 allows or requires the Internal Revenue Service to disclose or give the information shown on your tax return to others as described in the Code. For example, we may disclose your tax information to the Department of Justice to enforce the tax laws, both civil and criminal, and to cities, states, the District of Columbia, and U.S. commonwealths or possessions to carry out their tax laws. We may disclose your tax information to the Department of Treasury and contractors for tax administration purposes; and to other persons as necessary to obtain information needed to determine the amount of or to collect the tax you owe. We may disclose your tax information to the Comptroller General of the United States to permit the Comptroller General to review the Internal Revenue Service. We may disclose your tax information to committees of Congress; federal, state, and local child support agencies; and to other federal agencies for the purposes of determining entitlement for benefits or the eligibility for and the repayment of loans. We may also disclose this information to other countries under a tax treaty, to federal and state agencies to enforce federal nontax criminal laws, or to federal law enforcement and intelligence agencies to combat terrorism.

Please keep this notice with your records. It may help you if we ask you for other information. If you have questions about the rules for filing and giving information, please call or visit any Internal Revenue Service office.

We Welcome Comments on Forms

We try to create forms and instructions that can be easily understood. Often this is difficult to do because our tax laws are very complex. For some people with income mostly from wages, filling in the forms is easy. For others who have businesses, pensions, stocks, rental income, or other investments, it is more difficult.

If you have suggestions for making these forms simpler, we would be happy to hear from you. You can send us comments from *IRS.gov/forms*. Click on "More Information" and then on "Give us feedback." Or you can send your comments to Internal Revenue Service, Tax Forms and Publications Division, 1111 Constitution Ave. NW, IR-6526, Washington, DC 20224. Do not send your return to this address. Instead, see the addresses at the end of these instructions.

Although we can't respond individually to each comment received, we do appreciate your feedback and will consider your comments as we revise our tax forms and instructions.

Estimates of Taxpayer Burden

The following table shows burden estimates based on current statutory requirements as of November 2016, for taxpayers filing a 2016 Form 1040, 1040A, or 1040EZ tax return. Time spent and out-of-pocket costs are presented separately. Time burden is broken out by taxpayer activity, with recordkeeping representing the largest component. Out-of-pocket costs include any expenses incurred by taxpayers to prepare and submit their tax returns. Examples include tax return preparation and submission fees, postage and photocopying costs, and tax preparation software costs. While these estimates do not include burden associated with post-filing activities, IRS operational data indicate that electronically prepared and filed returns have fewer arithmetic errors, implying lower post-filing burden.

Reported time and cost burdens are national averages and do not necessarily reflect a "typical" case. Most taxpayers experience lower than average burden, with taxpayer burden varying considerably by taxpayer type. For instance, the estimated average time burden for all taxpayers filing a Form 1040, 1040A, or 1040EZ is 13 hours, with an average cost of $210 per return. This average includes all associated forms and schedules, across all preparation methods and taxpayer activities. The average burden for taxpayers filing Form 1040 is about 15 hours and $280; the average burden for taxpayers filing Form 1040A is about 8 hours and $90; and the average for Form 1040EZ filers is about 5 hours and $40.

Within each of these estimates there is significant variation in taxpayer activity. For example, nonbusiness taxpayers are expected to have an average burden of about 9 hours and $120, while business taxpayers are expected to have an average burden of about 22 hours and $430. Similarly, tax preparation fees and other out-of-pocket costs vary extensively depending on the tax situation of the taxpayer, the type of software or professional preparer used, and the geographic location.

If you have comments concerning the time and cost estimates below, you can contact us at either one of the addresses shown under *We Welcome Comments on Forms.*

Estimated Average Taxpayer Burden for Individuals by Activity

Primary Form Filed or Type of Taxpayer	Percentage of Returns	Average Burden					Average Cost (Dollars)**
		Average Time (Hours)					
		Total Time*	Record Keeping	Tax Planning	Form Completion and Submission	All Other	
All taxpayers	100	13	6	2	4	1	$210
Primary forms filed							
1040	69	15	7	2	4	1	280
1040A	19	8	2	1	3	1	90
1040EZ	12	5	2	***	3	1	40
Type of taxpayer							
Nonbusiness****	70	9	3	1	3	1	120
Business****	30	22	12	4	5	1	430

*Detail may not add to total time due to rounding.

**Dollars rounded to the nearest $10.

***Rounds to less than one hour.

****You are considered a "business" filer if you file one or more of the following with Form 1040: Schedule C, C-EZ, E, or F or Form 2106 or 2106-EZ. You are considered a "nonbusiness" filer if you do not file any of those schedules or forms with Form 1040 or if you file Form 1040A or 1040EZ.

Order Form for Forms and Publications

 You can view and download the tax forms and publications you need at IRS.gov/forms You can also place an order for forms at IRS.gov/orderforms to avoid having to complete and mail the order form.

The most frequently ordered forms and publications are listed on the order form. You will receive two copies of each form, one copy of the instructions, and one copy of each publication you order. To help reduce waste, please order only the items you need to prepare your return.

How To Use the Order Form

Circle the items you need on the order form. Use the blank spaces to order items not listed. If you need more space, attach a separate sheet of paper.

Print or type your name and address accurately in the space provided on the order form to ensure delivery of your order. Enclose the order form in an envelope and mail it to the IRS address shown next. You should receive your order within 10 business days after we receive your request.

Do not send your tax return to the address shown here. Instead, see the addresses at the end of these instructions.

Mail Your Order Form To:

Internal Revenue Service
1201 N. Mitsubishi Motorway
Bloomington, IL 61705-6613

▲ *Cut here* ▲

Save Money and Time by Going Online!
Download or order these and other forms and publications at IRS.gov/forms

Order Form

Please print.

Name

Postal mailing address   Apt./Suite/Room

City   State   ZIP code

Foreign country   International postal code

Daytime phone number
(   )

Circle the forms and publications you need. The instructions for any form you order will be included.

Use the **blank spaces** to order items not listed.

1040	Schedule F (1040)	1040-V	4868	8959	Pub. 505	Pub. 551	Pub. 946
Schedule A (1040)	Schedule H (1040)	1040X	5405	8960	Pub. 523	Pub. 554	Pub. 970
Schedule B (1040A or 1040)	Schedule J (1040)	2106	6251	8962	Pub. 525	Pub. 575	Pub. 972
Schedule C (1040)	Schedule R (1040A or 1040)	2441	8283	8965	Pub. 526	Pub. 583	Pub. 4681
Schedule C-EZ (1040)	Schedule SE (1040)	3903	8606	Pub. 1	Pub. 527	Pub. 587	
Schedule D (1040)	Schedule 8812 (1040A or 1040)	4506	8822	Pub. 334	Pub. 529	Pub. 590-A	
Form 8949	1040A	4506-T	8829	Pub. 463	Pub. 535	Pub. 590-B	
Schedule E (1040)	1040EZ	4562	8863	Pub. 501	Pub. 547	Pub. 596	
Schedule EIC (1040A or 1040)	1040-ES (2017)	4684	8917	Pub. 502	Pub. 550	Pub. 915	

Use your QR Reader app on your smartphone to scan this code and get connected to the IRS Forms and Publications homepage.

Major Categories of Federal Income and Outlays for Fiscal Year 2015

Income and Outlays. These pie charts show the relative sizes of the major categories of federal income and outlays for fiscal year 2015.

Income

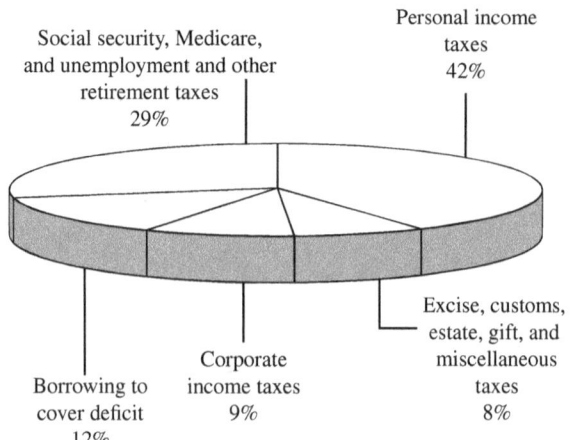

Social security, Medicare, and unemployment and other retirement taxes
29%

Personal income taxes
42%

Excise, customs, estate, gift, and miscellaneous taxes
8%

Corporate income taxes
9%

Borrowing to cover deficit
12%

Outlays*

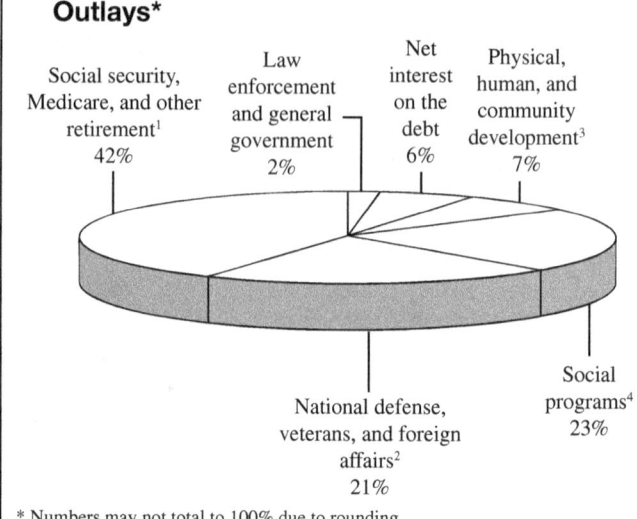

Social security, Medicare, and other retirement[1]
42%

Law enforcement and general government
2%

Net interest on the debt
6%

Physical, human, and community development[3]
7%

Social programs[4]
23%

National defense, veterans, and foreign affairs[2]
21%

* Numbers may not total to 100% due to rounding.

On or before the first Monday in February of each year the President is required by law to submit to the Congress a budget proposal for the fiscal year that begins the following October. The budget plan sets forth the President's proposed receipts, spending, and the surplus or deficit for the federal government. The plan includes recommendations for new legislation as well as recommendations to change, eliminate, and add programs. After receipt of the President's proposal, the Congress reviews the proposal and makes changes. It first passes a budget resolution setting its own targets for receipts, outlays, and surplus or deficit. Next, individual spending and revenue bills that are consistent with the goals of the budget resolution are enacted.

In fiscal year 2015 (which began on October 1, 2014, and ended on September 30, 2015), federal income was $3.250 trillion and outlays were $3.688 trillion, leaving a deficit of $438 billion.

Footnotes for Certain Federal Outlays

1. **Social security, Medicare, and other retirement:** These programs provide income support for the retired and disabled and medical care for the elderly.

2. **National defense, veterans, and foreign affairs:** About 15% of outlays were to equip, modernize, and pay our armed forces and to fund national defense activities; about 4% were for veterans benefits and services; and about 1% were for international activities, including military and economic assistance to foreign countries and the maintenance of U.S. embassies abroad.

3. **Physical, human, and community development:** These outlays were for agriculture; natural resources; environment; transportation; aid for elementary and secondary education and direct assistance to college students; job training; deposit insurance, commerce and housing credit, and community development; and space, energy, and general science programs.

4. **Social programs:** About 17% of total outlays were for Medicaid, food stamps, temporary assistance for needy families, supplemental security income, and related programs; and 6% for health research and public health programs, unemployment compensation, assisted housing, and social services.

Note. The percentages shown here exclude undistributed offsetting receipts, which were $116 billion in fiscal year 2015. In the budget, these receipts are offset against spending in figuring the outlay totals shown above. These receipts are for the U.S. Government's share of its employee retirement programs, rents and royalties on the Outer Continental Shelf, and proceeds from the sale of assets.

2016 Tax Rate Schedules

The Tax Rate Schedules are shown so you can see the tax rate that applies to all levels of taxable income. Do not use them to figure your tax. Instead, see the instructions for line 44.

Schedule X—If your filing status is **Single**

If your taxable income is: Over—	But not over—	The tax is:	of the amount over—
$0	$9,275	.... 10%	$0
9,275	37,650	$927.50 + 15%	9,275
37,650	91,150	5,183.75 + 25%	37,650
91,150	190,150	18,558.75 + 28%	91,150
190,150	413,350	46,278.75 + 33%	190,150
413,350	415,050	119,934.75 + 35%	413,350
415,050	....	120,529.75 + 39.6%	415,050

Schedule Y-1—If your filing status is **Married filing jointly** or **Qualifying widow(er)**

If your taxable income is: Over—	But not over—	The tax is:	of the amount over—
$0	$18,550	.... 10%	$0
18,550	75,300	$1,855.00 + 15%	18,550
75,300	151,900	10,367.50 + 25%	75,300
151,900	231,450	29,517.50 + 28%	151,900
231,450	413,350	51,791.50 + 33%	231,450
413,350	466,950	111,818.50 + 35%	413,350
466,950	....	130,578.50 + 39.6%	466,950

Schedule Y-2—If your filing status is **Married filing separately**

If your taxable income is: Over—	But not over—	The tax is:	of the amount over—
$0	$9,275	.... 10%	$0
9,275	37,650	$927.50 + 15%	9,275
37,650	75,950	5,183.75 + 25%	37,650
75,950	115,725	14,758.75 + 28%	75,950
115,725	206,675	25,895.75 + 33%	115,725
206,675	233,475	55,909.25 + 35%	206,675
233,475	....	65,289.25 + 39.6%	233,475

Schedule Z—If your filing status is **Head of household**

If your taxable income is: Over—	But not over—	The tax is:	of the amount over—
$0	$13,250	.... 10%	$0
13,250	50,400	$1,325.00 + 15%	13,250
50,400	130,150	6,897.50 + 25%	50,400
130,150	210,800	26,835.00 + 28%	130,150
210,800	413,350	49,417.00 + 33%	210,800
413,350	441,000	116,258.50 + 35%	413,350
441,000	....	125,936.00 + 39.6%	441,000

Index to Instructions

Where Do You File? Mail your return to the address shown below that applies to you. If you want to use a private delivery service, see *Private Delivery Services* under *Filing Requirements,* earlier.

 Envelopes without enough postage will be returned to you by the post office. Your envelope may need additional postage if it contains more than five pages or is oversized (for example, it is over $\frac{1}{4}''$ thick). Also, include your complete return address.

IF you live in...	THEN use this address if you:	
	Are requesting a refund or are not enclosing a check or money order...	Are enclosing a check or money order...
Florida, Louisiana, Mississippi, Texas	Department of the Treasury Internal Revenue Service Austin, TX 73301-0002	Internal Revenue Service P.O. Box 1214 Charlotte, NC 28201-1214
Alaska, Arizona, California, Colorado, Hawaii, Idaho, Nevada, New Mexico, Oregon, Utah, Washington, Wyoming	Department of the Treasury Internal Revenue Service Fresno, CA 93888-0002	Internal Revenue Service P.O. Box 7704 San Francisco, CA 94120-7704
Arkansas, Illinois, Indiana, Iowa, Kansas, Michigan, Minnesota, Montana, Nebraska, North Dakota, Ohio, Oklahoma, South Dakota, Wisconsin	Department of the Treasury Internal Revenue Service Fresno, CA 93888-0002	Internal Revenue Service P.O. Box 802501 Cincinnati, OH 45280-2501
Alabama, Georgia, Kentucky, New Jersey, North Carolina, South Carolina, Tennessee, Virginia	Department of the Treasury Internal Revenue Service Kansas City, MO 64999-0002	Internal Revenue Service P.O. Box 931000 Louisville, KY 40293-1000
Connecticut, Delaware, District of Columbia, Maine, Maryland, Massachusetts, Missouri, New Hampshire, New York, Pennsylvania, Rhode Island, Vermont, West Virginia	Department of the Treasury Internal Revenue Service Kansas City, MO 64999-0002	Internal Revenue Service P.O. Box 37008 Hartford, CT 06176-7008
A foreign country, U.S. possession or territory*, or use an APO or FPO address, or file Form 2555, 2555-EZ, or 4563, or are a dual-status alien	Department of the Treasury Internal Revenue Service Austin, TX 73301-0215	Internal Revenue Service P.O. Box 1303 Charlotte, NC 28201-1303

*If you live in American Samoa, Puerto Rico, Guam, the U.S. Virgin Islands, or the Northern Mariana Islands, see Pub. 570.

www.ingramcontent.com/pod-product-compliance
Lightning Source LLC
Chambersburg PA
CBHW060009210526

45170CB00017B/2127